A HISTORY OF CLASSICAL MUSIC REHEARSAL
Francis Knights & Pablo Padilla

ISBN: 978-1-912271-99-3

Published by Peacock Press
Peacock Press, Scout Bottom Farm, Mytholmroyd,
Hebden Bridge HX7 5JS (UK).
+44 (0) 1422 882751

Cover photo: Maximilian Mopp (1885-1954), *Symphony*, print (early 1920s)

Book design by www.SiPat.co.uk

All rights reserved. No part of this publication may be reproduced, stored or transmitted in any form or by any means electronically or mechanically, by photocopying, recording, scanning or otherwise, without the permission of the copyright owners. © Peacock Press.

DEDICATED TO SCHOLAR AND PERFORMER
PROFESSOR PETER HOLMAN MBE

A HISTORY OF CLASSICAL MUSIC REHEARSAL

FRANCIS KNIGHTS & PABLO PADILLA

CONTENTS

Preface 1

Part 1 4
   From the Middle Ages to 1800

1. Introduction 5
2. Sources and Materials 17
3. Institutions and Employment 41
4. Performers and their Training 69
5. Conductors 95
6. Performance Practice 105

Part 2 128
   Romantic to Modern

7. The 19th century 129
8. Rehearsal in the 20th century 151
9. The Impact of Technology in the 21st century 171
10. Research into Rehearsal 177
11. Rehearsal in the Performing Arts 183
12. Conclusions 189
Bibliography 197
Index 217

PREFACE

The history of musical rehearsal remains a little-studied area, but the topic preserves much important and illuminating information about the ways in which musicians and composers over the past hundreds of years have prepared for performances, whether public, domestic or liturgical. The individual components involved in these processes can be surprisingly broad, including notation, transmission, education, employment, social hierarchies, venues, ensemble layout and even lighting; for many of these areas more questions can be asked than answered, but it is usually possible to outline the various plausible options that must have made actual music-making possible, even for challenging repertoire such as the Eton Choirbook.

From about 1800, documents, including letters, journals, memoirs, reviews, anecdotes and interviews, help to fill out the narrative of rehearsal history, and such information is eventually supported by sound recordings, but for the earlier period the data is scattered, very incomplete and much less clear. Accordingly, this book is divided into two, with a thematic approach for the pre-Romantic period, then a chronological narrative for the modern era. Following that, the rehearsal story is brought up to date with a consideration of what research has achieved in helping musicians to understand how to rehearse efficiently, then exploring the ever-increasing impact of technology on the sequence of learning and then combining separate parts, and lastly by comparing rehearsal practices in the other performing arts.

As far as possible, original sources are quoted, so that the evidence comes directly from players and listeners of the period. As music historian Adam Carse noted of the 18th century, contemporary documents about the orchestra 'are not many, nor very explicit, for those who wrote about music in the 18th century, like their 19th and 20th century successors, have always been more ready to devote their attention to individuals and their works than to corporate bodies and their playing'.[1] Equally, the (usually) private process of rehearsal simply did not need documenting by anyone, and in any case bore the same preparatory relation to the final performance as did composer's sketches to the final work.

'Rehearsal' is here to be understood as 'collective practicing', with musicians (whether pre-prepared or not) coming together in order to combine their individual parts into the complete work; it therefore encompasses everything from duet playing to full-scale opera and oratorio. The numbers of performers may vary, but the fundamental problem is universal: how to achieve the most accurate and secure rendition of a score within a limited time. The focus here is almost exclusively on classical music, where a fully-composed and notated work is turned into sound by performers. While there are some other genres (such as film music, some big band arrangements and even to an extent change ringing) that operate on the same principles, the difference between the classical tradition and those incorporating improvisatory or less structured elements (for example, jazz or gamelan) is that classical rehearsal involves the improving repetition of given material, rather than exploring freer live possibilities. Key to the process is some form of rehearsal-management direction, whether shared or hierarchical (compare a small and quasi-democratic chamber ensemble with an orchestral conductor), and with that comes the possibility of personal creative performing input, a process that increases greatly during the 19th century.

Much invaluable information about early rehearsal practices has been unearthed by numerous scholars living and dead, especially Adam Carse, Peter Holman, Beverly Jerold, Andrew Parrott, Richard Sherr and Rob Wegman, and our thanks go to all of them, and also to a number of people (including Roger Bowers, Tim Braithewaite, Matthew Gouldstone, Kerry McCarthy, Eamonn O'Keeffe and Caitlin Parry) for helpful conversations about aspects of rehearsal, or for assistance with citations. In addition, Pablo Padilla would like to thank Clare Hall, University of Cambridge, for hosting a research visit, where this work was begun, and to PASPA of DGAPA (UNAM) for financial support. Further additions to the Bibliography below will be made on www.francisknights.co.uk under 'Books' in due course.

---

1   Adam Carse, *The Orchestra in the XVIIIth century* (Cambridge, 1940), p.v.

PART 1
FROM THE MIDDLE AGES TO 1800

CHAPTER 1
INTRODUCTION

A working musician's life comprises mostly practice and rehearsal, but this world 'behind the curtain' has often left very limited traces in the historical record. The nature of the evidence for early rehearsal practice is fragmentary and dispersed; even from the beginning of the 19th century, when documentation of musical practices becomes much fuller, information about actual rehearsals, goals and results is relatively thin on the ground.[2] Circumstantial or other evidence for the earlier periods includes musicians' letters, institutional account books and disciplinary documentation, comments from theorists and descriptions from listeners, but for some key areas, nothing whatsoever is known. In interpreting both historical commentary and anecdote it is vital to remember two things: that 'the past is a foreign country; they do things differently there', in the words of novelist L. P. Hartley;[3] and that practice likely varied from century to century, within style and genre, and from country to country, city to city and individual to individual. Roger North, writing in about 1700, was dubious as to value of descriptive written records at all: 'grant that a man read all the books of musick that ever were wrote, I shall not allow that musick is or can be understood out of them, no more than the taste of meats out of cookish receipt books. And for this reason, in every age, the musick of that time seems best, and they say, Are wee not wonderfully improved? And so comparing what they doe know, with what they doe not know, they are as clear of opinion, as they that doubdt nothing.'[4] Accord-

---

2   See, for example, Gary W. Harwood and Gregory W. Harwood, 'Robert Schumann's Choice of Repertory & Rehearsal Planning in his Career as a Choral Conductor', *The Choral Journal*, li/2 (September 2010), pp.32-39, 42-51.
3   Leslie P. Hartley, *The Go-Between* (London, 1953), p.1.
4   John Wilson (ed), *Roger North on Music: Being a Selection from his Essays written during the years c.1695-1728* (London, 1959), p.283.

ingly, the thoughts of any one writer at one place at one time should not be presumed as having any wider application, at least not without careful thought.[5]

Extrapolation backwards from modern practice to the period before 1800 may therefore tell us rather little about past working methods; and a full and coherent historical narrative cannot be assembled from such disparate scraps of evidence that remain. Nevertheless, a consideration of the rehearsal and performance options for particular past repertoires in terms of place, personnel, education, availability of time, performing materials, aesthetics and so on may lead to a better understanding of how the musical sources of the past were turned into sound - and how well. As John Morehen noted, 'Of all the areas where there is a paucity of contemporary information, that of performance standards is perhaps the most frustrating'.[6] Much of the rehearsal information that survives ties in with current concerns about performance practice, 'the question of what, historically, [musicians] thought and did when turning the notated work into the musical event'.[7]

THE NATURE OF HISTORICAL EVIDENCE

Rehearsal technique was a skill that was very likely passed on informally through an apprenticeship model or on an observational basis: anyone taking a rehearsal themselves would have sat through dozens, probably hundreds of such occasions, and hopefully been able to learn the working sequence of events that provided the best result within the limited time available. Because of this, such systems would not need to have been written down, and indeed were not until the end of the 19th century, when amateur conductors needed to acquire these skills in order to work with newly-founded amateur choirs and orchestras. Similarly, as private events where musicians did not generally want to be seen 'in preparation',[8] there is very little in the way of definite iconography, although three related 18th-century paintings by Marco Ricci (1676-1730) represent opera rehearsals:[9]

---

5 See Francis Knights, 'Guidelines for the systematic evaluation of early music theorists', *National Early Music Association Newsletter*, iii/2 (Autumn 2019), pp.44-49.
6 John Morehen, 'The "burden of proof": the editor as detective' in John Morehen (ed), *English Choral Practice, 1400-1650* (Cambridge, 1995), pp.200-220 at 218.
7 Rob C. Wegman, 'From Maker to Composer: Improvisation and Musical Authorship in the Low Countries, 1450-1500', *Journal of the American Musicological Society*, xlix/3 (Autumn 1996), pp.409-479 at 442.
8 Schumann specifically did not want his rehearsals 'reported in the public newspapers'; Harwood and Harwood (2010), p.36.
9 These are illustrated and discussed in Peter Holman, *Before the Baton: Musical Direction and Conducting in Stuart and Georgian Britain* (Woodbridge, 2020), pp.222-227.

in one, several singers and a languid group of strings are gathered round a small harpsichord in what looks like a private house, and their casual demeanor indicates that this is a rehearsal not a domestic performance, despite all being formally dressed.

From the evidence, information needs to be carefully decoded to see what its nature is, in respect of the expertise of the writer, the reason they made such remarks, and to whom.[10] Even private letters, especially those between professional musicians – a prime source of useful material about rehearsal – might have been subject to some self-censorship: Leopold Mozart told Wolfgang to be careful what he writes concerning his Salzburg employer, as 'one of your letters might get lost or find its way into other hands'.[11] Elsewhere, contradictory views may have existed, only one side of which now survives: as an example of the former, at Archbishop Laud's visitation of Salisbury Cathedral in 1634 the canons gave opposing evidence about the standards of the music, one saying that the choristers were 'not well ordered or instructed in singing', while another claimed that 'the choristers are well ordered … all save two sing their parts perfectly'.[12] In 1617, Bishop Bayly noted that there were only a small number of choristers at Bangor Cathedral, while Thomas Martin (clerk of the grammar school) explained that he had 'taken paines this twelvemonth and more to teach the singing boys …[he] hath taught one boy perfectly … and hath brought up foure or five more boyes prettilye in the skill of music, hoping they will do well in time'.[13] That this was a forlorn hope is shown by a visitation return two years later, noting the cathedral had just one competent chorister. Even where documentation relating to quality is more robust, as in the papers of the Sistine Chapel unearthed by Richard Sherr and others,[14] with its fascinating detail of a choir at work, the relevance of these specific practices to any other institution, period or country is very uncertain indeed.

---

10 Knights (2019).
11 Emily Anderson (trans and ed), rev Stanley Sadie and Fiona Smart, *The Letters of Mozart and his family* (London, 3/1989), p.278.
12 Alan Mould, *The English Chorister: A History* (London, 2007), p.106.
13 Sally Harper, *Music in Welsh Culture before 1650: A Study of the Principal Sources* (London, 2007), p.303. Eleventh article of Bishop Bayly's visitation return to Bangor (1617), MS 22808, University of Wales, Bangor; Thomas Martin, *Letter to Bishop Bayly* (1617), MS 22808, University of Wales, Bangor; Thomas William Reynolds, *A Study of Music and Liturgy: choirs and organs in monastic and secular foundations in Wales and the borderlands, 1486-1645*, PhD thesis (Bangor University, 2002), p.147.
14 See especially Richard Sherr, *Music and Musicians in Renaissance Rome and Other Courts* (Aldershot, 1999).

Where rehearsal is mentioned at all, the lack of detail can be disappointing: a rare Cambrai Cathedral chapter document from May 1497 specifically mentions it as part of their arrangements, but the meaning is obscure, as 'rehearsal' is not the point being made: 'Wherefore because the vicars go behind the choir in summer without sufficient cause (unless they should be invited for the purpose of rehearsing motets), the canons order that henceforth they may not presume to go there, unless for said reason'. Whether 'behind the choir' (or quire) means literally that, or actually outside the building, is unknown.[15]

It is important to note that much of the evidence for rehearsal as an aspect of performance practice is in the form of negative comments; and such descriptions as survive tend to be at the extremes, either praising performers for their abilities, or complaining about poor tuning, ensemble and so on. There is relatively little sense of what 'ordinary' music-making might have been like, possibly due to its very normality.

PERFORMANCE QUALITY AND INTENTION

The fundamental fact of rehearsal is that there is never enough time, as Andrew Parrott noted in 1978; the two basic problems he identifies are 'those inherent in the music, and those inherent in the musicians',[16] but of course there are many other components affecting rehearsal and performance conditions. Probably the most frustrating documentary absence is a sense of what the quality of the outcomes might have been. The idea of a completely accurate performance was of course understood, but how often was it achieved? As Roger North noted, music 'demands little less than perfection in the performance, which is not alwaies found',[17] while in 1727 Ernst Gottlieb Baron drily observed that 'it sometimes happens that the compositions is good but the performance is bad'.[18] Without knowing the desired 'output' of a historical rehearsal, it is very difficult to judge the musical or technical 'input' that would have been required to make it happen.

---

15   Craig Wright, 'Performance Practices at the Cathedral of Cambrai 1475-1550', *The Musical Quarterly*, lxiv/3 (July 1978), pp.295-328 at 307.
16   Andrew Parrott, 'Rehearsal time', in John M. Thomson (ed), *The future of early music in Britain* (London, 1978), pp.34-37 at 36.
17   Cited in Robert Donington, *The Interpretation of Music* (London, 1989), p.118.
18   Ernst Gottlieb Baron, trans Douglas Alton Smith, *Study of the Lute* (Apros, CA, 2/2019), p.111.

A note-perfect performance was more likely in solo circumstances: Oxford composer Edward Lowe (c.1610-1682) wrote to a female keyboard pupil urging her to 'play thes Lessons in the Order Sett down Constantly once a day … keep your eye (as much as you can) in your Booke. If you chance to miss goe not from the Lesson, till you have perfected it. Above all, Play not too fast'.[19] One manifestation of performance precision was aimed at through the use of mechanical instruments during the 18th century: 'It Would Be without Error', wrote Marie-Dominique-Joseph Engramelle of such a device in 1775.[20]

Second, of the two main categories of rehearsal technique today (preparing the piece, or training the ensemble), there is relatively little historical evidence for the latter.[21] Perhaps aspects of tuning, blend, vowel colour and so on were tackled through the music itself, rehearsals over long periods of time producing an ensemble with an established and well-trained approach, but this might be a more modern conception. Practice could also have varied depending on the institutional nature or purpose of the music, whether secular, sacred or occasional. In addition, the complex and individual inter-relationships between rehearsal goals, the time available, the difficulty of the music and the skill of the performers cannot be known.[22]

Third, it is important to remember that modern ideas of scientific precision did not exist then, and that people were used to functioning using various approximations of (for example) time,[23] weights, measures and spelling; musical notation, in all its forms, may not have been seen as precisely prescriptive either. How were time (the length of a rehearsal, and the distribution of its tasks) or tempo measured by musicians? Even two centuries after the invention of the metronome, debates about correct tempi in some 19th century repertoire (especially Beethoven) are not settled. In addition, what now appears to be a 'fast' tempo for a performer of today may have been different in the past: Edmund

---

19 Christopher Marsh, *Music and Society in Early Modern England* (Cambridge, 2010), p.199.
20 See Rebecca Cypess, '"It Would Be without Error": Automated Technology and the Pursuit of Correct Performance in the French Enlightenment', *Journal of the Royal Musical Association*, cxlii/1 (2017), pp.1-29.
21 A reference from the German College in Rome (1611) that 'the *maestro di cappella* trains [the students] in various types of singing' is ambiguous in that respect; Noel O'Regan, 'The performance of Palestrina: some further observations', *Early Music*, xxiv/1 (February 1996), pp.144–156 at 149.
22 Stewart Gordon, *Mastering the Art of Performance* (Oxford, 2006), pp.6-7.
23 See Paul Glennie and Nigel Thrift, *Shaping the Day: A History of Timekeeping in England and Wales, 1300-1800* (London, 2011) and Gillian Adler and Paul Strohm, *Alle Thyng hath Tyme: Time and medieval life* (London, 2023).

Fellowes complained about the 'drawled' tempi of Tudor services in early 20th century British cathedrals,[24] but this is merely subjective and we have no way of knowing whether that tempo or present-day faster tempos were closer to 16th century practice, or why they might have differed.

PROFESSIONAL PUBLIC CONCERTS

For public concerts in particular, one major purpose of rehearsal was to maintain standards sufficient to prevent disasters of the kind recorded by Johann Friedrich Reichardt (1751-1814) at a concert in Vienna in 1808: a Gloria 'miscarried altogether' while a Sanctus was 'a complete failure in performance'.[25] Fortunately the concert included Beethoven's Piano Concerto No.4, 'terribly difficult, which Beethoven played astonishingly well in the fastest possible tempi', together with his symphonies No.5, 'very elaborate and too long' and No.6, 'filled with the liveliest images and the most brilliant ideas and figures'. Of the C minor symphony, Reichardt makes a point of mentioning that 'a cavalier sitting near us reported having observed at the rehearsal' that the busy cello part was 34 pages long; clearly, some were permitted to attend such rehearsals (see below).[26]

Burney recounts a performance in Italy where he was barely able to judge the quality of an under-rehearsed work: 'If there had been more frequent rehearsals of the Miserere of Leo, in 8 real parts, which Ansani had performed last year, 1781, at the Pantheon, by more than 40 voices, I can conceive, from such movements as were correctly executed, that the effects of the whole would have been wonderful'.[27] Fortunately, a poor rehearsal might not sabotage the success of an actual performance, as Mozart found in Paris in July 1778: of his new symphony (K297) for the Concerts Spirituel, he wrote, 'I was very nervous at the rehearsal, for never in my life have I heard a worse performance. You have no idea how they twice scraped and scrambled through it. I was really in a terrible way and would gladly have had it rehearsed again, but there was so much else to rehearse, there was no time left'. However, it was still performed to 'great applause'.[28]

---

24 Edmund Fellowes, *Memoirs of an Amateur Musician* (London, 1946), p.120.
25 Such disasters can occur even today, as in the well-known case in 1999 of pianist Maria João Pires, who had prepared a different piano concerto by Mozart than the one the Amsterdam Concertgebouw Orchestra began playing in the concert; clearly, there had been no rehearsal beforehand. Fortunately she was able to play the other work from memory.
26 Oliver Strunk, *Source Readings in Music History: IV The Classic Era* (London, 1981), p.164.
27 Charles Burney, ed Frank Mercer, *A General History of Music from the Earliest Ages to the Present Period*, 2 vols. (London, 1935), ii, p.728.
28 Anderson (1989), p.557. This was the day after his mother's death.

MUSIC BEFORE THE AGE OF SOUND RECORDING

Understanding the attitudes and practices of early modern musicians is now hampered by a particular and absolutely crucial technological watershed, that of sound recording. For earlier composers and musicians, their art existed in the moment, and was subject to all the errors that might occur in live music-making. However, these mistakes were as ephemeral as the sound of the music itself, and one cannot assume that they were of the same concern as to modern musicians, for whom live performance now aspires to the technical accuracy of a CD. Judging earlier musicians by these standards, and with the modern possibilities of repeated playback, may be to misunderstand the attitudes of the past. As Robert Philip observes in his important study, *Performing music in the age of recording*, 'Early recordings make it clear that standards of accuracy, tuning, clarity and precision were generally lower in the early twentieth century than they are today, and there is no reason to suppose that they were higher through the nineteenth century',[29] and this is reinforced in respect of tuning by Beverly Jerold: 'Probably the greatest catalyst in the transition to modern intonation standards was the advent of recordings, which made it more essential to sing and play in tune'.[30] Performing standards likely varied greatly in the past, from the excellent to the atrocious. It is also worth noting that modern professionals may have performed canonical works such as Bach's St Matthew Passion many hundreds of times, whereas in the composer's day they were only given a few times, with implications for the different nature and necessity of rehearsal then and now.

As well as these components of modern performance precision, which may have significantly affected modern (as compared to historic) rehearsal practice, even elements as fundamental as historical tempo may have been misunderstood from the sources.[31] This is potentially significant, as the conduct and technical demands of a rehearsal where accuracy-at-speed is a goal may well be different. One specific example comes from 17th century England, where

---

29 Robert Philip, *Performing music in the age of recording* (New Haven, 2004), p.13. See also Beverly Jerold, 'Choral Singing before the Era of Recording', *The Musical Times*, cxlvii/1895 (Summer 2006), pp.77-84.
30 Beverly Jerold, 'Intonation Standards and Equal Temperament', *Dutch Journal of Music Theory*, xii/2 (May 2007), pp.215-227 at 218.
31 See the discussions in Ephraim Segerman, 'Tempo and tactus after 1500', in Tess Knighton and David Fallows (eds), *Companion to Medieval and Renaissance Music* (London, 1992), pp.337-344 and Ephraim Segerman, 'A re-examination of the evidence on absolute tempo before 1700', *Early Music*, xxiv/2 (May 1996), pp.227-249 and xxiv/4 (November 1996), pp.681-690.

a pendulum-based tempo measurement instruction from Thomas Tomkins' posthumous 1668 *Musical Deo Sacra* collection[32] equates to a pulse which David Wulstan described as 'far too slow as the basic beat for Tudor music';[33] nearly all scholars and performers have agreed with him in ignoring it as a performance practice instruction or guide.[34] At the very least, experimentation along these lines is warranted for the modern musician, and consideration of how such performance decisions might have affected rehearsal practice.

In respect of historical understanding of their own notational practices, Rob Wegman posits simple rules of thumb that must have made practical interpretation of the complexity of 15th-century English polyphony possible; he also suggests that changing note values over the period have implications for performing tempo.[35] Tudor English scribes (and presumably performers too) were also sometimes tripped up by the mensural complexities of their own music,[36] and Giovan Tomaso Cimello tells a story of the composer Jean L'Heritier being mocked by his master Josquin for not understanding the notation of one of the latter's works.[37]

---

32 Thomas Tomkins, *Musical Deo Sacra* (London, 1668).
33 David Wulstan, *Tudor Music* (Iowa City, 1986), p.188.
34 Note that Tomkins gives a single tempo apparently suitable for all this music in his collection, not (as a modern musician would expect) a range dependent on mood, text, performing acoustics, performer ability or musical preferences. Some support for such tempi comes from an Oxford manuscript of c.1680, which includes works like Gibbons' Short Service with an ornate added organ part that implies much slower speeds than are usual today. See Francis Knights, 'A Restoration Version of Gibbons' Short Service', *Organists' Review*, lxxvi: 271 (June 1990a), pp.97-100 and 'Magdalen College MS 347: An Index and Commentary', *Journal of the British Institute of Organ Studies*, xiv (1990b), pp.4-9.
35 Rob C. Wegman, 'Concerning Tempo in the English Polyphonic Mass, c. 1420-70', *Acta Musicologica*, lxi/1 (January-April 1989), pp.40-65. See also Rob C. Wegman, 'Different Strokes for Different Folks? On Tempo and Diminution in Fifteenth-Century Music', *Journal of the American Musicological Society*, liii/3 (Autumn 2000), pp.461-505 and Ruth I. DeFord, *Tactus, Mensuration, and Rhythm in Renaissance Music* (Cambridge, 2015).
36 Roger Bray, 'Editing and performing *musica speculativa*', in Morehen (1995), pp.48-73.
37 Rob C. Wegman, '"And Josquin Laughed...": Josquin and the Composer's Anecdote in the Sixteenth Century', *The Journal of Musicology*, xvii/3 (Summer 1999), pp.319-357 at 321.

ETYMOLOGY

In English, the word 'rehearsal' comes from Middle English, with a sense of 'repeat aloud', while comparison of the Old French term *rehercier* (perhaps from *re-* 'again' + *hercer*, 'to harrow', from *herse*, 'harrow') also conveys the idea of repetition, as in their modern term *répétition*. However, in Italian (*prova*), Spanish (*ensayo*) and Portuguese (*ensaio*), the term is more related to the idea of a 'test'. This is true in German (*Proben*) too, but it can also be translated as *Einübung*, which is closer to the idea of 'practice'. In non-Western traditions, for instance Chinese, the term *Páiyǎn* is also associated with the idea of repetition ('row' … 'into play'). In any case, to 'rehearse' seems to be associated with the idea of repeating a process in order to improve it. This repetition element is explicit at Wells Cathedral in the 17th century, for example, where the teaching of the choristers was to be by 'manifold repetition as often as, when and whenever the doing so is of profit'.[38]

The earliest music dictionary in English offers this definition: 'REHEARSAL, an essay or experiment of some composition made in private, previous to the representation or performance in publick, to habituate the actors: or performers, and make them ready or perfect, in their parts; we say there is a new tragedy in *Rehearsal*, or the *Rehearsal* of a new Anthem, but for the latter we more usually say *Practice*'.[39] In 1755 Dr Johnson was more concise: 'Rehearsal. 2. The recital of any thing previous to publick exhibition',[40] the key components again being a preparatory act to a public performance.[41] However, in the history of the subject neither the 'private' first part nor the 'public' second part are always true. The working definition used in the discussions below makes a distinction between individual ('practice') and collective ('rehearsal') live music preparation for a subsequent event.

---

38 Jane Flynn, 'The education of choristers in England during the sixteenth century', in Morehen (1995), pp.180-220, p.181.

39 James Grassineau, *A Musical Dictionary. being a collection of terms and characters, As well Ancient as Modern. Including the Historical, Theoretical, and practical Parts of Music* (London, 1740), p.196. There is no entry for 'Practice'. The earliest English dictionary, Robert Cawdrey's *A Table Alphabeticall of Hard Usual English Words* (London, 1604) omits 'rehearsal' as a term, and gives *practising* as the definition of 'practique'. Further historical definitions are cited in Graham Strahle, *An Early Music Dictionary* (Cambridge, 1995).

40 https://johnsonsdictionaryonline.com.

41 The *Oxford English Dictionary* summarizes 'rehearsal' (in the musical/theatrical sense, there being several other meanings) as a 'practice performance'; https://www.oed.com/dictionary.

The word 'rehearsal' might also comprise some individual training, not for an ensemble but for someone to take part in an ensemble: at a grand Leipzig wedding of the mayor's son in 1618 (later censured for its extravagance by the town council) cantor Samuel Schein arranged a performance of his grand double motet *Singet dem Herrn*. This required large forces, but the visiting Naumburg town pipers were evidently unable to supply a timpanist and the records show that a local boy was trained up specially: 'a schoolboy who had been rehearsed by the cantor played the drums in this piece'.[42]

It should be remembered that some performing traditions, including areas of early polyphony, involve improvised or unwritten music rather than notated works, and the notion of 'rehearsal' in that instance acquires a completely different meaning. However, improvisatory techniques can still be collectively rehearsed in order to increase their coherence and chance of aesthetic success.

It is also possible that there existed brief 'instruction-only' rehearsals, at which performers were reminded of the running order of a concert or service just before it began,[43] told to watch out for problems that were likely to occur on the basis of previous experience, and solos were allocated,[44] but with no actual music-making taking place.

Very rarely indeed, helpful written rehearsal (or possibly performance-reminder) notes are found for the singers. Two cases from the papal choir in October 1568 remind the singers to listen out for an unusual entry, and how to solve a puzzle canon: in the Agnus Dei of the Missa *L'homme armé* by Pipelare 'there is a contralto over the bass which duplicates the bass at the tenth', and a motet by Jean Mouton 'called *Benedicamus Domino* has a part over the tenor which waits for two beats then begins a step higher than the tenor' (ex.1).[45]

---

42 Michael Maul, trans Richard Howe, *Bach's famous choir: the Saint Thomas School in Leipzig, 1212-1804* (Woodbridge, 2018), p.45.

43 See, for example, the table of services, actions and places in Frank Ll. Harrison, *Music in Medieval Britain* (London, 2/1963), p.106.

44 Some institutions appear to have had traditions of which sections might be done in reduced scoring, such as solo voices; see O'Regan (1996), pp.146-149.

45 Sherr (1999), IV, pp.91-92; the correct title in the manuscript is *Benedicam Domino*, and the puzzle canon is headed 'Aspetta el tempo et sarai contento' ('wait for the time and you will be happy') without giving the resolution pitch.

Ex.1. Jean Mouton, *Benedicam Domino* (from the manuscript Cappella Sistina 38), bars 17-22.

THE LIMITS OF HISTORICAL RECONSTRUCTION

Finally, a reminder that filling in any gaps in the historical record by borrowing from other times and places, however plausible this may sometimes seem, can take us in the wrong direction entirely. This is demonstrated by an intriguing project where artist John Conway and his colleagues reconstructed modern animals from their bones, in the same way as dinosaurs are presently depicted in paleoart.[46] The results were alarmingly inaccurate, and provide a cautionary tale for early music performers of today, as they try and reconstruct the sounds of history from the musical bones in the archive.

---

[46] John Conway, C. M. Kosemen, Darren Naish and Scott Hartman, *All yesterdays: unique and speculative views of dinosaurs and others prehistoric animals* (n.p., 2012).

CHAPTER 2
SOURCES AND MATERIALS

THE ORIGINS OF THE PUBLIC CONCERT

A little before the English Civil War, Puritan politician's wife Lucy Hutchinson recorded that composer Charles Coleman hosted semi-public rehearsal meetings with his colleagues at Richmond: 'the rest of the king's musicians often met at his house to practice new airs and prepare them for the king; and divers of the gentlemen and ladies that were affected with music, came thither to hear'.[47] The tradition developed further in Commonwealth Oxford and then in Restoration London, and the role of London violinist John Banister senior (1624/5-1679) in this – as noted by Roger North – was significant.[48] Such events spurred the idea of the public concert, which spread all over Europe during the 18th century; one critical change was when certain repertoire (for example, Handel's oratorios) began being performed in the provinces by conductors like William Hayes, leading to the formation of an early canon, and the rise of ensembles to play it.[49]

From the late 1730s individual concerts started being advertised in the British press,[50] as opera had been already, and such announcements of specified repertoire and performers now demanded that the rehearsed music was available

---

47   Walter L. Woodfill, *Musicians in English Society from Elizabeth to Charles I* (Princeton, 1953), p.238; and Andrew Parrott, *The Pursuit of Musicke: Musical Life in Original Writings & Art* (n.p., 2022), p.394.

48   Wilson (1959), pp.302-307; see also Peter Holman, *Four and Twenty Fiddlers: the violin at the English court, 1540-1690* (Oxford, 1995), pp.267-268 and 349-352.

49   Holman (2020), pp.92-96.

50   For numerous examples, see Donald Burrows, Helen Coffey, John Greenacombe and Anthony Hicks (eds), *George Frideric Handel: Collected Documents. Volume 3 1734-1742* (Cambridge, 2019).

and ready for the paying public on the date and time specified, as cancellation brought the risk of both financial and reputational damage – Haydn's cancelled opera *Orfeo* in 1791 (see below) may have cost the promoter as much as £20,000.[51]

HISTORICAL DESCRIPTIONS OF REHEARSALS

There are about a dozen surviving contemporary descriptions relating to early rehearsals, although not all of them appear to reference an actual event. The earliest come from a pair of satirical poems by composer John Redford (d.1547), organist of St Paul's Cathedral. They describe the pains of musical study from a singer's point of view, and the historian's difficulty is knowing how seriously to take these, either as complaints or descriptions. The first is the lament of choristers learning 'prick-song' (polyphony) under their 'cursyd master', presumably Redford himself: 'We shall pray to Cryst to amend hym'. The refrain is 'We lytle poore boyes abyde much woe', and the verses explain how they are beaten for their errors, even though they fear any replacement of their master would be even worse: 'Yet for to hang hym I wene it be not best, / For yf he were gone, we shold have another gest / As yll as he, for nowght they be all the hole nest'. Most interesting is the reference to the conductor's unreasonable standards: 'He sayth we syng starke nowght, when we make a ryght good noyse'.[52]

The second Redford poem is the narrative of a 'singyng man', who 'sondry partes oft have I soong', and is in praise of the Mean voice, the second voice down in a five-part texture and which is 'Above all partes most to excell'. The Mean must 'must make our melodye', and all must 'tyme and tune our songe / Unto the meane, where all partes lene, / All partes ar kept from syngyng wrong'. It also helps keeps alignment when the notes are 'To low, to hye, to lowde, to softe, / … To swyft, to slowe, to sealde, to oft' and when the voices are 'To few, to many at a part'.[53] The components mentioned are the music's range (or possibly performing pitch), the dynamics, the tempo and the size of the choir, showing the type of concerns present at a Tudor choir rehearsal.

---

51 Christopher Hogwood, *Haydn's visits to England* (London, 1980), p.34, and H. C. Robbins Landon (ed), *The Collected Correspondence and London Notebooks of Joseph Haydn* (London, 1959), p.115.
52 James Orchard Halliwell (ed), *The Moral Play of Wit and Science, and Early Poetical Miscellanies* (London, 1848), pp.62-65.
53 Halliwell (1848), pp.80-82. For discussions of voice types and sonorities, see Ellen T. Harris, 'Voices', in Howard Mayer Brown and Stanley Sadie (eds), *Performance Practice: Music after 1600* (Basingstoke, 1989b), pp.97-116 and Parrott (2022), pp.306-309; for modern 'early' vocal traditions, see Joe Bolger, *The disembodied voice of Early music singing*, PhD thesis (King's College London, 2021).

Lully's careful operatic rehearsal practice was reported by Le Cerf de la Viéville in 1705, some two decades after the composer's death: 'However experienced Lully's singers might have been from previous operas, whenever he gave them a new & difficult part he began by going over it with them in his room, before the full rehearsals. This is the way, following his example, that Beaupui played the character of Protée in *Phaëton*, which Lully had taught him gesture by gesture. Finally rehearsals began. He only allowed in the essential people: the author, director of machines and so on. He had the freedom to criticise & instruct his singers; he would come & peer down his nose at them, one hand raised over his eyes to help his short sight, & would not accept anything from them which was of poor quality'.[54]

A fourth source comes from 1738, and is none other than a theatrical (but fairly plausible) description of a Bach rehearsal – or possibly a performance – written by Johann Matthias Gesner, director of the Thomasschule: Bach is 'singing with one voice and playing his own parts, but watching over everything and bringing back to the rhythm and the beat, out of thirty or even forty musicians [*symphoniaci*], the one with a nod, another by tapping with his foot, a third with a warning finger, giving the right note to one from the top of his voice, to another from the bottom, and to a third from the middle of it – all alone, in the midst of the greatest din made by all the participants, and, although he is executing the most difficult parts himself, noticing at once whenever and wherever a mistake occurs, holding everyone together, taking precautions everywhere, and repairing any unsteadiness, full of rhythm in every part of his body – this one man taking in all these harmonies with his keen ear and emitting with his voice alone the tone of all the voices'.[55]

Johann Kusser adopted a similar painstaking approach as Lully (above), according to Mattheson (1739): 'He was tireless in teaching; he would invite to his home all those under his supervision, from greatest to least; he would sing & play to them every single note as he wanted it performed, & he did all this for each person individually, with such gentleness & charm that everyone loved him & became deeply indebted to him for his dedicated teaching. But when guiding turned to playing & to public performance or rehearsal, then nearly everything trembled & quaked before him, not only in the orchestra but on stage'.[56]

---

54   Parrott (2022), p.395.
55   Hans T. David and Arthur Mendel (eds), rev Christoph Wolff, *The New Bach Reader* (New York, 1998), pp.328-329.
56   Parrott (2022), p.395.

A brief description of Handel in action comes from Charles Burney, who played violin and viola in Handel's band when rehearsing at Lower Brook Street (Handel's home) and Carlton House (where the Prince of Wales lived) in about 1745: 'He was a blunt and peremptory disciplinarian on these occasions, but had a humour and wit in delivering instructions, and even in chiding and finding fault, that was peculiar to himself, and extremely diverting to all but those to whom his lash was laid'.[57]

Burney's later description of a rehearsal of Niccolò Jommelli's new opera *Demofoonte* at the Teatro di San Carlo in Naples in November 1770 gives some sense of what might be expected at an initial reading: 'This was the first rehearsal and the instruments were rough and unsteady, not yet being certain as to the exact time or expression, but as far as I am able to judge the composition is perfectly suited to the talents of the [singing] performers, who tho' all good, yet not being of the very first and most exquisite class are more in want of the assistance of instruments to mark the images and enforce the passion which the poetry points out'.[58] In Vienna in three years later Gluck told Burney about his experiences in preparing his *Orfeo ed Euridice* (1762) for performance, but did not give any details: 'Gluck recounted to me the difficulties he had met with in disciplining the band, both of vocal and instrumental performers, at the rehearsals of Orfeo'.[59]

At a Covent Garden rehearsal of Samuel Arnold's opera *The Castle of Andalusia* in 1782, violinist Thomas Carter, who was attending as a listener, breached etiquette by jumping onto the stage, and 'began to direct the band, applauding, grimacing, shutting his ears, and running backwards and forwards along the whole front of the orchestra – it being a rehearsal [with] full band. "That horn too sharp – very well, oboe – that passage again – piano Mr. Tenor –bravo Crescendo!"'.[60] The composer left in disgust. This vivid description of chaos is paralleled by that of François Raguenet (1702) on opera in France nearly a century earlier: 'How many times must we practice an opera before it's fit to be performed; this man begins too soon, that too slow; one sings out of tune, another out of time; in the meantime the composer labors with hand and voice

---

57 Parrott (2022), p.389-390.
58 Charles Burney, ed H. Edmund Poole, *Music, Men and Manners in France and Italy 1770* (London, 1974), pp.185-186.
59 Charles Burney, *The Present State of Music in Germany, The Netherlands and United Provinces* (London, 1773), i, p.286. Gluck also reportedly made his performers repeat passages twenty or thirty times; Parrott (2022), p.396.
60 Holman (2020), pp.284 and 288-289.

and screws his body into a thousand contortions and finds all little enough to his purpose',[61] while the chaos and subsequent breakdown of a Greek Orthodox service in Nenita ('a horrid noise and confusion') was described by painter and traveller Guuillaume-Joseph Grelot (1680, translated and published in English by Playford three years later).[62]

A further description comes from Anton Stadler's 'Musick Plan' of 1800, which includes a brief outline of how a rehearsal should proceed, from a primarily educational perspective. Each student, first having checked the tempo, time signature, key signature of the work and 'tuned his instrument properly' in preparation, needs to 'learn his part correctly by himself and practice it with his teacher', after which it can be combined with those of the other players, repeating the composition 'as long as it takes to attain the tempo and correct intonation', with the student perceiving 'where he has the dominant part or simply the ripieno', determining 'dynamic markings . . . and finally, if the opportunity permits, introduc[ing] him first to simple, well-sounding ornaments, for whose harmony and prompt arrangement one has likewise to give him comprehension and insight'.[63]

Probably the most alarming rehearsal tale is of one involving Haydn that was interrupted, as recounted in London's *Morning Chronicle* in the summer of 1791, where royal permission to use the new Haymarket opera house (the previous King's Theatre having burned down two years earlier) was not forthcoming at the last minute: 'The Theatre now stood, completed, and the orchestra was gathered together to rehearse the opera *Orfeo*. Haydn had distributed the parts, and hardly were forty bars played through, when persons in authority entered and in the name of king and parliament forbade the opera to take place in any fashion whatsoever, not even in the form of a rehearsal. *Orfeo* was, as it were, declared to be contraband, and the worst of it was that the performance of *all* operas in the Theatre was forbidden for the future'.[64] Haydn was sanguine, having already been paid his fee in full; and the opera was not actually premiered until 1951.

---

61 Strunk (1981), iii, pp.124-125.
62 David R. M. Irving, *The Making of European Music in the Long Eighteenth Century* (Oxford, 2024), pp.81-82.
63 Pamela L. Poulin, 'A View of Eighteenth-Century Musical Life and Training: Anton Stadler's "Musick Plan"', *Music & Letters*, lxxi/2 (May 1990), pp.215-224 at 220.
64 Hogwood (1980), pp.34-35. Opera had also been forbidden at the old Haymarket Theatre by the Lord Chamberlain in the winter of 1745, that time due to the Jacobite Rebellion; see Burrows et al. (2020), p.361.

That there were troublesome ensembles that directors had to deal with is certain: Georg Christian Friedrich Schlimbach (1805) complains of overworked town musicians who, after a few days of playing at peasant weddings, 'use Saturday morning for lugging their instruments home, often several miles. Then the cantor has to lead them in the afternoon rehearsal! Their heads are full of haze, their eyes full of sleep, their instruments full of dust. They are irritable and surly. Woe to the cantor if he - which under such conditions is unfortunately all too often necessary - is forced to remind them about tuning their instruments and playing in tune (never mind good execution)'.[65] Composers would always have needed to be aware of the state of their ensemble, and an instance of rehearsal planning (particularly in the composer's absence) can be seen in a letter Mozart wrote to his father from Salzburg in early 1781 about *Idomeneo*: 'I trust that the rehearsal of the three acts which took place today, January 13th, went very well. It will have been a long one, the more so if Act III was rehearsed for the first time. Act III ought to have been rehearsed by itself or at least at the beginning, before the orchestra got tired'.[66] Similarly, in the early 16th century Cardinal Wolsey allowed the smaller communities of Austin Canons to use organs (likely *alternatim*)[67] in order to spare their voices and support their devotions.[68]

One late 18th-century source strikes a curiously modern note in respect of 'why' rather than 'what' a rehearsal is, seeing it as the place 'where the music director makes the players aware of the "hidden intentions of the composer"'.[69] What sort of 'hidden intentions' composers might have had at that particular point in musical history is unclear, and it is not certain whether the writer Johann Samuel Petri (1782) was imagining these in analytical or interpretative terms. While the idea of the conductor as artistic interpreter of another composer's musical ideas seems relatively novel, a reference by Claudio Merulo in 1566 to the way Philippe Verdelot 'wanted [his madrigals] … to be performed' shows these ideas have a longer history than is usually realized.[70]

---

65 Cited in Jerold (2005), p.80.
66 Anderson (1989), p.708.
67 See Harrison (1963), pp.386-388 for this practice.
68 Harrison (1963), pp.215-216.
69 Johann Samuel Petri, *Anleitung zur praktischen Music* (Leipzig, 2/1782), p.181, cited in Bruce Haynes, *The End of Early Music* (New York, 2007), p.101. See also John Spitzer and Neal Zaslaw, *The Birth of the Orchestra: History of an Institution, 1650-1815* (New York and Oxford, 2004), p.386.
70 See Cristina Cassia, 'Authorship in sixteenth-century Italian printed keyboard music', in Andrew Woolley (ed), *Studies on Authorship in Historical Keyboard Music* (Abingdon, 2024), pp.32-56 at 36.

AUDIENCES AT REHEARSALS

Rehearsals could also be announced or reported on in the press, not so much with a view to encouraging public attendance (venue and time are rarely given) but as a trail for the event: for example, rehearsals for Handel's celebratory *Utrecht Te Deum* (1713) were noted in the London press,[71] as were those for his Fireworks Music (1749).[72] However, invited audiences did attend rehearsals, such as the 'many Persons of Quality of both Sexes' at the 1713 event, or the 'splendid Assembly' at the rehearsal of Handel's new Dettingen *Te Deum* at Whitehall Chapel in November 1743.[73] Rehearsal of Boyce's court odes in London 'usually took place at the Turk's Head Tavern in Greek Street or Gerrard Street, "to a crouded audience", according to one newspaper report' in 1763.[74] 'Silver ticket' opera subscribers in mid-18th century London gained admission to a certain number of performances per season (typically 50), plus the ability to attend rehearsals.[75] At the upper end of the scale, 800 people attended the rehearsal of the grand Widows' Concert in London on 31 May 1792, with 2000 at the performance itself.[76]

Such occasions cannot have had the stop-start structure of a professional musical rehearsal, so must have been in the nature of a dress rehearsal, or pre-performance of a nominal premiere or event. For example, Handel's virtuoso Italian oratorio for Easter, *La Resurrezione*, was rehearsed on 1, 2 and 7 April 1708, 'the last being a "dress rehearsal", held in the evening and probably in front of an audience';[77] the performance took place the following day. Public or semi-public rehearsals were sometimes known as 'general' rehearsals, as when Haydn's *Seasons* was performed twice in April 1800 (the second at court, with no less than the Empress Maria Theresa (1772-1807) as soprano soloist – 'much taste and expression, but a weak voice', according to the composer) before the public

---

71 Donald Burrows, Helen Coffey, John Greenacombe and Anthony Hicks (eds), *George Frideric Handel: Collected Documents. Volume 1 1609-1725* (Cambridge, 2013), pp.264 and 269; Holman (2020), p.86. Fiona Smith, *Original Performing Material for Concerted Music in England, c.1660-1800*, PhD thesis (University of Leeds, 2014) lists numerous references to rehearsals, but there is no information other than that they took place.

72 Donald Burrows, Helen Coffey, John Greenacombe and Anthony Hicks (eds), *George Frideric Handel: Collected Documents. Volume 4 1742-1750* (Cambridge, 2020), pp.662 and 677.

73 Burrows et al. (2020), p.131.

74 Smith (2014), p.212.

75 Elizabeth Gibson, 'Italian Opera in London, 1750-1775: management and finances', *Early Music*, xviii/1 (February 1990), pp.47-62 at 51.

76 Robbins Landon (1959), p.254.

77 Burrows et al. (2013), p.124.

performance in the Large Redoutensaal the following month.[78] Such traditions continued for many years, at least on an occasional basis: in a letter of January 1907 Gustav Mahler refers to a noon 'public and final rehearsal' of his third symphony in Berlin.[79]

Other such events were actually fundraisers, as in May 1747, where a collection at the rehearsal for the Festival of the Sons of the Clergy at St Paul's Cathedral, in the presence of the Prince and Princess of Wales and a 'very numerous and splendid Appearance of Gentlemen and Ladies', netted over £480, 'being the largest Sum ever made on the same Occasion'. This was taken further in Dublin that December, in a rehearsal that was ticketed: a benefit for Mercer's Hospital with music by Handel allowed those who had bought half-Guinea tickets to attend the 'Grand Performance' three days later, to be admitted, with 'a Part of the Tickets will be torn off' at the rehearsal, and the remainder retained for the concert.[80] The purpose may have been to allow patrons to hear some rarely-performed music twice. This pseudo-public process was apparently not known to Haydn (perhaps it was an English practice), as in a letter from March 1791 he describes the impresario Signor Gallini in London as having 'had the clever idea of arranging, one evening a few days ago, a dress rehearsal in such a manner as if it were the real opening night; he distributed four thousand tickets, and more than five thousand came. The opera, entitled Pyhro, by Paisiello, was very successful'.[81]

It is likely that musicians and eminent visitors would have been able to arrange to attend such events, as when Leopold Mozart went to a Milan opera rehearsal in June 1770. At other times, invited attendance was much more exclusive: in December 1780 Mozart wrote to his father from Munich of *Idomeneo* that the 'rehearsal went off extremely well. There were only six violins in all, but we had the requisite wind-instruments. No listeners were admitted except Count Seeau's sister and young Count Sensheim'.[82] For the rehearsals of Mozart's *Così fan tutte* in 1790 the composer invited just two friends, Haydn and the Viennese banker Michael Puchberg.[83]

---

78 Robbins Landon (1959), p.180.
79 Alma Mahler, trans Basil Creighton, *Gustav Mahler: Memories and Letters* (London, 1946), p.201.
80 Burrows et al. (2020), pp. 483 and 527-529.
81 Robbins Landon (1959), p.115.
82 Anderson (1989), pp.141 and 677.
83 Robbins Landon (1959), p.125.

MATERIALS FOR REHEARSAL AND PERFORMANCE

The physical medium of music changed greatly from the Middle Ages to the early Romantic period, especially after the invention of printing. The question of what was suitable also changed: 'late-medieval notation, with respect to both pitch and rhythm, was conceptually unsuited for use in score … composers neither had nor needed the visual control of simultaneities that modern scores give us',[84] and the growth of musical literacy (for example, at the Tudor court), changed practice from forms of vocal improvisation mainly to the reading of composed music.[85]

Manuscript copyists are subject to the quality of their exemplars, and the limitations of their own accuracy, skill and understanding; in general, errors are more likely to be introduced than corrected.[86] How copies were used is not always now understood, especially with regard to part-sharing: while two or three singers might be able to read from the same voice part in a Bach cantata,[87] it seems highly unlikely that twelve people could have read one piece in that number of parts from the tablebook format (parts facing outwards, to be read by performers gathered around it lying on a table) of British Library 31390.[88] Choirbooks, which could be very large indeed in order to be seen by all the members of an ensemble of up to 30 strong when placed on a lectern,[89] present their own particular difficulties and limitations for performers in terms of rehearsal techniques.[90] For all early formats, effective display and lighting is a concern.

---

84 Margaret Bent, '*Resfacta* and *Cantare Super Librum*', *Journal of the American Musicological Society*, xxxvi (1983), pp.371-391 at 376-777.

85 David Price, *Patrons and musicians of the English Renaissance* (Cambridge, 1981), p.2.

86 Formal checking procedures must usually have depended on the diligence of individual copyists, although some institutions may have had specific procedures, like those of the medieval English Chancery; see Michael T. Clanchy, *From Memory to Written Record: England 1066-1307* (Oxford, 2/1993), pp.130-131. See also Parrott (2022), pp.104-105.

87 See, for example, the practices outlined in Andrew Parrott, *The essential Bach choir* (Woodbridge, 2000), and the discussion in Andrew Parrott, *Composers' Intentions? Lost Traditions of Musical Performance* (Woodbridge, 2015), pp.317-320.

88 John Milsom, 'Sacred songs in the chamber', in Morehen (1995), pp.161-179 at 171.

89 There may also have been an alternative 'shelf' format, if that is the implication of the 'board in the nave from which the antiphon was sung' at New College, Oxford; Harrison (1963), p.159.

90 See Francis Knights and Pablo Padilla, 'Issues in the Historical Performance from Renaissance Choirbooks', *National Early Music Association Newsletter*, viii/2 (Autumn 2024), pp.15-66.

Producing manuscript music is very labour intensive, so it normally contains the content sufficient for a performer, but no more.[91] The apparent difficulty of using some early sources has led a number of modern scholars to suggest that there were alternative and different versions (all now lost) for actual use, an improbable concept at scale. Hugh Benham wonders whether some surviving choirbooks 'were library copies rather than "performing editions"; and indeed the few signs of actual use would seem to re-inforce this';[92] while Roger Bray notes 'Nearly all the manuscripts which survive today must have been library- or presentation-copies … Performing manuscripts must have been destroyed at some stage by religious zealots'.[93] These suggestions say more about our lack of understanding of historical rehearsal processes than they do about any purported missing sources.

The survival of sources to the present might have depended on their value (a highly decorated parchment choirbook would have been regarded as worth keeping as an artistic object even when the music in it was outmoded), on the type of binding, or the way in which it was stored. Single sheet copies did exist from the Middle Ages into the 18th century, but were exceedingly fragile (illus.1). Some of these later copies were 'single-occasion' loose parts, for particular events rather than repeated use. Scrolls and rolls[94] might be more robust in terms of eventual preservation, but binding sewn pages in leather-covered boards is far safer, as the survival numbers attest.

---

91 For example, manuscripts including *alternatim* polyphony usually omit the chant portions, or chant incipits in masses.

92 Hugh Benham, *Latin Church Music in England c.1460-1575* (London, 1977), p.22. For a unique bass voice-part fragment on large-format parchment which has been proposed as a 'rehearsal' copy from a choirbook, see Roger Bowers, 'University Library, MS Buxton 96', in Iain Fenlon (ed), *Cambridge Music Manuscripts 900-1700* (Cambridge, 1982), pp.114-117. Note that some autograph choirbooks have survived on the continent, suggesting very close links between composition, notational format and performance; see Jessie Ann Owens, *Composers at Work: the craft of musical composition* (New York, 1997), p.111.

93 Roger Bray, 'The Interpretation of Musica Ficta in English Music c.1490-c.1580', *Proceedings of the Royal Musical Association*, cxlvii (1970-1971), pp.29-45 at 33.

94 For an early 15th century example see Roger Bowers, 'Trinity College, MS o. 3. 58', in Fenlon (1982), pp.88-90, and for a late parchment example from 1580, see Iain Fenlon, 'King's College, MS Rowe 1', in Fenlon (1982), pp.137-139.

CHAPTER 2: SOURCES AND MATERIALS

Illus. 1. William Hogarth (1697–1764), 'The chorus' (1732), a satirical engraving showing the singers for the oratorio Judith by William Defesch (c.1680-1758)

CHOIRBOOKS AND PARTBOOKS

Choirbook format[95] was standard in a number of places in the early 16th century:[96] 'in 1524 all the polyphonic music at Magdalen College, Oxford was contained in choirbooks, nine of which had been bought between 1518 and 1524'.[97] King's College, Cambridge – the sister institution to Eton – had in 1529 '5 great bokys wyth rede lether conteynynge the most solemne anthems off v partes' which sound very similar to the Eton Choirbook ('a grete ledger of pricke song ii folio'), but it also had numerous sets of partbooks (both paper and parchment) in sets of three to six.[98] In other words, there was only one book per voice part to share, so (as with a choirbook) the 16 choristers would all have had to crowd round one volume, probably on a small lectern (by comparison, the choirbook now at Caius College, Cambridge, is an enormous 72 x 49 cm).[99] No pre-Reformation Cambridge choir sources have survived, but as partbooks tend to be relatively small (two manuscripts of c.1590 from the Petre collection now in the Essex Record Office are rather larger than usual, but are still only about A4 oblong)[100] how they can have been used collectively in rehearsal and performance is unclear. Memorization at some level (see below) seems a likely part of the solution.

Choirbooks were very valuable, but how they were stored when not in use is unknown – at Madgalen College, Oxford, six printed hymnals were 'chained in the choir',[101] for example, which is one way of securing material from loss, if not damage. Despite the practical limitations of choirbooks, thes English sources contain some of the most complex music of the period, from the esoteric *Musica Speculativa* tradition, such as Lloyd's *O quam suavis*[102] and Fayrfax's *O quam glorifica* (his DMus exercise) and *Albanus* masses.[103]

---

95 Choirbooks as performing sources are discussed in detail in Knights and Padilla (2024).
96 For a rare early example of c.1440, see Roger Bowers, 'University Library, Pembroke College MS 314', in Fenlon (1982), pp.103-106.
97 Benham (1977), p.24, Harrison (1963), p.166; see p.431 for the 1522 inventory.
98 Harrison (1963), pp.162, 432-433.
99 Geoffrey Chew, 'The Provenance and Date of the Caius and Lambeth Choir-Books', *Music & Letters*, li/2 (April 1970), pp.107-117.
100 Francis Knights, 'Observations on two 16th century music manuscripts belonging to Sir John Petre', *The Consort*, lxxv (Summer 2019), pp.22-41.
101 Harrison (1963), p.167.
102 The Cambridge manuscript names no composer but includes a motto *Hoc fecit matres maris* ('Matres maris made this'), possibly a way of anonymizing a DMus submission; in modern times it has been attributed to Chapel Royal Lay Clerk John Lloyd (or Flude) (c.1475-1523); see Roger Bowers, 'University Library MS Nn. vi. 46', in Fenlon (1982), pp.118-122.
103 Bray (1995), pp.48-73. In fact, some of the music is unperformable as presented in the surviving sources, and needs an 'edition' to be usable, as happened with the contemporary copy made of *O quam glorifica*.

Paper partbooks (individual musical parts, usually gathering groups of pieces by composer or genre) were the most common format, and were relatively cheap to make, as well as being easy to manage in performance and convenient to store. Unlike choirbooks, their downside is that individual volumes from a set could be damaged or lost, rendering the whole set unusable. This likely happened quite often (and many surviving 16th and 17th century sets are now incomplete) and was recognized as a danger: at Trinity College, Cambridge in 1664, when George Loosemore (organist 1660-82) found that a manuscript set of 'Grace-songs which wee use upon our Solemne Feast-daies' by his predecessor Robert Ramsey (organist 1628-42) was incomplete he composed new settings of the same texts, noting in a handwritten dedication that 'by the unhappie losse of one book, or part, [Ramsey's] acurate parries, and labours, is lost and become uselesse'.[104]

One of the principal practical difficulties in working with separate parts is that while the ear can confirm that a player or singer *is* or *is not* aligned with the harmony and rhythm of the other parts, listening to find out where one *should be* in the latter case is very difficult without seeing the music of the other performers (and assuming *they* are all in the right place).[105] Much rehearsal time can be spent 'learning' the sound of the whole work in order to understand the harmonic and other context of a performer's own part, and this is especially important where there is no score to consult.[106]

Renaissance composition itself usually occurred via temporary physical formats,[107] and very few early scores have survived. A 1570 letter of Palestrina to the Duke of Mantua noted that he had scored up a motet in order to 'examine it more closely' (*per meglio contemplarlo*);[108] but the idea of creating a score

---

104 See Francis Knights, 'The historic chapel music manuscripts at Trinity', *Trinity College Annual Report* (2007), pp.55-59 at 56.

105 For one experiment working with facsimile material, see Floris Schuiling, '(Re-)Assembling Notations in the Performance of Early Music', *Contemporary Music Review*, xxxix/5 (2020), pp.580-601.

106 Technology is now making it possible for individuals all to have just such an overview. For example, the Britten Sinfonia now perform from iPads, meaning everyone can see the score, there are no physical page turns and full overhead lighting is not needed; the principal gain is that less rehearsal time is needed. See Jessica Duchen, 'Who needs a conductor?', *Sunday Times*, Culture magazine (16 July 2023).

107 The most thorough explanation of the process can be found in Owens (1997), ch.5; see also Milsom (2008) and Knights and Padilla (2024).

108 Cited in Edward E. Lowinsky, 'On the Use of Scores by Sixteenth-Century Musicians', *Journal of the American Musicological Society*, i/1 (Spring 1948), pp.17-23 at 17. See also Owens (1997), p.292 and Anne Smith, *The Performance of 16th-Century Music* (Oxford, 2011), ch.9.

from parts in order to rehearse or help understand it for performance seems to be nowhere else mentioned in the period,[109] although this must have been an essential part of compositional study for students. A 1555 competition between Andrea Festa and Benedetto Spinone to see who had composed a better additional voice to two five-voice madrigals by Willaert and de Rore (and judged by Willaert himself, together with singers from St Mark's, Venice) took place through performance audition rather than scoring up of the supplied parts, even though the composing itself must have occurred through such scoring up.[110]

MUSICAL SOURCES AND MISTAKES

Inaccurate manuscripts in circulation were regarded both as unfair on the reputation of a composer, and a justification for publication: Byrd notes that previous copies of motets in his *Cantiones Sacrae* I (1589), 'owing to the carelessness of scribes in making copies, had suffered a certain amount of error',[111] while Handel's preface to his Eight Suites for keyboard (1720) complains that 'Surrepticious and incorrect copies of them had got abroad'.[112] Whether there really were substantial numbers of inaccurate manuscript copies circulating is sometimes doubtful, but such claims certainly helped validate the composer-authenticated print version.

The level of care that could be taken over accuracy is shown in two letters from composer Benedetto Pallavicino, who had agreed to proofread a set of (now-lost) Magnificats published by Angelo Gardane in Venice in 1586: 'I will go over the manuscript and printed copies minutely, and will not fail to correct all the important errors'.[113] With some manuscripts, such as *Will Forster's Virginal Book* (London, 1624), the copyist went over his work carefully and made a very large number of corrections from the exemplars.[114] Printed copies were not always preferred to manuscript: Rosenmüller in 1682 noted shortcomings such as the individually-stemmed semiquavers and demisemiquavers used in moveable type.[115]

---

109 It is possible that 16th and 17th century Anglican organbooks may have had rehearsal as a partial purpose, due to their short-score format.
110 Owens (1997), p.55.
111 Alan Brown (ed), *Byrd: Cantiones Sacrae I (1589)*, Byrd Edition 2 (London, 1988), p.xxi.
112 Burrows et al. (2013), p.519.
113 Sherr (1999), XVII, p.124.
114 Jon Baxendale and Francis Knights (eds), *Will Forster's Virginal Book* (Tynset, 2023).
115 Parrott (2022), p.476.

Where source errors were located during rehearsal, it is not known what was done to correct or understand these; corrections to manuscript and print copies that look as though they are performer additions seem rather rare, and that may be because writing materials (whether pencil,[116] or pen and ink)[117] were not available in the rehearsal space, especially if that was also the performance venue, for example a cathedral. Nor it is certain who would have been responsible or have had the authority for annotating material in this way, if it was even permitted. Some errors (for example, inaccurate numbers of bars' rest in a long sectional votive antiphon,[118] as can be found in the Eton Choirbook) would have made the work unusable – at least without the musicians being able to discover the exact nature of the error, and remember the correction – but source indexes rarely contain any annotations which might indicate to future users that there were such 'unperformable' works in a collection. Modern editors of course make all such corrections in their published scores, thus erasing the traces what must have been a very real problem for the musicians of the past.

In respect of errors in Bach's hurriedly-copied cantata sources (for example, Cantata 111, 'Der Herr ist mein getreuer Hirt' of 1731) (illus.2),[119] Alfred Dürr pondered whether, with respect to the parts, 'In view of the number of extant mistakes, we must, in fact, raise the question of whether there were any rehearsals at all'.[120] Martin Geck and Alfred Mann suggested that Johann Abraham Birnbaum's published 1738 defence[121] (possibly partly drafted by Bach) against the criticisms by Johann Adolph Scheibe of the excessive difficulty of Bach's vocal compositions is related to the composer's own experience of inadequate performances ('lack of an able presentation').[122] While Bach manuscript sources do indeed indicate that

---

116 Pencils were likely rather rare: the earliest mass-produced graphite pencils came from Nuremberg as late as 1662.

117 See Owens (1997), pp.135-136 for writing materials.

118 See Harrison (1963), pp.81-88 and 295-344 for the votive antiphon tradition. Examples of a composer's own rest-counting errors by Cipriano de Rore are noted by Owens (1997), p.249.

119 For Bach's copying process, see Robert L. Marshall, *The Compositional Process of J. S. Bach*, 2 vols. (Princeton, 1972).

120 Alfred Dürr, 'Performance Practice of Bach's Cantatas', *American Choral Review*, xxix/3-4 (Summer and Fall 1987), pp.25-34 at 29; see also Alfred Dürr and Traute M. Marshall, 'De vita cum imperfectis', *Bach*, lii/2 (2021), pp.212-225. Martin Geck and Alfred Mann, 'Bach's art of church music and his Leipzig performance forces: contradictions in the system', *Early Music*, xxi/4 (November 2003), pp.558-571, worry about the practical utility of Bach's source materials, but without coming to any firm conclusions.

121 David and Mendel (1998), pp.338-348.

122 Geck and Mann (2003), p.569. See also Beverly Jerold, 'Bach's Lament about Leipzig's Professional Instrumentalists', *Bach*, xxxvi/1 (2005), pp.67-96. Don L. Smithers, in "The Original Circumstances in the Performance of Bach's Leipzig Church Cantatas, "Wegen Seiner Sonn- und Festtägigen Amts-Verrichtungen"', *Bach*, xxvi/1-2 (Spring-Summer 1995/ Fall-Winter 1995), pp.28-47 at 44, makes a distinction between correctable minor details (including actual wrong notes) and missing notes, rests or even bars.

notated 'corrections were rarely or never made in rehearsal',[123] Dürr is in error supposing that necessary emendations could not have been mentally marked for the performance, rather than actually written in.

Finally, a musician would have to know or judge whether something unusual in the performing material was actually a mistake or not (consider a 17th-century performer working with what Burney called 'Dr Blow's crudities'):[124] are such things to be judged by a performer as an intentional composer decision, a composer error, a miscopying,[125] or a copyist's error?

ARCHIVES AND STORAGE

Storage space for valuable musical manuscripts was likely to have been a concern. The choirbook lectern in Gaffurius' 1512 engraving (illus.3) appears to have a (lockable?) cupboard below, paralleled in the St Omer accounts for 1494/5, which refer to payment for making 'an oak cupboard bearing a lectern, placed at the end of the choir on the side of monseigneur the provost, [in which] to place the books of discant that are in the choir'.[126] Care and storage (and cataloguing) of music is also mentioned in the draft instructions for Haydn (1765), fairly newly arrived at Esterházy, from Prince Nicolaus: he was to 'deliver the necessary music for each service to the schoolmaster Joseph Diezl, put it in their proper order after the service, and have it returned to, and stored in, the cupboard wherein it belongs, so that nothing will be taken away or miscatalogued'.[127] It is not clear from this whether the music was provided in advance for the performers; a further reference to Diezl (a tenor in the choir, and responsible for it) having to appear 'in the choir-loft a quarter of an hour before the service begins' might suggest not. However, in respect of Boyce's court ode rehearsals in London at about the same time, Fiona Smith suggests that performer names on the wrappers of sets of parts indicate they could have received their music for distribution to their colleagues in advance.[128] This

---

123 Dürr (1987), p.28.
124 Burney (1935), ii, p.353.
125 See, for example, Robert Carver's motet *O bone Jesu* a19, where he was working at the limits of his technical ability in that many voices; Harrison (1963), p.344. For a story about a singer having difficulty reading a composer's own manuscript corrections, see Owens (1997), p.163.
126 Andrew Kirkman, *Music and Musicians at the Collegiate Church of St-Omer: Crucible of Song, 1350-1550* (Cambridge, 2020), p.133.
127 Robbins Landon (1959), p.5.
128 Smith (2014), p.260.

Illus. 2. J. S. Bach, *Der Herr ist mein getreuer Hirt*, BWV111 (1731), Duetto, autograph score (excerpt). The manuscript becomes increasingly untidy as Bach rushed to finish copying (Bach Digital)

additional key level of pre-rehearsal preparation is almost entirely absent from the earlier historical record (compare Stadler, above); however, Handel (1744) is recorded as wanting to get the vocal parts (at least) out early, to 'give them their parts in time to be perfect in every one of them'.[129]

SOURCE COLLECTIONS AND PERFORMING REPERTOIRE

With rare exceptions, for the earlier periods it is not possible to link musical sources with the working repertoire chosen from them; there are few markings or corrections that indicate actual use, and no music lists to correlate. Some institutions had far more music copied than they would have been able to use, or in some cases been capable of singing, as in the collection of some 300 works compiled from the 1630s for the small new chapel choir at Peterhouse, Cambridge.[130] The majority of source collections do not therefore represent a precise performing repertoire, and must be considered with care when considering issues of rehearsal or performance practice.[131]

REHEARSAL LETTERS AND BAR NUMBERS

Navigating within a movement or section in rehearsal is both difficult and slow without clear points of reference, yet it seems that historical performers either had no choice but to repeat sections from the beginning each time there was a problem, or else had some other methods of negotiating the content, in the absence of a score for consultation. In the latter case, there are a number of options for finding one's way around shorter works, none of which seems ideal: singers who knew a text well (for example, mass or antiphon sections) might have been able to pick up the music from the first appearance of a new word phrase; performers without barlines in their partbooks could have counted forward from the start or back from the end in breves, for some distance; repeat or refrain sections (for example, recapitulations or da capos) could have been located; and distinctive passages (significant changes of key or dynamics, or the beginning of imitative passages) could have been referenced.[132] This would

---

129 Parrott (2022), p.395.
130 Anselm Hughes, *Catalogue of the Musical Manuscripts at Peterhouse Cambridge* (Cambridge, 1953); Francis Knights, 'Thomas Wilson, *Organista Petrensis*', *Early Music Performer*, 1 (April 2022), pp.16-29.
131 See Morehen (1995), p.212.
132 Location by text or counting breves is mentioned in one theory source (see Bonnie J. Blackburn, Edward E. Lowinsky and Clement Miller (eds), *A Correspondence of Renaissance Musicians* (Oxford, 1991), pp.119-120), and may have been quite common; Owens (1997), p.54.

Illus. 3. Franchinus Gaffurius, Practica musicae (Venice, 1512); this frontispiece engraving appears in the Venice edition but not the 1496 Milan original.

have become much more difficult where a performer's part (for example, the horns) had long passages of rests intersecting with any such start point. In Pliny the Elder's *Natural History* (77 AD), being able to locate something in a longer document is the very definition of an index: 'They will not need to read right through ... but only look for the particular point that each of them wants, and will know where to find it'.[133] It is curious that musicians did not think in the same practical terms for millennia.

The origins of actual rehearsal letters in orchestral parts comes surprisingly late, and one wonders how performers had previously managed to find their way around long movements in rehearsal without such cues – the new system enabled quicker access in substantial Romantic symphonic and other movements. The first use of cue letters in music is found in Enriquez de Valderrábano's *Libro de musica de vihuela* (1547), which link sections of the vocal part at the top of the page with the vihuela accompaniment at the bottom.[134] In 1825 Thomas Busby had suggested numbering every twenty bars of scores and parts to avoid 'beginning the whole movement a second time',[135] but this concept did not become a reality until the publication of Beethoven's *Grosse Fuge*, Op.133 of 1827 (illus.4), where rehearsal letters were 'added by Beethoven's friend Karl Holz at the request of the composer and his publisher Mathias Artaria ... Rehearsal letters can be found in orchestral scores by Mendelssohn and Spohr from the early 1830s, but none are known from the 1820s in scores by these or other composers'.[136] Actual bar numbers in chamber or orchestral parts seem to be a 20th-century practice.[137] All such rehearsal aids are now seen as essential: Thomas Lloyd writes that 'There is nothing more important for an efficient rehearsal than making sure the parts, choral scores, and full score have uniform rehearsal numbers'.[138]

---

133 Dennis Duncan, *Index, A History of the* (London, 2021), pp.5-6.
134 Illustrated in Owens (1997), p.53. Cue letters in Vivaldi's 'Four Seasons' (Op.8/1-4, 1725) are actually references to the lines of the poems associated with the music.
135 Thomas Busby, *Concert-room and Orchestra Anecdotes* (London, 1825), vol.ii, p.134.
136 Barry Cooper, 'Rehearsal Letters, Rhythmic Modes and Structural Issues in Beethoven's Grosse Fuge', *Nineteenth-Century Music Review*, xiv/2 (August 2017), pp.177-193.
137 Bach and some other composers such as Zelenka certainly counted bars for structural or copying reasons, but did not use them as a way of negotiating the rehearsal content; see Ruth Tatlow, *Bach's numbers: compositional proportion and significance* (Cambridge, 2016).
138 Thomas Lloyd, 'When the Orchestra Arrives', *The Choral Journal*, xl/5 (December 1999), pp.35-46 at 39. This article provides a very useful practical guide to the realities of modern rehearsal.

Illus. 4. Ludwig van Beethoven, Grosse Fuge, Op.133, First edition (Vienna, 1827), p.11 showing letter 'C'.

REHEARSAL FOR AUDITIONS AND PROOF-READING

One further purpose for rehearsal was interim feedback for a composer: a test-reading of the music. One characteristic Josquin anecdote describes the process: 'Whenever he had composed a new song, he gave it to the singers to be sung, and meanwhile he walked around, listening attentively whether the concordant sound came together well. If he was dissatisfied, he stepped in: "Be silent," he said, "I will change it!"'.[139] In opera, different singers, staging and circumstances could lead to very different versions of the same work, as with Monteverdi's *L'Incoronazione de Poppea*. Handel, a frequent reviser of large-scale works in particular, made numerous revisions in his oratorios and operas. For the former, these tended to arise after performances, or were dependent on the availability of particular soloists each time (consider the different versions of *Messiah*), but for operas these are more likely to have occurred during the longer rehearsal process – where Handel was also subject to the whims and demands of his diva soloists: arias deleted, replaced or inserted, and so on. The working scores of works such as *Tamerlano* (1724), *Poro* (1731) and *Belshazzar* (1744), for example, contain some cuts that may have been a response to experience in bringing the work to stage, such as the length of incidental music required to cover a scene change, or the appropriate dramatic purpose of a *da capo*.[140]

A different type of 'audition' process is described in a letter Mozart wrote to his father from Paris in September 1778 about a potential new opera commission, for which he wanted a guaranteed performance, because 'What happens in Paris, as you probably know, is this :– When the opera is finished, it is rehearsed and if those stupid Frenchmen do not like it, it is not performed – and the composer has had all that trouble for nothing'.[141]

---

139 Cited in Wegman (1999), p.330.
140 See J. Merrill Knapp, 'Handel's *Tamerlano*: The Creation of an Opera', *The Musical Quarterly*, lvi/3 (July 1970), pp.405-430, Graham Cummings, 'Handel's Compositional Methods in His London Operas of the 1730s, and the Unusual Case of "Poro, Rè dell'Indie" (1731)', *Music & Letters*, lxxix/3 (August 1998), pp.346-367 and David Ross Hurley, 'Handel's Recomposed Return Arias and Romantic Attraction in Alexander Balus', *Journal of the American Musicological Society*, lxix/3 (Fall 2016), pp.651-698. Comparable and timed information for cuts is found for Galuppi's *La clemenza di Tito* in Turin; Margaret R. Butler, 'Time management at Turin's Teatro Regio: Galuppi's *La clemenza di Tito* and its alterations, 1759', *Early Music*, xl/2 (2012), pp.279-289.
141 Anderson (1989), p.613.

Another and more unusual purpose of a rehearsal is mentioned in a letter from Leopold Mozart in Milan in December 1770, where Wolfgang's new opera *Mitridate, re di Ponto* had its 'first rehearsal with instruments … held in order to discover whether the score had been copied correctly'.[142] This presupposes that the ensemble could sight-read the music more accurately than the copyist could copy it, so it may instead refer to a test as to whether all the parts were complete and the music was in the right order; either way, this seems a very inefficient way of proceeding. It also reinforces Leopold's general worries about the accuracy of professional copyists, as shown in a letter to his son from Salzburg seven years later: 'It is far too laborious to have your compositions copied from the score, and a thousand mistakes will creep in unless the copyist works the whole time under your supervision'.[143]

Finally, there is also the possibility that some works were created for the private enjoyment of musicians in rehearsal, rather than for actual performance: Elizabeth Eva Leach imagines of the ingenious double-texted song *Je me merveil/J'ay pluseurs fois* by the late 14th-century composer Jacob de Senleches, featuring two singers complaining about the state of contemporary music-making: 'So are we left thinking that this song, for all its cleverness, did its greatest cultural work in the rehearsal room? Did it serve only the social interaction of its singers? Is it just some kind of singers' in-joke?'.[144] And in the 15th century, Tinctoris records having silently read ('inspected', 'examined') vocal polyphony on his own, for enjoyment and education.[145]

---

142 Anderson (1989), p.174.

143 Anderson (1989), p.319.

144 Elizabeth Eva Leach, 'Nature's forge and mechanical production: Writing, reading and performing song', in Mary Carruthers (ed), *Rhetoric Beyond Words: Delight and Persuasion in the Arts of the Middle Ages* (Cambridge, 2013), pp.72-95 at 86.

145 Rob C. Wegman, 'Johannes Tinctoris and the "New Art"', *Music & Letters*, lxxxiv/2 (May 2003), pp.171-188 at 174.

CHAPTER 3
INSTITUTIONS AND EMPLOYMENT

ENSEMBLE SIZES

Documents such as account books, payment lists, registers and statutes sometimes indicate the nominal sizes of musical ensembles, which could range from just four singers (as at one small 16th-century Oxford college),[146] to an opera orchestra of 60 or more. In the earlier periods, the meaning of lists of singers need to be understood with great care; they may include (or omit) minor canons who could have been contributing to the music;[147] they may name both choristers and adult singers who were no longer active, or absent or ill or even dead (for example, three choristers at King's College, Cambridge died in 1532 alone);[148] and they may not include additional voluntary performers such as instrumentalists[149] or indicate whether a person on the books for one role was actually undertaking a different one (a Lay Clerk playing the organ, for example). The full lists therefore indicate a theoretical maximum number of performers, which likely often fell short - there

---

146 See Francis Knights, 'The Choral Foundation of Corpus Christi College, Oxford', *The Organ*, lxx/275 (Winter 1991), pp.10-14.
147 James Saunders, *English Cathedral Choirs and Choirmen, 1558 to the Civil War: An Occupational Study*, PhD thesis (University of Cambridge, 1997), p.66.
148 Roger Bowers, 'Chapel and Choir, Liturgy and Music, 1444-1644', in Jean Michel Massing and Nicolette Zeeman (eds), *King's College Chapel 1515-2015: Art, Music and Religion in Cambridge* (London, 2014), pp.259-286 at 266.
149 Some London churches booked and paid additional singers for major feasts; Harrison (1963), pp.198-199.

is even an archival reference to three men singing Palestrina's four-part motet *Nos autem*.[150] The impact of this on rehearsal and performance effectiveness would have depended on the quality of those absent relative to the quality of those present, but it is safer to assume lower numbers than high. One partial exception is the lists of performers actually present at an event, such as for livery payments for royal funerals,[151] though here it is not certain what role some of the older and quasi-retired musicians might actually have undertaken.

The idea of instrumentalists 'within' a choir, or singers able to do double duty, who might be invisible in the records, may require further investigation. An engraving in Tylman Susato's *Liber primus missarum quinque vocum* (Antwerp, 1546) shows a solitary sackbut accompanying a choir,[152] and the tradition of a bass instrument combined with voices is also found in Spain, with the *bajón* (dulcian). This seems an excellent solution to the problem of providing a fixed pitch and a firm bass line, and was also found elsewhere. It may have been more widespread than the documentation and iconography at first suggests: one of the Gonzaga chapel choir 'basses' in 1586 was actually a trombonist;[153] a bass singer at the German College in Rome in 1589 used to send a trombonist as a deputy;[154] and the 17th-century Chapelle-Musique in Paris employed 'basses able to play the serpent'.[155] However, for Tudor England John Stevens argued that there were musical status issues between vocalists and instrumentalists which would have prevented such practice there: 'the very idea of a singing-man playing, say, a shawm is ludicrous ... the instrumentalist was of considerably lower rank'.[156]

Numerous cathedral and collegiate choir personnel or office lists survive for the Tudor and Stuart period, showing sizes varying between six choristers and a dozen or so adult singers to 16 choristers and at least as many adults (the number of active musicians is often unclear, with some priests possibly being part of

---

150 Graham Dixon, 'The performance of Palestrina: Some questions, but fewer answers', *Early Music*, xxii/4 (November 1994), pp.666–676 at 669.

151 See the lists in Andrew Ashbee, *Records of English Court Music*, 9 vols. (Snodland/Aldershot, 1986-96).

152 Reproduced in Brown and Sadie (1989a), p.194.

153 A letter notes 'there were two basses. One is a trombone'; Seishiro Niwa, '"Madama" Margaret of Parma's patronage of music', *Early Music*, xxxiii/1 (February 2005), pp.25–38 at 33.

154 Dixon (1994), p.670; O'Regan (1996), p.150.

155 Marcelle Benoit, 'Paris, 1661-87: the Age of Lully', in Curtis Price (ed), *The Early Baroque Era* (Basingstoke, 1993), pp.239-269 at 247; the serpent was sometimes used to double plainchant in 17th and 18th century France.

156 John Stevens, *Music and Poetry in the Early Tudor Court* (Cambridge, 2/1979), pp.312 and 318.

the choirs, as noted above).[157] However, all that can be inferred from this is that the numbers were intended to be sufficient to carry out their musical duties. Sometimes small ensembles operated a rota system to cover their numerous services: the pre-Reformation lists of voices and organists for Leconfield Castle choir indicate a maximum of 17 singers: 6 boys, and ATB disposed 4/4/3 (several lists are given, but the numbers do not agree exactly). The daily Lady Mass was sung by four men, and the full choir appears to have been needed daily for Matins, High Mass, Evensong and Compline.[158]

Large ensembles were known, although it is not certain how, when or even if their full forces were heard in combination: Lassus in Munich had at his disposal some 90 musicians, including 16 boys, five or six castrati, 13 altos, 15 tenors, 12 basses and 30 instrumentalists, while Christian IV in Denmark in c.1590 had at least 61, including 23 singers and 38 instrumentalists (remarkably, 23 of whom were trumpeters).[159] From the late 17th century onwards, special events sometimes fielded more than a hundred performers – Quantz (who played in it) reports that the 1723 premiere of Fux's coronation opera *Costanza e Fortezza* in Prague fielded a cast of 100 and an orchestra of 200, so many that *Kapellmeister* Antonio Caldara 'had to beat time'.[160]

STIPENDS

Payment for professional performers was very variable over the period, but was often subject to a decline in real value over time – inflation was a major problem in Tudor England, for example – and the (insufficient) remuneration often provided almost certainly had an impact on the performers' attitude to their work, both professionally and musically: '*Pitifull-poor-Wages*' led to '*Dead-heartedness, or Zeal-benumb'd-Frozen Affections*', according to Thomas Mace.[161] In the worst case, a 16th or 17th-century Lay Clerk's salary in an Eng-

---

157 Peter Le Huray, *Music and the Reformation in England, 1549-1660* (London, 1967), pp.14-17 summarizes what is known, from a variety of documentary sources; see also Harrison (1963), section IV.
158 Harrison (1963), p.173, Peter Giles, *The History and Technique of the Counter-Tenor* (Aldershot, 1994), pp.28-29 and Roger Bowers, 'To chorus from quartet: the performing resource for English Church Polyphony, c. 1390-1559', in Morehen (1995), pp.1-47 at 35-37.
159 K. Dawn Grapes, *Dowland* (Oxford, 2024), p.111
160 Holman (2020), p.33.
161 Thomas Mace, *Musick's Monument, or a Remembrancer of the best Practical Musick ...* (London, 1676), p.25.

lish cathedral might be at the lower end of a labourer's wages,[162] so all the documented complaints about poor behaviour and absenteeism should be read in this light. Because of financial hardship, some musicians took on extra work, which could be musical, administrative or even from an 'inferior trade' (Mace mentions barbers, shoemakers and tailors).[163]

PRACTICE SCHEDULES

Some sources give reasonable detail in respect of the musical responsibilities of the Director of Music: in 1477 the Chapter Acts of Lincoln Cathedral noted that William Horwood was to instruct the choristers 'in the science of singing', which is listed as 'playnsonge, pryksonge, faburdon, Diskant, and cownter as well as in playing on the organ, and especially those whom he shall find apt to learn the clavycordes',[164] while James Crawe's Lincoln appointment in 1539 as Song Master and Organist uses almost the same terms: he was 'duly and diligently to instruct chorister boys, both in the science of singing, viz. playnsonge, prykyd songe, faburdon, diskante, and counter, and also in playing the organs in the Cathedral'.[165] These choristers were (and are) a source of future organists in Britain, the instrument being rarely available outside church environments until the Civil War.[166] It is interesting to note that the requirement for lay clerks to be sufficiently proficient in 'pricksong' (polyphony), at Lincoln (1483), Ripon (1503) and York (1507),[167] for example, ties in with the newly-complex multi-voice and large-scale counterpoint of the contemporary Eton Choirbook-type repertoire. Whether these musical demands required better singers, or whether better-trained singers made such new musical demands possible, is uncertain.

---

162 Saunders (1997), p.161; see pp.130-140 for information on terms and stipends.
163 Saunders (1997), pp.141-142; Mace (1676), p.25. Magnus Williamson, *The Eton Choirbook: Its Institutional and Historical Background*, DPhil thesis (University of Oxford, 1997), p.363 also notes additional non-musical roles at Eton College.
164 For a table of the skills taught to pre-Reformation choristers, see Flynn (1995), p.182.
165 David G. T. Harris, 'Musical Education in Tudor Times (1485-1603)', *Proceedings of the Musical Association*, 65th session (1938-1939), pp.109-139 at 117 and 119; see also Harrison (1963), pp.8-9. For the comparable arrangements in a French institution, see Kirkman (2020).
166 For a list of known players before the English Civil War, see Francis Knights, 'A Register of British keyboard makers, composers, copyists and players, c.660-1630', *National Early Music Association Newsletter*, vii/2 (Autumn 2023), pp.25-108.
167 Bowers (1995), p.33.

CHORISTERS' MUSIC LESSONS

The 1513 indenture from Durham Cathedral noted that choirmaster Thomas Ashwell was to give the boys music lessons 'with assiduous care and as be best knows how ... take pains to teach them both to play the organ and to acquire a knowledge of plain chant and harmonized chant by practising plain-song, prick-note, faburden, descant, s[qu]arenote and counterpoint. He shall give them lessons carefully and adequately four times a day on all ferial days, that is, twice in the morning and twice in the afternoon, and shall hear their renderings, keeping from them nothing of his knowledge in these matters'.[168] Perhaps this represented a choristers' rehearsal before each sung service in the pre-Reformation liturgy, or a mixture of theory lessons and rehearsals. Comparison can be made of Anglican practice a century later, as at Chichester Cathedral in 1610 Master of the Choristers Thomas Weelkes was instructed to 'bestow three hours at the least in every day of teaching the choristers'; a 1616 regulation made clear this was now extended to two hours before Matins at 10 am and two hours before Evensong at 4 pm, but it returned to being two hours and one hour a year later.[169] However, whether this represented three/four hours of purely musical tuition and rehearsal is uncertain, as the choristers would also have learned grammar and some of the other material familiar to Jacobean schoolboys, and this might have been included in the teaching remit. At King's College, Cambridge, the boys went to a grammar school in town for two hours each morning for separate instruction in the 1590s; their education within College was probably therefore exclusively musical.[170]

---

168 David Knowles, *The Religious Orders in England: Volume III, The Tudor Age* (Cambridge, 1971), pp.17-18. The reference to 'keeping from them nothing of his knowledge' is interesting, as Thomas Mace complains about teachers who were '*Very Sparing* in ... *Imparting* much of *Their Skill* to their *Scholars*' (Mace (1676), p.40). Paul O'Dette agrees that performers 'appear to have been ... protective of their personal practices' ('Teaching Historical Lute Technique in the 21st Century: Exceptions to the Normal Rules of Renaissance Lute Fingering', in John Griffiths and Sigrid Wirth (eds), *Teaching & Studying the Lute* (n.p., 2022), pp.23-42 at 23); see also Pat O'Brien, 'Just how secret were those Muses?', *Lute Society of America Quarterly*, xlii/1 (2007), pp.11-14 and Karel Davids, 'Craft Secrecy in Europe in the Early Modern Period: A Comparative View', *Early Science and Medicine*, x/3 (2005), pp.341-348. It should be remembered that guilds could be more about *restricting* than *promoting* activity in, or knowledge of, their subject; Woodfill (1953), pp.8-15.

169 David Brown, *Thomas Weelkes: a Biographical and Critical Study* (London, 1969), pp.34, 37 and 40; see also Mould (2007), p.58-60. At Durham Cathedral in 1563, prayers for all were at 6 am for 'almost halfe an houre', with Matins at 9 am and Evensong at 3 pm, Saunders (1997), p.22. For the tuition and training of musicians and singers in England, see Saunders (1997), pp.117-120.

170 Bowers (2014), p.276.

Records from the Thomasschule in Leipzig 1574 show that music classes took place for an hour after lunch four days a week, though whether this was theory or actual repertoire is unknown.[171] The 18th-century regulations for Cambrai note the choristers' daily programme from getting up until bedtime, with the 'Rehearsal of the pieces for the Mass' after breakfast, a music lesson before supper and after supper a 'Rehearsal for Matins and the daily office, the obits, and the Office of the BVM for the next day';[172] such rehearsal of the services for the following day was also found in Tudor institutions (see below).[173] The same was true of some concert performances: Dittersdorf, describing Gluck directing a band in Vienna in 1753, reported that at such private academies, 'a rehearsal was always held the previous evening so that everything, especially new items, would be orderly & accurate'.[174]

John Lilliat, an 'irreverent, turbulet spirit', who succeeded Thomas Weelkes at Chichester, did not teach the choristers 'to sing true, neither to time true, tune true, or vowel true, nor yet for the true wyndinge of the note … which is to the great annoyaunce to them that heare them in the Churche of God'. In other words, the boys could not sing in time or tune, breathe correctly or pronounce words properly.[175] That this list of requirements for the choristers was standard is seen from William Bathe's *A Briefe Introduction to the Skill of Song* (1600): his 'Ante Rules of Song' are '1. To prepare for Naming the Notes: Practise to sunder the Vowels and Consonants, distinctly pronouncing them according to the manner of the place; 2. To prepare for Quantitie: Practise to have the breath long to continue, and the tongue at liberty to run; 3. To prepare for Time: Practise in striking to keep a just proportion of one stroke to another; 4. To prepare for Tune: Practise to have your voice clear, which when thou hast done, learn the rules following: The skill of song doth consist in four things – Naming, Quantitie, Time, Tune'.[176] It is interesting that breathing technique is mentioned, 'to have the breath long to continue', as this rarely mentioned in early choral contexts (with regard to actual breath-mark notation in wind music, the earliest examples seem to be by Michel Blavet (1700-68)).[177]

---

171 Maul (2018), p.23. A 1592 document shows that this had slightly changed by that date; Maul (2018), pl.5.

172 Alejandro Enrique Planchart, 'Choirboys at Cambrai in the Fifteenth Century', in Susan Boynton and Eric Rice (eds), *Young Choristers 650-1700* (Woodbridge, 2008), pp.123-145 at 128; see also Sandrine Dumont, 'Choirboys and *Vicaires* in the Maîtrise of Cambrai: a socio-anthropological study (1550-1670)' in Boynton and Rice (2008), pp.146-162 at 152.

173 Harris (1938), p.112.

174 Parrott (2022), p.395.

175 Saunders (1997), pp.195-196.

176 William Bathe, *A Briefe Introduction to the Skill of Song* (London, 1600). See also see Flynn (1995).

177 Lewis Emanuel Peterman, 'Michel Blavet's Breathing Marks: A Rare Source for Musical Phrasing in Eighteenth-Century France', *Performance Practice Review*, iv/2 (Fall 1991), article 4.

A 1737 document from the Jesuit Cappella in Cracow provides a daily rota for student musicians, from 5 am to about 7 pm, which includes instrumental lessons and practice, singing, musical handwriting, memorization and accompaniment, spread throughout the day – over six hours of music in total.[178] Cathedral schools or schools attached to ecclesiastical institutions were then almost the only source of musical education, apart from private teaching. National conservatoires did not spread across Europe until the early 19th century, and before then the lack of formalized early musical education was felt by a number of musicians, including Roger North: 'it is an unhappiness in England that there are not musick schools for young people to be taught, as well as reading and wrighting schools'.[179]

REHEARSAL SPACES

One interesting question is whether rehearsals took place in the same space as performances. Then as now, a variety of practices certainly existed; in some cathedrals today the full rehearsal is in the quire, whereas with others it is in a drier Song School or smaller room. Preparing to perform in a large building by rehearsing in a small room is a challenge, but the clarity of the latter may be an advantage in rehearsal. Historically, many large churches and cathedrals were so busy with a continuous round of services that previous access would not always have been possible. In terms of the qualities a resonant space gives, Roger North summarizes it well: an advantage for 'Church Musick' is 'a spacious church, repleat with eccho, the very extent of which gives liberty to the sounds, as well as to soften, as to intermix'. Further, he says this kind of music would not 'be so good in a chamber, for there the harmony would appear more broken, and all the roughness and defects of the voices be perceivable than in the church'.[180] Quantz (1752) was also aware of these differences, and gave advice on repertoire selection and performance style, depending on whether the performing space was resonant or not.[181] Writing two centuries earlier, Giovanni Camillo Maffei (1562) took a different view, that resonance enables a singer to hear themselves back: 'Select a practice area with a good echo so that you can judge the quality of what you have just sung'.[182] Those who misjudged the spaces suffered, as Leopold noted to his daughter in a letter of March 1785:

---

178 Parrott (2022), p.133.
179 Wilson (1959), p.238
180 Wilson (1959), p.268.
181 Johann Joachim Quantz, trans Edward R. Reilly, *On Playing the Flute* (London, 1966), p.200.
182 Cited in Timothy J. McGee, *Medieval and Renaissance Music: A Performer's Guide* (Aldershot, 1990), p.56.

singer Madame Lange's loud notes were excessive for a room but her 'delicate passages' were too quiet for the theatre.[183]

Sometimes, as with a Song School, institutional spaces were set aside for music practice and rehearsal: at Douai in 1620, 'Four rooms in the college were set aside for music. Notably – and with some implications for composer Hugh Facy's later work at Douai – three of these rooms were used for instruction in singing (of which two were set aside for instruction in psalmody and plainchant)'.[184] This is unusually specific in terms of musical types, and the reason may be the specific educational materials (instruments, scores, blackboards,[185] charts and so on) located in each room.

Lastly, private houses were also used for rehearsals, space permitting (illus.5),[186] and there are records of such at Handel's own Brook Street house in January 1744 (when Mary Delaney was a guest), March 1749 and April 1749, among others. Two were for oratorios and the last for the Fireworks Music, so clearly the full ensembles could not have been present.[187] A contemporary description of the house of the early 17th-century Florentine nobleman Jacopo Corsi says it was 'always open, like a public academy, to everyone who had intelligence or talent in the liberal arts ... Entertainments with parade floats (*cocchiate*), celebrations and ballets accompanied by music were arranged and rehearsed there. Recitative style for use on stage was born there through the labour of Ottavio Rinuccini, celebrated poet, and Jacopo Peri, great master of harmony'.[188]

ENVIRONMENT AND LIGHTING

The choice of actual performing space would have been determined by liturgical, commercial or practical concerns, but their associated rehearsal spaces and times might sometimes have been selected for reasons of good light. The

---

183 Anderson (1989), p.889.
184 Andrew Cichy, 'Lost and found: Hugh Facy', *Early Music*, xlii/1 (February 2014), pp.95-104 at 97.
185 For a 1501 illustration of a music blackboard in class, see Owens (1997), p.83.
186 The *studiolo* may have been one particular private space for aristocratic rehearsal in Italy, and also for some kinds of domestic performance; see Tim Shephard, 'The Studiolo, Identity, and Music', in *Echoing Helicon: Music, Art and Identity in the Este Studioli, 1440-1530* (2014), pp.4-29.
187 Burrows et al. (2020), pp.151, 645 and 677.
188 Cited in John Walter Hill, 'Florence: Musical Spectacle and Drama, 1570-1650', in Price (1993), pp.121-145 at 135.

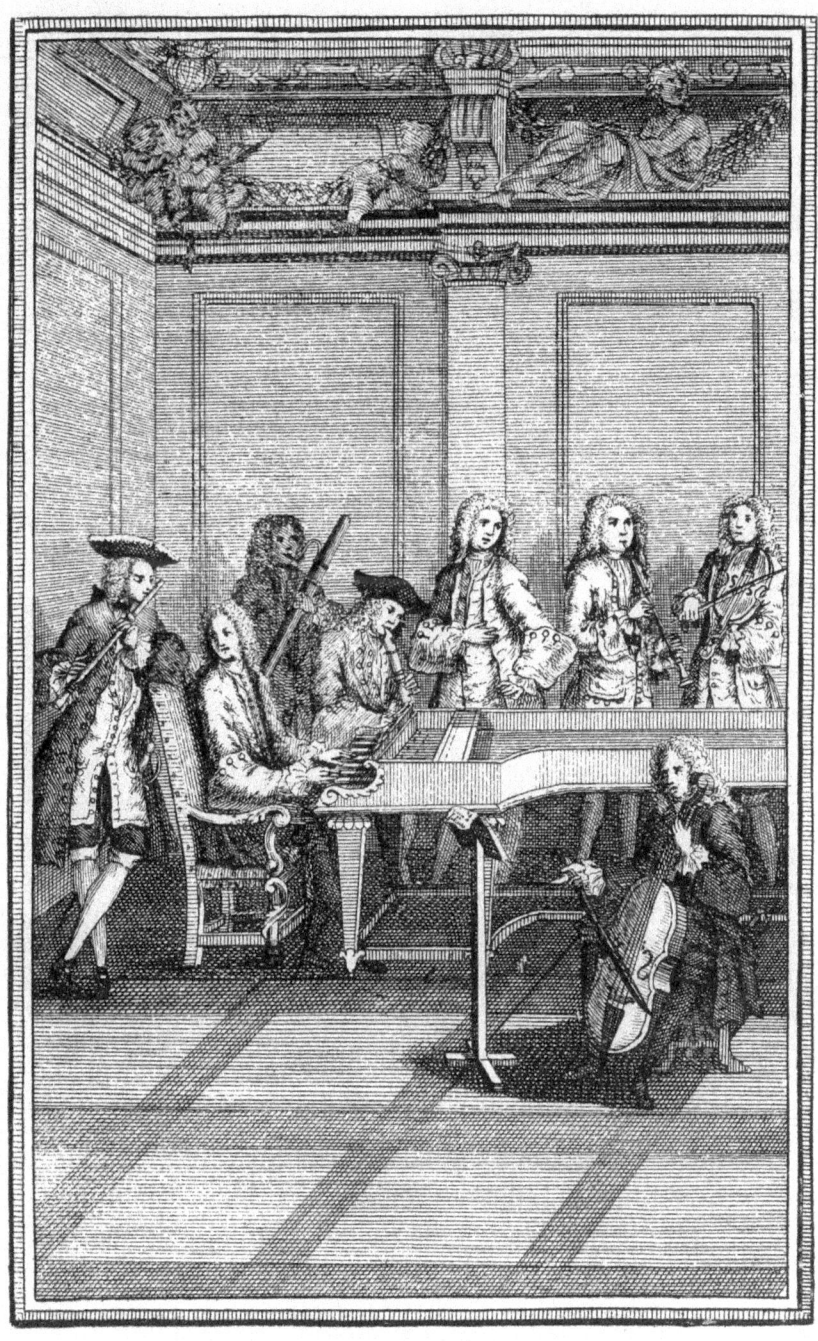

Illus. 5. Singer with an instrumental ensemble, from Peter Prelleur, *The Modern Musick-Master, or The Universal Musician* (London, 2/1731), frontispiece.

tradition of monastic or quasi-monastic night services would have accustomed musicians to sometimes working with relatively little or no light: 'The psalter and canticles, which the boys were to have memorized, were chanted without the aid of written sources, often in total darkness'.[189] The effect on the eyesight of musicians is not known – the history of pre-modern eyesight problems does not appear to have been written, although spectacles were an (expensive) medieval invention[190] – but it is likely that many events, such as the evening antiphon at Eton College, were held at times when candles were needed to compensate for the absence of daylight. This was a significant expense, whether tallow or the more expensive wax candles (sometimes called 'church candles') were used, and the cost of lighting large rooms such as theatres could be quite considerable.[191] Reading at a distance hand-copied music by flickering candles would have posed particular challenges in complex music, such as the Eton repertoire, with its bi-coloured text underlay.[192]

It is also possible in some places that the temperature, either high or low, at different times of year affected what was done and where. In Manila in 1665, 'They do not sing the pater-noster nor the *Pax Domini* nor even the Preface, because it is very hot in this country';[193] while in the colder parts of northern Europe in winter, a freezing church may have led to truncated or hasty rehearsals and even services.

EMPLOYMENT, RECRUITMENT AND REQUIREMENTS

An institution's musical resources, in terms of staff and materials, must have been determined by a combination of music requirements and funding, as well

---

189 Boynton and Rice (2008), p.10.
190 Data on the importation of spectacles and spectacle cases from 1380-1537 can be found in Stuart Jenks (ed), 'The London Customs Accounts', *Hansischer Geschichtsverein Lübeck*, lxxiv (2016-2023), 45 vols. At Pamplona Cathedral in 1646 the *bajón* Gorriti was described as 'very old & not much use, as his eyesight is very poor' ; Parrott (2022), p.366.
191 Judith Milhous, 'Lighting at the King's Theatre, Haymarket, 1780-82', *Theatre Research International*, xvi/3 (1991), pp.215-236. See also Simon Eliot, 'Reading by Artificial Light in the Victorian Age', in Matthew Bradley and Juliet John (eds), *Reading and the Victorians* (London, 2015), pp.15-30 and Lee Prosser, 'Experiments with historic light in Kensington Palace's early eighteenth-century interiors', in Christine Casey and Melanie Hayes (eds), *Enriching Architecture: Craft and its conservation in Anglo-Irish building production, 1660-1760* (London, 2023), pp.138-159.
192 See Knights and Padilla (2024), pp.53-55.
193 David R. M. Irving, *Colonial Counterpoint: Music in Early Modern Manila* (Oxford, 2010), p.180.

as liturgical need in the case of church music (for the latter, adult singers were likely drawn from the ranks of former choristers, they being almost the only ones with the specialist musical knowledge necessary). Ensembles, whether cathedral, opera or orchestral, grew and shrank over the decades depending on the desire of the authorities to fund music, of wealthy individuals to support expensive cultural projects, and on external circumstances such as wars. The change of a monarch, duke, bishop or dean could result in the instant dismissal of an entire musical department, or the creation of one where there had been none. Musicians must always have felt at the mercy of such circumstances, though possibly less so in those ecclesiastical environments where statutes determined both employment numbers and duties.

It must be remembered that the nominal choir sizes reflected in financial and other accounts represent a numerical maximum, as singers might have been absent (see below), ill, or busy with other duties: in pre-Reformation practice in England, 'At High Mass on Sundays and festivals a substantial proportion of the choir was engaged about the ceremony of the service and thus unable for much of its duration to participate in the singing'.[194] In 1515 Ramsey Abbey needed at least fourteen monks at High Mass in order that two were available to sing the chant. Chorister numbers in Britain increased towards the end of the 15th century, which Roger Bowers sees as reflecting a move to five-part polyphony,[195] and costly changes like this determined by purely musical needs are likely to have received mixed responses from the authorities at times.

A principal difficulty in recruitment was the advertising of vacancies; the arrival of newspapers towards the end of the 17th century made this easier, but previously an institution would have had to let potential musicians know of a vacancy by local word of mouth (easier in a large city, where the musicians knew each other), or by writing to organizations elsewhere. At the Sistine Chapel, for example, 'When a place became vacant, usually on account of a death, the maestro had to organize the recruitment of the new singer. Advertisements were printed, and displayed in the main churches of Rome and the main Italian cathedrals. In 1652 those selected were Bologna, Florence, Naples and Venice. Any unmarried singer could apply; there were various auditions, with a special programme devised by the maestro, the Dean of the singers and a few senior members of the cappella. The whole college voted for each candidate; to be admitted, a singer needed to gain two-thirds plus one of the votes

---

194 Bowers (1995), p.34. Practice in the cathedrals of Scotland, Wales and Ireland has been relatively neglected by modern scholars, but see Harrison (1963), pp.14-17, 26-27 and 37-38.
195 Bowers (1995), p.31.

cast'.[196] Singers were sometimes specifically invited, or international diplomatic networks used for talent spotting. In one case this created a serious diplomatic incident, with singer Jean Cordier spirited away from Naples to Milan.[197]

Where there was difficulty getting voices, choirs could be seriously under strength for periods of time: in 1558 Exeter Cathedral had three instead of ten Lay Vicars, although the number was restored fairly soon afterwards.[198] A sense of declining quality during the early Elizabethan period was registered by composer Thomas Whythorne in 1567; he thought that the stock of competent church musicians would 'soon be worn out'.[199] The same complaint was made by Roger North at the end of the 17th century: 'it is very hard to get voices to make a Quire'.[200]

Agreement between institutions and musicians became increasingly formalized over time, at least as far as surviving documentation implies. For example, a detailed set of sixteen regulations survives from the important church of S. Petronio in Bologna in 1658: these *Ordinari* were drawn up by the incoming *maestro di capella* Mauritio Cazzati (1626-78), and actually printed.[201] They specified the activities of the 35 musicians (22 singers, disposed SATB 4/6/6/6, eight strings, two trombones, a theorbo and two organists) at the church.[202] In summary, they were required to 'give of their best in divine service', be present as required, obey the *maestro*, and pay a series of graded fines for absence or lateness. The new regulations proved contentious with some of the undisciplined musicians already in post, and one of those excluded under the new arrangements took his revenge by initiating a decade-long polemic argument about numerous contrapuntal 'errors' he identified in a published Kyrie by the *maestro*; by 1671 Cazzati had had enough of all this and departed to work for the Gonzagas in Mantua.

---

196 Jean Lionnet, 'Performance Practice in the Papal Chapel during the 17th Century', *Early Music*, xv/1 (February 1987), pp.3-15 at 4.
197 Klaus Pietschmann and James Steichen, 'Musical institutions in the fifteenth century and their political contexts', in Anna Maria Busse Berger and Jesse Rodin (eds), *The Cambridge History of Fifteenth-Century Music* (Cambridge, 2015), pp.403-426 at 421.
198 Saunders (1997), p.90.
199 Saunders (1997), p.116.
200 Wilson (1959), p.270.
201 Ursula Brett, 'The Polemics of Imperfection', *The Consort*, lxxviii (Summer 2022), pp.71-94 at 73-74.
202 A cornett is also mentioned elsewhere in the regulations.

In 1691 the Scuolo dello Spirito Santo in Venice created a job specification for a five-year music director post, and their priorities in terms of giving exact numbers of singers and instrument types, but not repertoire, are interesting: the 'maestro di cappella is obligated to have sung, entirely at his expense, on the three days of Pentecost, at the usual hours, mass and vespers on each day. On the first day [this should be done] with twelve singers [selected] from the best of the Cappella di San Marco, that is, three sopranos, three altos, three tenors, and three basses, [and] with three organs, a violone, two violas da gamba, four violins, four violas, two cornetti, a theorbo, and a trumpet, and also these instrumentalists shall be among the best of the said Cappella. And on the two subsequent days, there should be one eighth fewer singers and one third fewer instrumentalists than on the first day. In each of the said masses there should be motets and sonatas as is usually done'.[203]

The statutes of Charles V's and Philip II's chapels note contractual regulations for the singers which suggest there had been previous difficulties, as in item 14: 'the verse and the Alleluia must be sung every day from now on as it was done on holy days until today, and the children's master has to make them sung by each singer, and they have to stand in order without mixing up, and none of them can refuse to sing the said duet or trio, or anything that suits the said service, when the master asks them, at the risk of receiving the given punishment, unless they have a legitimate reason'.[204]

Paid rehearsal would have been a given for full-time musician employees, but records from the early 18th-century Haymarket Orchestra in London provide rare evidence of contractual payments for freelancers' rehearsals: those leading musicians who got 25 shillings per performance also received '5 shillings per Practice'.[205] The additional costs for rehearsal attendance perhaps explain the restricted numbers of such events.

At some institutions a singer's role might involve additional tasks, as at Chichester Cathedral in 1589, where the Chapter saved on copyists' fees by giving paper to each of the Lay Vicars to copy their 'owne parte'.[206]

---

203 Jonathan Glixon, '*Far il buon concerto*: Music at the Venetian Scuole Piccole in the Seventeenth Century', *Journal of Seventeenth Century Music*, i/1 (1995), section 3.4.
204 Cited in Philippe Canguilhem, 'Singing upon the Book according to Vicente Lusitano', *Early Music History*, xxx (2011), pp.55–103 at 99.
205 Holman (2020), p.218. Low payment for rehearsals continued to be a sore point in the early 19th century; see Christina Bashford, *Public Chamber-Music Concerts in London, 1835-50: Aspects of History, Repertory and Reception*, PhD thesis (King's College, London, 1996), i.
206 Saunders (1997), p.41.

PROFESSIONAL AUDITIONS

At the audition for the organist's position at Málaga Cathedral in 1552, the candidates were examined through practical tests: 'a choir-book was placed before each, opened at random, and the sight and score-reading ability of each was tested'.[207] With regard to the latter skill, Bermudo confirms that it is possible and indeed desirable to be able to play polyphony at the keyboard by reading all the voices from separate partbooks simultaneously.[208] The greatest professional challenge that survives is in the remarkable Twenty Tests for Applicants for the post of Choirmaster at Toledo Cathedral in 1604, as successor to Alonso Lobo:[209] candidates had to improvise free counterpoint on a plainsong and on any voice of mensural music; add an additional improvised voice to music in two, three and four parts; be fluent in the Guidonian hand to indicate pitches, while singing a different voice; add a cantus firmus, and in syncopation; add imitation at the second, fourth and the fifth; direct singers from a choirbook, being able to demonstrate all the voices; give cues to the singers for correct entries instead of them counting rests; notice when a voice is missing in the texture; and understand canon, fugue and composition. The four named candidates were Francisco de Bustamante (from Coria), Juan Sisear (Valladolid), Diego de Bruceña (Burgos) and Lucas Tercero (León); none was appointed.

Auditions for instrumentalists are also recorded, though less frequently; for example, members of the Bassano family at Queen Elizabeth's court were appointed to '"try and examine" which of two candidates was "the more skilful and efficient musician in all manner of musical instruments"'.[210] In 1769 one Pfaffe, auditioned for the rank of *Stadtpfeifer* in Leipzig by Johann Friedrich Doles, played 'the following either passably or well: A piece for horn; A trio on the violin; A *concertirenden* chorale on the *Zugtrompete*; A simple chorale on the discant, alto, tenor and bass trombones; The *concertirenden* chorale again on the double bass'.[211] Both of these accounts are a reminder that single-instrument specialization is a 19th-century phenomenon, and earlier apprenticeship processes might involve mastering (to some extent) many different instruments.[212] Quantz reported that 'The first instrument I had to learn was the

---

207 Cited in Smith (2011), p.5

208 See Owens (1997), pp.48-50.

209 See https://www.cacophonyhistoricalsinging.com/post/the-twenty-tests-for-applicants-for-the-post-of-choirmaster-at-toledo-cathedral-in-1604, and Canguilhem (2011).

210 Woodfill (1953), p.42

211 Jerold (2005), pp.91-92.

212 For early 18th-century Germany, see Jerold (2005), pp.67-96.

violin, for which I appeared also to have the most desire and capability. Then followed the oboe and trumpet. These three instruments occupied most of my efforts during my years of training. But I was not exempted from learning the other instruments, such as cornett, trombone, Waldhorn, recorder, bassoon, German double bass, violoncello, viola da gamba, and who knows how many others that a true town musician must be able to play. Because of being spread so thin with all these different instruments, it is certainly true that one always remains a bungler on each. Nevertheless, one does come to learn their characteristics, which is almost indispensable knowledge for composers, particularly those working with church music'.[213] Haydn – who was reputed to play most instruments – even tactfully gave an impromptu timpani lesson to the 18-year-old George Smart during a rehearsal in London in 1794.[214]

PERFORMER ATTENDANCE REGULATIONS

Attendance is a crucial aspect of ensemble efficiency, and numerous records attest to singer absences in particular. What arrangements were made for deputies (as in modern practice) is hardly known, nor whether in some traditions missing voices might be replaced by instruments (as mentioned above) or covered by an organ accompaniment. A well-organized institution could arrange formal cover for absence, as at València, where another musician was instructed to 'play the cornett to cover all of Vicente Úbeda's absences and illnesses'.[215]

One piece of evidence does exist for the proportion of attendances, which Rob Wegman has calculated from payment records for the Guild of our Lady at Bergen op Zoom: two singers, Jacob Obrecht and 'Reynier with the hump', averaged attendance at three-quarters of services in 1483/4.[216] However, because these were per-service payments and not a salary, it is not possible to say whether this level of attendance was what had been agreed, or represents any level of non-attendance (Obrecht's career disciplinary record was far from exemplary, rendering the latter a distinct possibility). The question of what to do when not enough singers were available was also raised at Bergen op Zoom in 1499/1500: the high-profile evening *Salve Regina*, 'commonly attended by all the noble-

---

213 Cited in Jerold (2005), p.75.
214 H. Bertram Cox and C. L. E. Cox (eds), *Leaves from the Journals of Sir George Smart* (London, 1907), p.3.
215 Mireya Royo, 'Instruments in the liturgy of the Real Colegio Seminario de Corpus Christi, València, in the 17th century', *Early Music*, xlix/1 (February 2021), pp.35–48 at 40.
216 Rob Wegman, *Born for the muses: the life and Masses of Jacob Obrecht* (Oxford, 1994), p.81.

men and foreigners who are staying in the city' was regularly short of the agreed number of singers Obrecht was supposed to bring with him, so the authorities suggested that it would be better for reputational reasons not to perform the *Salve* at all than have it done in 'great confusion'.[217] Some institutions seemed to respond to such problems more casually: at San Rocco in Venice a 17th-century document records a request for an additional soprano, as their only one was 'often missing at the offices and other services, leaving the oratory without a soprano ... especially in processions and other important occasions ... with an extra soprano, if one is missing the other can supply'.[218]

In England, the New Foundation cathedral statutes issued by Henry VIII prohibited absence from residence for the choirmen even for a single day or night without permission. Attendance at every service was also compulsory, although some institutions like Norwich Cathedral (1566) allowed 40 days' holiday per year, and such regulations seem to have been widely breached, in nay case.[219] At Wells Cathedral in 1597, Vicar Choral Richard Mewe was eventually dismissed, having been absent for more than six months.[220] Absenteeism was rife at Chichester Cathedral at the end of the 16th century, both of choir and clergy, and in 1595 they could not always muster enough singers even for the Sunday services. Vicar Choral John Mead there missed no fewer than 183 services in late 1618, so clearly someone was keeping careful score; in 1610 a per-service absence fining system (*iis vid*, a significant amount) had been instituted by the demanding new bishop Samuel Harsnett, evidently to little effect.[221]

Fines or threats in respect of absenteeism were also not uncommon on the continent: at St Omer in June 1483 'the vicars Guillaume Didier and Gerardus de Vledrezelle were admonished to be present by the day of the next patronal feast or be sacked',[222] singers at Évora Cathedral in 1565 were fined for errors ('The singer who makes a mistake in what he sings in solo or in trios, or in a duo, will lose ten *réis*'),[223] while the València chapel records for 1644 note an

---

217 Wegman (1994), p.305.
218 O'Regan (1996), p.153.
219 Saunders (1997), p.62. Larger choirs could presumably operate a rota system to allow for both daily services and individual holidays; the surviving repertoire of music for men's voices only shows that choristers also got time off, either by design or for illness.
220 Le Huray (1967), p.42.
221 Brown (1969), pp.29 and 34.
222 Kirkman (2020), p.81.
223 João Pedro d'Alvarenga, 'On performing practices in mid- to late 16th-century Portuguese church music: the "cappella" of Évora Cathedral', *Early Music*, xliii/1 (February 2015), pp.3-21 at 8.

unspecified fine for non-attendance by a cornett player ('if he misses any date he will be fined from his salary of 90 pounds').[224] As a response to 'obvious proof of negligence of duty among certain members of the band', in 1802 Prince Nicolaus II at Esterházy specified a fine of 'one Gulden per person' for any of his performers absent without a 'proper excuse'.[225]

LENGTH OF SERVICE, AND PENSIONS

Frequent rehearsal and performance by a team of musicians who worked well together was understood to produce better results: Bottrigari (1594) mentions the excellence of the San Vito musicians, saying 'perfection of concord in an ensemble is born in the long association of singers and players'.[226] Some surviving payment records can be used to calculate lengths of service for English cathedral musicians: at Durham the Lay Clerks averaged about 19 years between 1558-1637, and the numbers for Ely (1561-1655) were similar. The recorded maximum service was 33 years, although this was very long. The Westminster Abbey numbers (1558-1645) are much lower, averaging 8 years and with a maximum of 13, perhaps suggesting that alternative musical opportunities were more easily found in London.[227]

At Eton College, during the critical time when the Eton Choirbook was being compiled, there were increasing numbers of long-serving singers: William Yong, Thomas Kendall and William Ketyll all appear in the early 1490s, and left in around 1517-19, 1525 and 1526-28 respectively: Magnus Williamson notes that 'Clerkships lasting between 28 and 35 years (Ketyll's possibly as long as 40 years), were exceptional' but 'by the mid-1500s, half of the clerks or more had worked alongside each other for five years or more. In this sense, it is possible to talk of the clerks as a team, with a particularly long-serving and experienced nucleus: an important advance on the situation, pre-1490'.[228] It is important to remember that while extended periods in a role would have increased both musical experience and repertoire familiarity, it was no guarantee of aspiration towards increased standards by the Lay Clerks, as Morley complained: 'for the most part, you shall find amongst them, that let them continue never so long

---

224 Royo (2021), p.38.
225 Landon (1959), p.207.
226 Stras (2018), p.237.
227 Saunders (1997), Table 4, pp.215-216.
228 Williamson (1997), pp.347-348; he also suggests that higher payments were given to long-standing members, which may have aided retention of experienced singers.

in the church, yea though it were twentie years, they will neuer studie to sing better then they did the first day of their preferment to that place'.[229]

Long service was likely to conclude with ill health, a decline of the voice or hearing problems, as the archives attest: at the Scuola di San Marco in Venice in 1460, it was recorded that the 'singers are worn out like old men … these men are weakened and unsuitable',[230] while one of the York Waits dismissed in 1584: as well as being 'oft drunk and is at diverse times troubled with the falling sickness', he suffered from 'hearing imperfect or almost deaf as that he is not sufficient to serve his place'.[231] Palestrina also had sight problems at the end of his life, although it does not appear to have affected the quantity of his composing.[232] Bass Ugo Miglietti moved from Margaret of Parma's ensemble to San Giovanni in Laterano in Rome; but according to Scipione Gonzaga (1586), he was 'not a man to be counted on, because he has a ruptured vein in his chest'.[233]

The absence of formal pension schemes before the 20th century sometimes led to musicians being either paid off, or else kept on without doing duty. One example of the former was the dismissed York Wait mentioned above who, being 'a poor old man', was pensioned off at 26 shillings and eight pence annually.[234] Remarkably, the Durham Cathedral records indicate that Lay Clerks Nicholas Hobson and William Murray were still nominally in office at more than eighty and ninety years old respectively.[235]

There was also an informal and occasional 'pension' scheme in England for choristers whose voices had broken: as their voices went much later than modern boys and as university starting age was usually lower, it was sometimes possible to keep a few on the books (known informally as 'dry choristers') to bridge this gap, even though they were no longer singing. This included at least eleven boys at King's College, Cambridge, in the 1580s and 90s.[236]

---

229 Thomas Morley, *A Plaine and Easie Introduction to Practicall Musicke* (London, 1597), p.179. Whether the better-paid full-time singers of the Tudor period had similar attitudes is not recorded.
230 Jonathan Glixon, 'Music at the Venetian Scuole Grandi, 1440-1540', in Iain Fenlon (ed), *Music in Medieval and Early Modern Europe: Patronage, Sources and Texts* (Cambridge, 1981), pp.193-226 at 196.
231 Woodfill (1953), p.88.
232 Owens (1997), p.293.
233 Niwa (2005), p.33.
234 Woodfill (1953), p.88.
235 Saunders (1997), p.126.
236 Bowers (2014), p.275.

Within an institution, success could lead to promotion that even straddled music and other professions: Craig Wright lists no fewer than 13 positions an ambitious young musician might eventually work his way through on his way from choirboy to Canon at St Aignan in Paris.[237] The York statutes noted the possibility of a progression from chorister to thurifer, sub-deacon, deacon and vicar,[238] while at Eton, singer George Kendall was successively clerk (1496-), organist (1502), Informator (1506) and finally chaplain (1509).[239] At Oxford, Richard Davy moved from Master of the Choristers to ordained priest to chaplain of the Boleyn family.[240] Music offered a form of social mobility, and some lucky sons of Tudor workmen and craftsmen could rise very respectably through music within the hierarchies of the early modern class system.[241] William Crane, successor to Cornysh as Master of the Children in Henry VIII's Chapel Royal, acquired significant additional roles outside music and became a rich man.[242] Two centuries later, Charles Burney rose from humble beginnings to considerable wealth and musical and social status, earned through his own efforts rather than through patronage.

MUSICIANS' BEHAVIOUR

Tensions between clergy and musicians have a very long history, and surviving written texts usually derive from the former, often as hostile witnesses and referencing animal noises by way of mockery. One early account paints a vivid picture of the performance of polyphony (and apparently including a falsettist): in a sermon by Augustinian monk Johannes Hübner in around 1400 but derived from a 12th-century text, the preacher asks, 'whence so many monstrous songs in church? This one sings under, that one sings against, another sings above, yet another divides and chops certain notes in the middle; now the voice is strained, now cracked, now battered, now broadened in a more dispersed noise, and sometimes, I am ashamed to say, it is forced into horse-like whinnying; and at times, having lost its manly vigour, it is sharpened with

---

237 Craig Wright, 'Antoine Brumel and patronage at Paris', in Fenlon (1981), pp.37-60 at 47.
238 Harrison (1963), p.9.
239 Williamson (1997), p.377.
240 Stevens (1979), p.305. Note however that there were several Richard Davys, whose biographies may have become confused; see David Skinner, 'Davy [Davys], Richard', www.oxfordmusiconline.
241 Woodfill (1953), p.244. See also Heinrich W. Schwab, 'The Social Status of the Town Musician', in Walter Salmen (ed), trans Herbert Kaufman and Barbara Reisner, *The Social Status of the Professional Musician* (New York, 1983), pp.33-59 and Kirkman (2020), ch.2.
242 Stevens (1979), pp.315-316.

the thinness of a woman's voice. Meanwhile, the whole body is moved about with histrionic gesticulations, the lips are twisted, the eyes rolled about; they play with their arms, and curlings of fingers accompany all single notes'.[243] In 1496 Savonarola described 'a singer with a big voice who appears to be a calf and the others cry out around him like dogs, and one can't make out a word they are saying'.[244] The poor sound of one 17th-century Exeter Cathedral Lay Clerk gave rise to a tale recorded about a 'countrey woman' found crying after a service, who told him to his face that 'when she heard him sing, she called to mind her mare that was lately dead & dying made just such a noise as he did in his singing'.[245] In view of these descriptions, the question may be asked whether an ensemble's director had much control of the sounds individual singers made, or saw vocal blend and balance as part of a rehearsal goal? Was rehearsal just for learning pieces to a sufficient level of accuracy, or for training (in the modern sense) an ensemble too?

As well as such dislike of music in church itself, complaints about the behaviour and morals of singers they employed have a long history. Erasmus called them the 'dregs of humanity', one of his contemporaries objected to them actually being paid (1523),[246] while reformer Martin Bucer complained that choirs sang too quickly, part of a catalogue of errors indicating their lack of devotion.[247] Such rushing is also referenced in a Cambrai Cathedral document from February 1504, where 'The deacon, scholaster, and sires Brillet, Bacheler and Dumont, along with the master of the grand mestier, are appointed to urge both the great and lesser vicars to sing and psalm more slowly'. The problem continued there, and similar ineffectual comments about tempo were made in 1514, 1544, 1547 and 1551.[248]

The idea of the necessity of dignified behaviour by singers in church appears repeatedly in the early modern period: according to notes made by papal Master of Ceremonies Johannes Burckard in around 1500, the duties of the *Magister capellae* were, in summary, to 'diligently see to it that the singers sing the

---

243 Rob C. Wegman, '"Musical Understanding" in the 15th Century', *Early Music*, xxx/1 (February 2002), pp.46-66 at 55.
244 Cited in Wegman (2002), p.57.
245 Saunders (1997), p.75.
246 Daniel Trocmé-Latter, 'Thieves, Drunkards, and Womanisers? Perceptions of Church Musicians in Early Reformation Strasbourg', in R. Gerald Hobbs and Annie Noblesse-Rocher (eds), *Bible, Histoire et Société: Mélanges offerts a Bernard Roussel* (Turnhout, 2013), pp.383-399 at 384, 387.
247 Trocme-Latter (2013), pp.390-391 and 395.
248 Wright (1978), p.312.

canonical hours nocturnal and diurnal at the due times and with due reverence and silence'.[249] On Christmas Day 1553, the traditional ceremony of the Boy Bishop took place in Gloucester Cathedral and chorister John Stubs preached the sermon, taking the opportunity to scold the bad behaviour of his own colleagues, the boy singers: 'rashly thei cum into quire without any reverence; never knele nor cowntenaunce to say a prayer or Pater-noster, but rudely squat down on ther tayles and justle wyth ther felows for a place; a non thei startes me owt of the quire agayne and owt agayne, and thus one after an other, I kannot tell how oft nor wherfor, but only to gadd and gas abrode, and so cum in agayne and crosse the quere fro one side to an other an never rest'.[250]

At Chichester Cathedral the singers' offences included threats of violence, drawing a knife in a brawl, quarrelling, drunkenness, slander, absenteeism, bringing dogs into church, and going bowling instead of attending the service.[251] The Chapter books at Wells Cathedral from the 1590s to 1609 bear out these same complaints about fornication, indiscretion, absenteeism, frequenting taverns, gambling and so on,[252] while at Salisbury in 1454 they played tennis or went drinking.[253] The nefarious activities of Thomas Weelkes at Chichester are well known, and finally being officially declared a 'common drunkard and a notorious swearer and blasphemer' in 1616 he was dismissed the following year. However, he seems to have been readmitted despite not mending his ways at all, dying in 1623.[254]

It was easier to identify a problem than to persuade the musicians to improve, as Thomas Harrold at St Paul's Cathedral lamented to Bishop Bancroft in 1598: disciplinary 'disorders have been most of them complained at every visitation, and yet continue in their old irregularity'.[255] In 1628 John Earle (Fellow of Merton College, Oxford, and Bishop of Salisbury after the Restoration) complained in his book *Microcosmographie* of drunkenness among church singers: 'The Common singing-men in Cathedral Churches are a bad Society, and yet a Company of good Fellowes, that roare deep in the Quire, deeper in the

---

249 Richard Sherr, 'The papal chapel in the late fifteenth century', in Busse Berger and Rodin (2015), pp.446-462 at 447.
250 Harris (1938), p.119.
251 Brown (1969), pp.28-31.
252 Le Huray (1967), pp.41-44.
253 Harrison (1963), p.8.
254 Brown (1969), pp.34-44.
255 Le Huray (1967), p.44; for a survey of the topic, see Saunders (1997), ch.6.

Taverne'.[256] John Brown (1763) took the view that having low-class lay singers rather than clerical voices (as in France) resulted in a lack of 'Dignity of Character' in cathedral music, instead having a 'Band of Lay-Singers, whose Rank and Education are not of Weight to preserve their Profession from Contempt'.[257]

The behaviour of certain organists continued to be a concern well into the Georgian era, with reports of John Alcock's (Lichfield Cathedral) 'scandalous and indecent behaviour' – this accusation was a part of a three-way battle between organist, singers and clergy, with Alcock said to perform 'Splenetic Tricks upon the Organ to expose or confound the performers'. A similar musical feud took place between organist William Walond and the Dean at Chichester Cathedral at the end of the 18th century.[258]

DISCIPLINE AND DISMISSAL

Bad behaviour, whether musical or disciplinary (absenteeism, alcoholism, fornication) is recorded in many places besides Britain, and the Cambrai Cathedral documents called the *monitiones vicariorum* list consequent punishments, ranging from bread and water to imprisonment.[259] Another form of punishment is recorded in the Cambrai archives: when tenor Adam le Grand came to Matins of Epiphany 'attired as a woman' in 1508 he had to stand upright during all the canonical hours for a certain number of days.[260] At Wells in 1504 John Braddon had to process into the cathedral with a candle and say the penitential psalms,[261] while in 1601 Vicar Choral Richard Marwood was punished by having to copy out church music for months, under the direction of the Precentor.[262] Chapel Royal countertenor Thomas Loughton murdered his wife in 1638, 'for which he was deprived of his place in ye Chappell';[263] it is not known whether he received any further criminal sanction.

---

256 Jerold (2006), p.77.
257 John Brown, *A dissertation on the rise ... and corruption of poetry and music* (London, 1763), p.214; cited in Jerold (2006), p.77.
258 Holman (2020), pp.50-53 and 48-49; for Alcock, see Philip Marr, *The Life and Works of John Alcock (1715–1806)*, PhD thesis (University of Reading, 1978).
259 Dumont (2008), pp.160-161.
260 Wright (1978), p.295.
261 Harrison (1963), p.8.
262 Le Huray (1967), p.42.
263 Giles (1994), p.49.

Discipline of the boys often involved a tradition of physical chastisement: the early 10th-century monk Odo of Saint-Maur said 'if the boys commit any fault in the psalmody or other singing, either by sleeping or such like transgressions [let them be beaten] with pliant and smooth osier rods'.[264]

While those in employment could be dismissed in the case of serious disciplinary infractions, rather than just punished or fined, some institutions also made allowance to remove those who were no longer of sufficient standard: a Cambrai Cathedral document from August 1544 notes that 'those unsatisfactory singers who lose their voices should be dismissed',[265] while at the Scuola di San Rocco in Venice in 1531, the players of harp, lute and viol 'who served very badly' were replaced.[266] At another institution in that city, the Scuola della Misericordia, the entire choir was dismissed in 1540, 'because of their bad manner of singing, without any harmony and sweetness, singing in contempt of all rules, and with great dishonour in general to all'.[267] The companies of Waits of Nottingham. Ipswich, Leicester, Manchester and Coventry were also dismissed wholesale by their employers between 1578-1635, mostly for reasons of fractiousness or incompetence.[268] It might be assumed that threats of dismissal would have helped musicians to take their rehearsal and performance duties more seriously, but how this sanction was viewed is uncertain. Correct institutional appointment processes also needed to be followed in the first place: in 1571 three papal singers were fired for having been improperly admitted.[269]

OPERA REHEARSAL TRADITIONS

Opera existed both as commercial public entertainment, and – for wealthy aristocrats who could afford to build or maintain their own theatres – at court or in palaces.[270] The latter venues were private, but court functionaries and guests presumably combined to provide sufficient audiences for the series laid on by, for example, Haydn at Esterházy from 1763-88, where there were as many as 150

---

264 Giles (1994), p.26.
265 Wright (1978), p.312.
266 Glixon (1981), p.202.
267 Glixon (1981), p.203.
268 Woodfill (1953), p.88.
269 Sherr (1999), IV, p.87.
270 Michael F. Robinson, *Opera before Mozart* (London, 3/1978), pp. 24-25.

performances a year.²⁷¹ Both public and private opera seasons saw productions given in rotation: the surviving lists for Covent Garden and the King's Theatre in London for 1734-35 show the lengths of a run, and the gaps between revivals.²⁷² The tradition on parts of the continent may have been more demanding, and similar to Elizabethan theatre practice (see below): writing from Munich in December 1774 Leopold Mozart notes that they had the same procedure there as in Salzburg – works 'cannot be performed more than twice in succession, for otherwise attendance would be poor. So for two or three weeks other operas have to be performed and then the first one may be trotted out again, just as is done in the case of plays and ballets. Thus the singers know the parts of at least twenty operas which are performed in turn, and at the same time they study a new one'.²⁷³ During the Venetian 1701-2 Carnival season, at a time of war and with many opera venues closed, there were a 'mere four operas' staged in 24 days.²⁷⁴ In France, by contrast, Diderot claimed in *Rameau's Nephew* (and with some with literary exaggeration) that opera runs could last far longer: 'In the past, pieces like *Tancrède, Issé, Europe galante, Les Indes,* and *Castor* or *Les Talents lyriques*, used to run for four, five, six months. There was no end to the performances of a piece like *Armide*'.²⁷⁵

Letters from Milan between Mozart father and son in late 1770 about the latter's new opera *Mitridate, re di Ponto* for the Teatro Regio Ducale ('very large and splendid', according to Burney, illus.6)²⁷⁶ enable a partial reconstruction of the preparation order and content of an Italian opera, extracted from dateable comments such as 'The second rehearsal of the recitatives is taking place today … the first went so well'.²⁷⁷ Recitative rehearsals (of which three may have been usual)²⁷⁸ were likely for the performers only, although Leopold (1780) on a later occasion implies to Wolfgang that even there listeners were present: 'It is true

---

271 H. C. Robbins Landon, 'The Operas of Haydn', *New Oxford History of Music*, vii (Oxford, 1973), pp.172–199.
272 Burrows et al. (2019), pp.305. For the 'Second Academy' season in London in 1730-31, see Cummings (1998), p.356: seven works, with between six and 16 performances.
273 Anderson (1989), p.249.
274 Bruno Forment, 'An enigmatic souvenir of Venetian opera: Alessandro Piazza's "Teatro" (1702)', *Early Music*, xxxviii/3 (August 2010), pp.387-401 at 395.
275 Denis Diderot, trans Kate E. Tunstall and Caroline Warman, *Rameau's Nephew/Le Neveu de Rameau* (Cambridge, 2/2016), p.74.
276 Charles Burney, cited in Stanley Sadie and Neal Zaslaw, *Mozart: The Early Years 1756-1781* (Oxford, 2006), p.214.
277 Anderson (1989), pp.173-176.
278 Leopold Mozart (1772): 'During the last few days we have had three rehearsals of the recitatives'; Anderson (1989), p.220.

that at a rehearsal where the eye has nothing to engage it, a recitative immediately becomes boring; but at the performance, where between the stage and the audience there are so many objects to entertain the eye, a recitative like this is over before the listeners are aware of it'.[279] It is possible that a three- rather than two-week preparation process is indicated (the recitative rehearsals may not have been the starting point), although there must have been instances where this was truncated and adjusted, as in the same city in January 1773: Leopold wrote that the *primo tenore* was 'only engaged a week before the performance'.[280]

8 December	Second recitative rehearsal
15 December	'first rehearsal with instruments', with 16 instruments, the 'small orchestra'
17 December	'first rehearsal with full orchestra', 60 players, in the *sala di ridotto*
21 December	Recitative rehearsal
19 December	'first rehearsal in the theatre'
22 December	second rehearsal in the theatre
24 December	dress rehearsal
26 December	first performance, to 'general applause'
27 December	second performance

As well as separate recitative (and probably soloist, and chorus) rehearsals, sectional instrumental rehearsals also took place in Italy for the concertino; they are described as being later discontinued.[281] While some production information can be gleaned from surviving scores and parts, even very rare documents such as prompt copies provide relatively little additional information, and say nothing about the rehearsals that made the productions possible.[282] The composition and rehearsal process in Italy could become very compressed, and in the early 19th century William Thomas Parke noted that composers 'considered the overture to an opera of so little consequence that they generally left it till the last moment, and I have frequently known that scarcely time has been allowed for the copyist to get it ready for the last rehearsal'.[283]

---

279 Anderson (1989), p.696.
280 Anderson (1989), p.223.
281 Holman (2020), p.274.
282 Judith Milhous and Robert D. Hume: 'A Prompt Copy of Handel's *Radamisto*', *The Musical Times*, cxxvii/1719 (1986), pp.316–321.
283 William Thomas Parke, *Musical Memoirs* (London, 1830), vol.i, p.268.

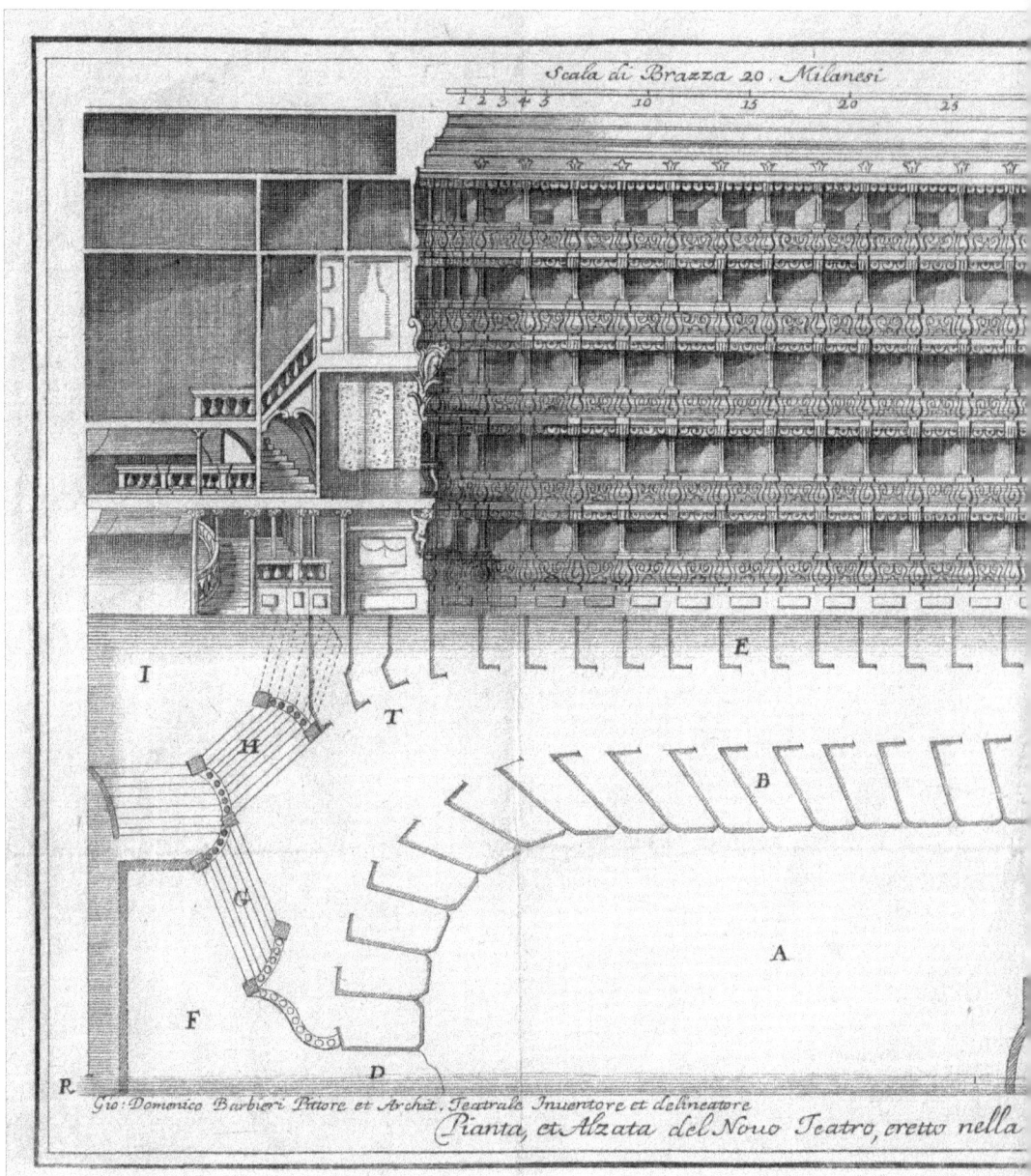

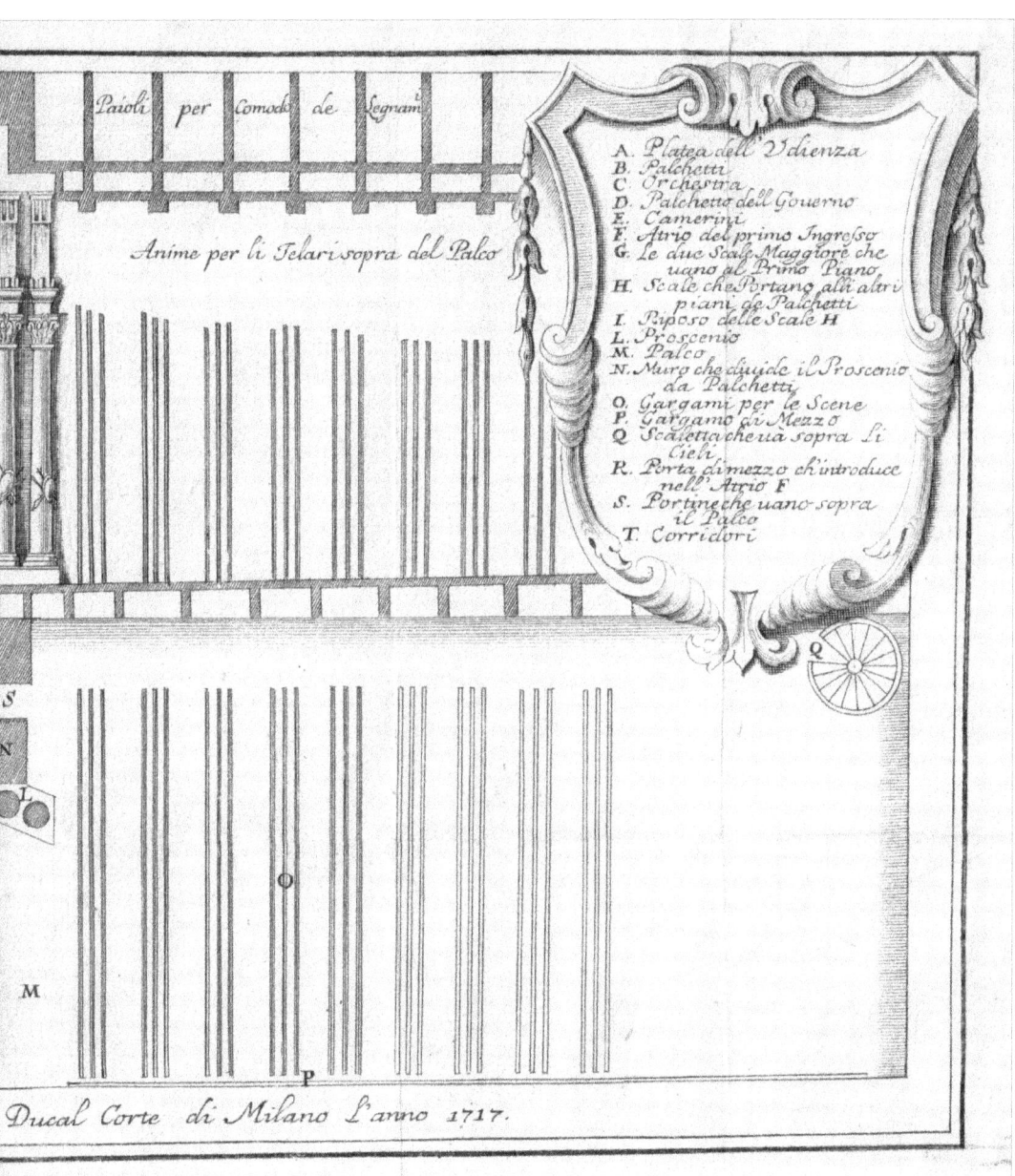

Illus. 6. Two-view cutaway drawing of the Teatro Regio Ducale, Milan (*Descrizione di Milano*, 1737).

CHAPTER 4
PERFORMERS AND THEIR TRAINING

LISTENING AND HEARING

For much of the early modern period, musical traditions were relatively local, and even professional musicians were not always aware of the standards and styles that existed elsewhere. This both deprived them of good models, and the knowledge of how things were done differently (and better) elsewhere. In 1780 Johann Adam Hiller lamented that 'The poor condition of our church and theater music is related to yet another disadvantage ... Talented young people never have the opportunity to hear something excellent, which could serve as a model for imitation'.[284] However, travel was to become easier the following century, and the newly-appointed organists of Norwich (1821) and Salisbury (1869) cathedrals each undertook considerable national tours to hear and learn from other institutions. The latter, John Richardson, even published an account of his travels, including many comments praising the choirs and organs he heard.[285] Enthusiastic amateurs also left records of their musical travels, including Lieutenant Hammond and Francis North in the 17th century.[286]

---

284 Cited in Beverly Jerold, 'Fasch and the Beginning of Modern Artistic Choral Singing', *Bach*, xxxv/1 (2004), pp.61-86 at 70.
285 Francis Knights, 'John Richardson's Cathedral Tour of 1869', *The Organ*, lxix/272 (Spring 1990), pp.8-12.
286 L. G. Wickham Legg (ed), *A Relation of A Short Survey of 26 Counties* (London, 1904); Wilson (1959), pp.38-41.

How people thought about and described music varied according to time, place and tradition. While some modern studies of the historical listener provide useful perspective,[287] for the earlier periods the idea of performance criticism or description is essentially absent: Christopher Page points out that 'very little medieval writing has yet been discovered which records a personal or impressionistic reaction to music',[288] Craig Wright asks, 'How much in specific terms do we truly know about tempo, dynamic levels, pitch, and, perhaps the most important, vocal production – about the nature or quality of the sound of the voice of a court or cathedral singer?',[289] while Nikolaus Harnoncourt suggests that pre-20th-century audiences were more interested in the work itself than its performance.[290] This latter observation seems plausible for a pre-canonical era, though Quantz was certainly aware of the reverse: if audiences 'listen more for the sake of judging the performer than of enjoying the music, they voluntarily deprive themselves of the greater part of the pleasure that they might experience'.[291]

PERFORMANCE DESCRIPTIONS

One actual description of a music event, the consecration of Florence Cathedral in 1436, for which Dufay composed his motet *Nuper rosarum flores*, is notable both for its florid language and its lack of musical detail: 'everywhere there was singing with so many and such various voices, such harmonies exalted even to heaven, that truly it was to the listener like angelic and divine melodies; the voices filled the listeners' ears with such a wondrous sweetness that they seemed to become stupefied'.[292] Such generalizations tend to be produced by non-expert listeners or non-musicians, and their value as evidence

---

287 See Shai Burstyn, 'In quest of the period ear', *Early Music*, xxv/4 (November 1997), pp.692–701, Shai Burstyn, 'Pre-1600 music listening: a methodological approach', *The Musical Quarterly*, lxxxii (1998), pp.455–465, Wegman (2002) and Tim Carter, 'Listening to music in early modern Italy: some problems for the urban musicologist', in Tess Knighton and Ascensión Mazuela-Anguita (eds), *Hearing the city in early modern Europe* (Turnhout, 2018), pp.25–49.

288 Christopher Page, *Discarding images: reflections on music and culture in medieval France* (Oxford, 1993), p.xxii. For 15th-century music aesthetics, see Rob C. Wegman, 'Sense and Sensibility in Late-Medieval Music: Thoughts on Aesthetics and "Authenticity"', *Early Music*, xxiii/2 (May 1995), pp.298-312. Stevens (1979), p.235 suggests that the 'public music of the late Middle Ages … was functional rather than expressive'.

289 Wright (1978), p.295.

290 Nikolaus Harnoncourt, trans Mary O'Neill, *Baroque Music Today: Music as Speech* (Portland, 1988). For early 'listeners', see James H. Johnson, *Listening in Paris: a cultural history* (Berkeley, 1995) and William Weber, 'Did People Listen in the 18th Century?', *Early Music*, xxv/4 (November 1997), pp.678-691.

291 Quantz (1966), p.298.

292 Wegman (2002), p.53.

is quite limited. In January 1483 one listener at the Abbey of Saint Aubert in Cambrai noted the monks 'played the organ and sang more splendidly than I had ever heard',[293] while the English Chapel Royal was described by the Venetian ambassador Pasqualigo: 'We attended High Mass which was chaunted by the Bishop of Durham, with a superb and noble descant choir'; in 1515 his colleague Sagudino was at Richmond Palace, where 'High Mass was sung by his majesty's choristers, whose voices are really divine than human: they did not chaunt but sung like angels (*non cantavano ma jubilavano*), and as for the counter-bass voices, they probably have not their equal in the world'.[294] In Italy, the Duke of Ferrara said of the Christmas High Mass of 1591 that he 'had never heard a more beautiful mass than this one'.[295]

Reports from professional musicians were not always much more specific, but carry more weight: Mozart (a severe critic of others' performances), writing to his father from Vienna in April 1784 about his just-completed Piano Quintet K452, was able to give full credit to the unnamed performers of 'the best work I have ever composed … how beautifully it was performed'.[296]

In general, it seems easier to find praise of individual solo singers than of ensembles,[297] and perhaps standards and expectations were different in each case. Precentor John Borne of Canterbury (d.1420) had 'the most excellent voice of any monk in the kingdom',[298] while in 1455 in Venice, visitors heard a 'young English woman who sang so sweetly and pleasantly that it seemed not a human voice, but divine',[299] and Thomas Coryat (1577-1617), visiting the same city, also noted the quality of the solo voices: 'there were three or four so excellent that I think few or none in Christendome do excelle them, especially one, who had such a peerless and … supernaturall voice … that I think there was never a better singer in all the world'.[300] In Rome in 1770 Burney heard a daughter of the fashionable painter Pompeo Bartoni, who 'sings divinely with more grace, taste and expression than any female in public or private I ever heard'.[301]

---

293 Wright (1978), p.306.
294 Harris (1938), p.122; Giles (1994), p.30.
295 Laurie Stras, *Women and Music in Sixteenth-Century Ferrara* (Cambridge, 2018), p.302.
296 Anderson (1989), p.873.
297 For example, in Giles (1994), ch.3 and 4.
298 Harrison (1963), pp.189-190.
299 Wegman (2002), p.49.
300 Thomas Coryat, *Coryat's Crudities* (London, 1611), cited in Ellen Rosand, 'Venice 1580-1680', in Price (1993), pp.75-102 at 83.
301 Burney (1974), p.149. Her name is not given by Burney, but was either Rufina or Maria Benedetta.

MUSIC EDUCATION

The use of young musicians in the Medieval church meant that educational responsibility was held by local monasteries, cathedrals and churches, who created formal and informal schools for music and other education. In addition, training could be provided for the adults, as in vocal and notational training organized for nuns, using the Guidonian hand.[302] A further group of young musicians were orphans, and music could be a significant part of the activity of orphanages such as the Santa Maria della Visitazione degli Orfani in Rome[303] or the Ospedale della Pietà in Venice; the Italian music conservatoire tradition appears to have later emerged from these.[304] Burney (1773) notes that the musical directors of such Italian orphanages (which had included distinguished musicians such as Legrenzi, Rovetta, Vivaldi and Hasse) saw their roles as compositional and administrative: 'the maestro di capella only composes and directs ... and attends all the rehearsals and public performances'.[305]

From the end of the 18th century there were formal music conservatoires in Italy, followed by Paris (1795), Prague (1811), Graz (1815), Vienna (1817), London (1822) and so on. Other projects included Anton Stadler's 'Musick Plan' of 1800, which was unusual in that the curriculum was designed from scratch by one person.[306] The spread of such institutions provided a model of good practice (seen, for example, in the very influential teaching material generated from the Paris Conservatoire in the early 19th century). However, Nikolaus Harnoncourt has argued that the conformity of the conservatoire system has since produced some pernicious effects with regard to the absence of some freedom and local traditions available to earlier musicians.[307]

While the possibility of a musical career would have entirely depended on musical talent, allied with education (only those who could read, read music and had access to musical instruments for study, for example), it is interesting to think what proportion of the population as a whole this number might have represented. It is possible that this was not large, perhaps thousands in a pop-

---

302 Anne Bagnall Yardley, 'The Music Education of Young Girls in Medieval Nunneries', in Boynton and Rice (2008), pp.49-67 at 59.
303 Noel O'Regan, 'Choirboys in Early Modern Rome', in Boynton and Rice (2008), pp.216-240 at 233.
304 Burney gave an account of the Naples Conservatoire in 1770; Burney (1974), pp.162-164.
305 Burney (1974), p.77.
306 Poulin (1990), p.216.
307 Harnoncourt (1988), p.25.

STANDARDS AND COMPETENCE

Given the patchy historical record of early modern performers, and the extreme difficulty of some of the music they played, modern writers have taken a variety of views about the technical standards of the past. Harnoncourt suggested that 'We must assume that leading musicians of all periods have been able to perform the most difficult works of the composers of their own times',[308] while Jerold notes that 'Today's historically-informed performances mirror the view that eighteenth-century musicians were our equal in technique and musicianship, and that they performed with great refinement. To all appearances, this has not been documented, but simply presumed'.[309] Clearly, those with the talent, time and inclination (and expert tuition) could achieve extremely high standards individually, and Quantz's recommendation for a beginner flautist to practice for four hours a day – which is 'neither too much nor too little' – should give modern musicians pause for thought.[310]

The standards of historical choristers certainly 'varied widely, for while some institutions strove to engage boys from far and wide with pure voices, others sought to educate the poor of the surrounding region'.[311] Similarly, their social status is likely to have varied considerably between traditions, countries and centuries; the anonymous Elizabethan author of *The Praise of Musick* (1586) describes cathedral choristers as being 'of the poore and beggerly sort, whose parents are not able to pay any thinge for their learninge'.[312] The choristers at Salisbury Cathedral in 1602 were 'by reason of their want of knowledge and practice in the church songs and music' unable 'to sing surely and perfectly but [did] often miss and fail and [were] out in their singing',[313] while of the quiristers (choristers) at Winchester College in 1631, it was said 'Only two or three

---

308 Harnoncourt (1988), p.17.
309 Jerold (2004), p.61.
310 Quantz (1966), p.118.
311 Boynton and Rice, 'Introduction: Performance and Premodern Childhood', in Boynton and Rice (2008), pp.1-18 at 9.
312 Flynn (1995), p.198.
313 Woodfill (1953), p.146.

can sing'.[314] Ludovico Viadana (1602) in Italy also had a poor opinion of young singers: 'boys, for the most part, sing carelessly, and with little grace'.[315] Nevertheless, some virtuoso Tudor music written for trebles, such as the five-part Magnificat (c.1510) by William Cornysh (ex.2), shows that there must have existed choristers of a very high standard.[316]

Ex.2 William Cornysh, *Magnificat*, final duo for Treble and Mean

---

314 'Dotted Crotchet' [Frederick George Edwards], 'Winchester College. Seinte Marie College of Wynchestre', *The Musical Times*, xlv/736 (1 June 1904), pp.360-369.

315 Strunk (1981), iii, p.62.

316 Mould (2007), p.50.

Where detailed institutional records exist, the picture they paint can be alarming: the proportion of substandard singers in the 16th-century papal choir may have approached 40%, according to Richard Sherr, with individual voices described as 'terrible', 'harsh, 'hoarse', 'dissonant', 'almost bearable' or 'has no voice'; however, some 'do not have good voices but are good musicians'. In terms of their moral character, one singer is 'the worst kind of heretic', one a 'gambler' and another has 'fled because of debts'. The highest vocal praise in a 1565 list made for the Cardinals' Commission is the single laconic word 'acceptable', although a 1573 list is more generous to one tenor at least: Mattia Bianco has 'a very good voice'.[317]

Monteverdi's letters include comments about his auditions of singers that make it clear be believed musical reliability to be crucial: 'he sings his part very surely in motets' (1610); 'as a singer he is very reliable' (1627).[318] The quality of training must always have been very important, and students were dependent on the skill, experience and affordability of their teacher, if they even had one. Mozart writes from Mannheim in November 1777 about the composer Cannabich's daughter Rosa, whose left hand has been ruined, and she does 'what she does, because no one has ever shown her any other way'.[319] However, certain places were very well equipped with music teachers, of whatever quality, and Leopold Mozart (1778) stated that 'in *Naples alone* there are at least three hundred maestri'.[320]

The standard of singers on the continent (apparently generally poor) often comes in for criticism: choral singing 'was filled with screaming from the most wretched voices' (Reichardt, 1785);[321] while in Italy 'all the *musici* [castrati] in the churches at present are made up of the refuse of the opera houses, and it is a very rare thing to meet with a tolerable voice upon the establishment of any church in Italy' (Burney, 1770).[322]

Professional instrumentalists could also be poor: in October 1777, a letter from Mozart describes a concert including the Munich violinist Charles Albert Dupreille (1728-1796) 'who could not play four bars in succession without

---

317 Sherr (1999), XIV, pp.608, 612, 614 and 617.
318 Denis Arnold and Nigel Fortune (eds), *The New Monteverdi Companion* (London, 1985), pp.26 and 66.
319 Anderson (1989), p.374.
320 Anderson (1989), p.492.
321 Cited in Jerold (2006), p.79.
322 Burney (1974), p.164. For the background to these comments, see John Rosselli, 'The Castrati as a Professional Group and a Social Phenomenon, 1550-1850', *Acta Musicologica*, lx/2 (May-August 1988), pp.143-179.

going wrong. He could not find his fingering and he knew nothing whatever about short rests',[323] while Jean-Jacques Rousseau's satirical *Letter of a Symphonist to his Comrades in the Orchestra* (1753) notes the decline of orchestral playing in France, now that 'we do not play much in tune or stay together very well'.[324] The question of overall ensemble standard relative to the quality and ability of individual performers is an interesting one; Burney's remark about the Mannheim orchestra being 'an army of generals' may represent an ideal rarely achieved[325] – but note that an anonymous account from 1785 of a crushed and noisy audience busy playing cards and wandering around while the same Mannheim band played is hard to reconcile with modern ideas of performing precision.[326]

INSTRUMENTS

The use of instruments in church varied from denomination to denomination, and clergy and others that objected to either their sound or cost found plenty of evidence from centuries of past ecclesiastical critics to censure their use: writing before the Civil War, Puritan lawyer William Prynne wondered why 'hath the church so many organs and musical instruments? To what purpose, I demand, is that terrible blowing of bellows, expressing rather cracks of thunder than the sweetness of the voice?',[327] while John Vicars complained of '*Roaring-Boyes*, tooting and squeaking *Organ-Pipes*'.[328]

Elsewhere, at about the same time but very different in its appreciation of the mix of voices and instruments, the complex interplay of voices and instruments could even be contractually specified for specific services, as in the *Constituciones* of the *Real Colegio* at València: 'in the Salve sung on Saturdays, after the organ has played a little, the service will begin with the antiphon *Ad honorem* in polyphony, followed by the Salve, one verse on the organ, and the other sung by the choir in plainchant, and then the *gozos*, Gaude Virgo, etc.,

---

323 Anderson (1989), p.300.

324 Beverly Jerold, 'Fontenelle's Famous Question and Performance Standards of the Day', *College Music Symposium*, xliii (2003), pp.150-160 at 157.

325 Burney (1773), i, p.93.

326 Quoted in Peter Walls, *History, Imagination and the Performance of Music* (Woodbridge, 2003), pp.72-73. For all the other sorts of goings-on during opera performances in early 18th-century Italy, see Forment (2010) and Parrott (2022), pp.273-274.

327 Cited in Le Huray (1967), p.52.

328 John Vicars, *Gods arke overtopping the worlds waves* (London, 1646), p.184.

with the organ playing one verse, and the other verse with the choir in polyphony; then the instrumentalists will play, immediately followed by the organ, and then a polyphonic motet for the feasts of our Lady will be sung. When the motet has finished, the cornetts will play, bringing the Salve to an end with the verse *Monstra te esse matrem*, which will be chanted by the two *capiscoles* and the responses will be chanted'.[329]

Other practical factors about instruments and instrumentalists may have had a significant impact on rehearsal practice. For example, were instrumental doublings of voices determined by the conductor in advance or in rehearsal?[330] Were such choices made for musical decisions, for practical ones (supporting the choir) or just in order to make sure all the lines were covered? How were different tuning systems and pitch differences accommodated? Who owned the instruments (for example, was the very large royal collection of Henry VIII to an extent a 'loan' set?),[331] where were they kept, who moved them about, who maintained them[332] and how were they accessed for individual practice? Were there separate rehearsals for instrumentalists? Who (if anyone) was responsible for choices about technical matters such as bowing?[333] Was uniformity of ensemble tone, volume or articulation a concern?

---

329 Royo (2021), pp.37-38. For these documents, see also Greta Olson, 'Required early seventeenth-century performance practices at the Colegio-Seminario de Corpus Christi, Valencia', *Studies in Music*, xxi (1987), pp.10–38 and Mireya Royo, *La Capilla del Colegio del Patriarca: vida musical y pervivencia de las Danzas del Corpus de Juan Bautista Comes (1603–1706)*, PhD thesis (University of Oviedo, 2015).

330 See, for example, the scoring allocations made by Augsburg cantor Adam Gumpelzhaimer (1559-1625) in copies of printed multi-choir works by Giovanni Gabrieli; Richard Charteris, 'Giovanni Gabrieli's *Sacrae Symphonae* (Venice, 1597); Some rediscovered partbooks with new evidence about performance practice', *Early Music*, xxiii/3 (August 1995), pp.487-498.

331 A list is transcribed in Raymond Russell, rev Howard Schott, *The Harpsichord and Clavichord* (London, 2/1973), pp.155-160.

332 Accessing consumables like replacement reeds and strings may sometimes have been a problem, particularly when they needed to be imported: a 1607 letter in the Hatfield House records notes that 'My Lord's instruments are unstrung, and … this half year none will come over'; Richard Charteris, 'Jacobean Musicians at Hatfield House, 1605-1613', *Royal Musical Association Research Chronicle*, xii (1974), pp.115-136 at 117.

333 For the application of Georg Muffat's rules on bowing, see Walls (2003), pp.151-152; Corelli also demanded regular bowing (Parrott (2022), p.396). The study of later performance annotations has been undertaken by the CHASE (Collection of Historical Annotated String Editions) project, https://mhm.hud.ac.uk/chase.

KEYBOARD ACCOMPANIMENT

The prevalence of keyboard accompaniment also varied during the Renaissance and Baroque; at some times and places this involved a simple doubling of vocal parts that was suitable both for rehearsal and performances,[334] whereas elaborated examples were intended primarily for performance.[335] Keyboard accompaniment material from the pre-Civil War era can be very sketchy in nature, such as in the early 17th-century Batten organ book (Tenbury 791), outlining the highest and lowest voices rather than providing a keyboard reduction of all the vocal parts.[336] The information provided is usually sufficient to infer the harmony (and therefore to support the singers in rehearsal in performance, even where their inner voice was not included), whereas 18th century formats sometimes also provide cues, registration, ornamentation or figured bass to assist the player further. Thomas Mace (Lay Clerk of Trinity College, Cambridge, for many years) approved the use of the organ in terms of helping with both ensemble and tuning: 'the *Organ* stands us in stead of a *Holding, Uniting-Constant-Friend*; and is as a *Touch-stone*, to try the certainty of *All Things*; especially the *Well-keeping* the *Instruments* in *Tune* &c'.[337] Viadana (1602) supported keyboard accompaniment for his music too: 'If anyone wants to sing this kind of music without organ or clavier, the effect will never be good; on the contrary, for the most part, dissonances will be heard'.[338] The implication of the second phrase may be that an accompaniment prevents (or covers) singers' errors.

However, whether manuscript organ parts were intended for rehearsal, or both rehearsal and performance, is not always certain, and this relates to rehearsal venues and to whether (for example) cathedral song schools even had keyboard instruments in them.[339] In Britain during the 16th and 17th centuries the

---

334 See the various options outlined by Italian theorists in Augusta Campagne and Elam Rotem, *Keyboard Accompaniment in Italy around 1600: Intabulations, Scores and Basso Continuo* (Basel, 2022).

335 For a Restoration example from Oxford, see Knights (1990a) and Knights (1990b).

336 Rebecca Herissone, 'To fill, forbear, or adorne': The Organ Accompaniment of Restoration Sacred Music (Aldershot, 2006). John Morehen, 'Ornaments in organ scores' (unpublished essay, c.1968) even wonders whether the absence of keyboard ornaments in such scores might have meant that they 'were generally used as conductor's copies and that they were not actually used to play from'.

337 Mace (1676), p.242; he is discussing the consort organ at this point.

338 Strunk (1981), iii, p.62.

339 None of the twenty or so surviving English virginals has a known institutional provenance, for example; see Donald H. Boalch, rev Charles Mould, *Makers of the Harpsichord and Clavichord, 1440-1840* (Oxford, 3/1995), now superseded by https://boalch.org.

matter is also complicated by varying pitch standards between (for example) a rehearsal keyboard and a church organ (based on 10' not 8' pitch).[340] In 1549 Eton had 'one litle paire of orgaynes in the Scholem^rs Chamber' in addition to the main chapel organ, while Magdalen College, Oxford had a second small organ in 1488-89,[341] as did New College, Oxford in 1488,[342] and likely a Dallam chamber organ in the 1660s.[343] It does seem likely that stringed keyboards or small organs were kept in at least some rehearsal venues, but the recorded presence of an organ did not mean that it was actually usable: at Durham Cathedral in 1589 the quire organ 'had not worked for many years', but was repaired by William Smith (c.1550-1604).[344]

Modern performance of Renaissance polyphony is almost entirely *a capella*, but this probably did not reflect general historical practice, and some like Beverly Jerold have suggested that some form of accompaniment was in fact common.[345] The Sistine Chapel did not use organ at that time (although one was installed later),[346] but that unaccompanied choral practice did exist sometimes within the Anglican tradition is shown by Roger North's complaint about psalmody, that 'where the organ is not used which keeps the quire upright, the chanting is scandalous, such a confused din as no one living not pre-instructed could guess what they were doing'.[347]

Another form of keyboard accompaniment was provided by score reading, and Albrechtsberger (1790) provides an early published discussion of this skill,[348] which must always have been necessary for composers and players rehearsing an opera from a full manuscript score. The importance of this ability was to

---

340 See Andrew Johnstone, '"As it was in the Beginning": Organ and Choir Pitch in Early Anglican Church Music', *Early Music*, xxxi/4 (November 2003), pp.506-525.
341 Harrison (1963), p.167; there were three by 1531-32.
342 Harrison (1963), p.160.
343 Williamson (1997), p.132 and David Force, 'A Holding, Uniting-Constant Friend': The Organ in Seventeenth-Century English Domestic Music, PhD thesis (The Open University, 2019), p.99.
344 Saunders (1997), pp.142-143.
345 Beverly Jerold, 'Why Most *a cappella* Music Could Not Have Been Sung Unaccompanied', *The Choral Journal*, xl/7 (February 2000), pp.21-27. See also Parrott (2015), ch.16.
346 Jerold (2000), p.27: in 1784 'Christian Carl Rolle mentions that the singers of the papal chapel were accompanied by organ, but not instruments'.
347 Wilson (1959), p.269.
348 Johann Georg Albrechtsberger, ed Ignaz von Seyfried, trans Sabilla Novello, *J. G. Albrechtsberger's Collected Writings on Thorough-Bass, Harmony, and Composition, for Self-Instruction* [Vienna, 1826] (London, 1855), pp.254-256.

diminish with the creation of cheap printed vocal scores from the end of the 18th century, the orchestral parts having been reduced to a keyboard accompaniment.[349] For expert keyboard players, the same skill of condensing scores at sight obviated the need for notated figured bass. A few references exist of implied or specified keyboard-only accompaniment in initial opera rehearsals: a letter from Leopold Mozart in Milan in September 1772 mentions of a newly-completed Wolfgang work that 'The choruses were rehearsed yesterday, but without the instruments',[350] while in London in the 1820s the accompanying instrument was named as 'the composer's piano-forte'.[351]

PLAYING BY EAR

Even with accurate source material, musicians needed to understand incomplete parts, such as unfigured bass lines: Giovanni Piccioni (1610) expected expert organists to play from an unfigured bass 'correctly by ear and by art';[352] this is perfectly possible with experience, but initially will result in the right-hand chords lying behind the beat.

MEMORIZATION

Socrates, as reported by Plato in the *Phaedrus* (c.370 BC), was concerned about the use of writing, as 'it will create forgetfulness in the learners' souls, because they will not use their memories; they will trust to the external written characters and not remember of themselves. The specific which you have discovered is an aid not to memory, but to reminiscence',[353] and he was correct in

---

[349] See Elena Pons Capdevila, *Arranging the Canon: keyboard arrangements, publishing practices and the appropriation of musical classics, 1770-1810*, PhD thesis (Royal Holloway, 2017). The quality of such arrangements was variable, and that for Mozart's *Die Entführung aus dem Serail*, for example, was described in 1791 as having 'ruined' the work; Cliff Eisen, *New Mozart Documents* (London, 1991), p.41. The keyboard intabulation tradition was of course much older, but the extent to which such material served explicitly for rehearsal is not known. See Thomas Neal, 'Between Practice and Print: Performing Palestrina's *Missarum liber quartus* (1582) with Alessandro Nuvoloni's *Basso principale co'l soprano* (1610)', in Marcello Mazzetti (ed), *Basso Continuo in Italy: Sources, Pedagogy and Performance* (Turnhout, 2023), pp.105-139.

[350] Anderson (1989), p.199.

[351] Holman (2020), p.309.

[352] Donington (1989), p.291.

[353] Benjamin Jowett (trans), *The dialogues of Plato* (Oxford, 3/1892), p.484. For a discussion of the changing historical relationship between memory and notated text in the Middle Ages, see Clanchy (1993).

that memorization abilities diminish with lack of use. In historical societies where literacy was not universal, the role of memory was far more important than it is today, and the Tudor school system, for example, was built on 'colossal amounts of memorization'; John Donne would routinely compose his very lengthy sermons on paper, then memorize them for delivery.[354] Musicians were also able to commit substantial amounts of repertoire to memory by design – or by accident.[355] For example, Fray Motolinia's *Historia de los Indios* describes how an old friar taught young indigenous boys numerous prayers through Gregorian chant, noting that 'if the pages get mixed up or the books fall while they are singing this does not prevent them from singing on without the slightest error'.[356] At Notre Dame in Paris (1313) singers were expected to know the antiphoner and psalter by heart.[357] However, it was not until the 19th century that musicians (especially soloists) outside the church or opera house routinely began to memorize repertoire.[358] In terms of locating rehearsal start points, memorization of course makes matters even more cumbersome.

Where memory did fail, assistance could be found: in November 1498 the choir of Cambrai Cathedral was not able to sing the *Salve Regina* chant uniformly, so the music was 'painted on a tablet that was affixed to the wall of the chapel of the Trinity' so that they could see it: 'Because the vicars are frequently discordant when singing the Salve regina, one is to be made in large notes and placed against the wall following the example of the Alma that is before the horologe'.[359]

A large memorized repertoire was obviously an unusual matter of note in classical music: the *Concerto delle donne* in Ferrara could perform more than 330 madrigals 'by heart';[360] while writing from Paris in May 1778 Mozart mentions a composition-pupil daughter of the Duc de Guines who played the flute and harp, 'has a great deal of talent and even genius, and in particular a marvellous memory, so that she can play all her pieces, actually about two hundred, by heart'.[361]

---

354 Katherine Rundell, *Super-Infinite: The Transformations of John Donne* (London, 2022), p.223.

355 For a discussion of the historical importance of memory to musicians, see Smith (2011), pp.15-18 and Boynton and Rice (2008), p.10.

356 Robert M. Stevenson, *Music in Mexico: A Historical Survey* (New York, 1952), p.55.

357 Parrott (2015), p.16.

358 Jennifer Mishra, 'A Century of Memorization Pedagogy', *Journal of Historical Research in Music Education*, xxxii/1 (October 2010), pp.3-18.

359 Wright (1978), p.304.

360 Claude V. Palisca, *The Florentine Camerata: Documentary Studies and Translations* (New Haven, 1989), p.121.

361 Anderson (1989), p.538.

PERFORMER ERRORS

The principal purpose of rehearsal today is the elimination of individual and collective mistakes: Mary Ellen Cavitt calculates that 'error correction may consume almost half (49%) of all rehearsal time'.[362] In the entirely 'live' music environment of the past, performance errors (as in wrong notes) passed by very quickly, and it cannot be assumed that players would have had the same text-critical attitude to accuracy as today. In addition, few institutions seem to have specifically punished musical errors (the Sistine Chapel being an obvious exception, see below), as the 'rituals' of performance were not inviolate. This is in stark contrast with Aztec sacred music traditions: 'Training of an extremely rigid kind was prerequisite to a career in music since music itself was always thought of as a necessary adjunct to ritual, absolutely perfect performances – such as only the most highly trained singers and players could give – were constantly demanded … Imperfectly executed rituals were thought to offend rather than to appease the gods, and therefore errors in the performance of the ritual music – such as missed drumbeat - carried the death penalty'.[363]

In the monastic tradition, those making errors had to kneel and acknowledge their mistakes, according to the Benedictine rule, and at Syon Abbey there was a categorization of such errors in reading or singing, although musical errors were all listed as the lowest ('light'), rather than the fourth ('most grievous'), which covered violence, lechery and so on.[364] The acknowledgement of rehearsal errors by individual singers is still common choral practice in British cathedrals, where 'a finger or hand [is raised] to acknowledge his or her mistake so long as it is not catastrophic enough as to have caused a complete breakdown in the musical texture'.[365]

Remarkably, Luigi Zenobi gives as one of his eight qualities needed to be a 'secure' singer the ability to, 'on meeting with an error on the part of the composer or the copyist, [know] how to improvise a remedy to the error while singing and find his way back without help from others'.[366] A example of this process might be found in the very curious description of Stephano Vanneo (1531), who invites his reader to admire and 'observe the parts of an accom-

---

362 Mary Ellen Cavitt, 'Descriptive analysis of error correction in instrumental rehearsals', *Journal of Research in Music Education*, li/3 (2003), pp.218–230 at 228.
363 Stevenson (1952), p.18.
364 Yardley (2008), pp.61-62.
365 Leach (2013), p.94.
366 Cited in Smith (2011), p.136; see also p.138.

plished singer, who when he feels that he is producing a dissonant progression, at once little by little and so discretely, that it can scarcely be recognized and detected, either flattens or sharpens it, until a consonant and sweet progression strikes the ears'.[367]

The fining-for-mistakes system of the papal choir described by Richard Sherr and others is remarkable in that it sometimes specifies the musical error that resulted in the fine. Not coming in during polyphonic entries was one infraction, as well as getting the pitch wrong or having a voice missing. In November 1583, for example, one singer called Bellucius was fined 'because Cesare Bellucius in the Gloria in excelsis which he was supposed to sing, did not sing, and because of the dissonance was the cause of great subversion'.[368] In 1594 'at Mass the sopranos allowed a three-part section to begin, the Benedictus qui venit, which started with an alto, and they allowed the alto to sing for about 20 beats before any of the sopranos decided to start'.[369] In 1700 the four-part *Missa paris vocibus* by Vincenzo Pellegrini (c.1562-1630) was put on the music list but with the wrong set of solo singers present (STTB), and 'Great disharmony came from this mistake, it never having occurred that a mass was sung without the contralto part' (this implies the work had not been rehearsed, otherwise this would have been noticed). Four singers were fined in 1728 for 'having altered the pitch taken from the senior singer in the motet, which caused much disharmony'. Later two singers simultaneously began the motet *O magnum* a tone apart, 'which caused the senior singer to stop singing, which caused certain confusion'.[370] These are familiar sorts of transgressions in choral singing today, even with scores being used, but the question of whether these Sistine Chapel mistakes occurred *after* the music had been rehearsed correctly, or whether they were a result of no rehearsal having taken place, is unknown. Fining singers would have seemed fairer in the first instance.

A parallel English instance of error penalties can be found in the Acts of the Dean and Chapter of Westminster, 1560-1609 (chapter minutes of 12 October 1561): 'Item it is decreed that everie Saterdaie their shalbe a quire chapitor wherat shalbe one of the prebendaries, before whom all the quire shall appere for redresse of faultes in the weeke before committed'. Whether these 'faultes' were purely musical or also included behaviour issues is unknown. The *Book of Perditions* mentioned in John Strype's *Annals of the Reformation* was more

---

367 Donington (1989), p.137.
368 Sherr (1999), XIII, p.457.
369 Lionnet (1987), p.7.
370 Sherr (1999), XIII, pp.454-455.

explicit in the latter respect, covering the 'Default of such as were absent, or negligent in the Week before'.[371]

The necessity of rehearsal partly depends on the regularity of performance, as well as the size of repertoire, without even taking into account the ability of performers. In Vienna in the early 1770s, Burney reported that 'there is hardly a church or monastery in Vienna where a musical mass is not performed each morning … the churches are very full every day'.[372] As can be seen from the very rare 1680 music list surviving from Durham Cathedral,[373] full choral services there took place twice daily, and this seems to have been normal practice in the major Anglican cathedrals until the 20th century. In these circumstances, core repertoire would be known very well, the 'house style' of performance was a given and there would be no need to rehearse standard material such as responses and psalms.

GETTING LOST

It is interesting to consider the possible 'catch-up' mechanisms that singers of complex polyphony working from parts had at their disposal when they became lost through miscounting or other errors. These include the location of recognizable harmonic features (for example, structural points such as cadences), distinctive melodic turns, imitative and sequential passages and, of course, referring to the text. These resources would have become more effective if the piece was already known or had already been rehearsed, which is one additional reason why rehearsals might have been important: not only to prevent mistakes, but provide a 'safety net', given that there will always be some errors. All of these resources are more effective if the ensemble's rhythmic precision is maintained, so that the underlying beat can be quickly identified.

For one example of rhythmic complexities that would have made ensemble precision a challenge when working from a choirbook, see a passage from the Credo of Fayrfax's *Missa O Quam Glorifica* (ex.1), where the two mensurations used (C and O, differing between the voices, and called 'double mensuration' by Roger Bray)[374] are transcribed as 6/4, and shown here without barlines. While

---

371 John Strype, *Annals of the Reformation*, 4 vols. (London, 1709-25), p.113.
372 Cited in Harnoncourt (1988), p.151.
373 See Brian Crosby, 'A Service Sheet from June 1680', *The Musical Times*, lxxi/1648 (June 1980), pp.399-401.
374 Bray (1995), p.49.

the underlying pulse is maintained (only) in the tenor, the part is at the bottom of its register, and the text is a melisma, so it is very unlikely this could have provided a solid metrical foundation. All of the other voices are syncopated, and it would have taken a great deal of practice to achieve metrical clarity here, when no one voice part knew exactly what the others were doing.

Ex. 3. Fayrfax, *Missa O Quam Glorifica*, Credo, 'bars' 86-90, Treble, Mean, Contratenor, Tenor and Bass. Clefs modernized, melismatic text underlay '[de-] ce- [lis]' omitted

PERFORMANCE ANXIETY

One of the modern purposes of rehearsal is to give confidence to players that they know the music well enough to play it creditably in public. However, the actual concepts of stage fright and musical perfectionism may be relatively modern: remarkably, the first published discussion of this former problem was by Adolph Kielblock in 1891, in a book called *The Stage Fright or How to Face an Audience*.[375] Andrew Steptoe notes that performance anxiety's 'cognitive disturbances centre around worries concerning potential catastrophes, performance quality and exaggerated beliefs about the importance of any particular

---

375 Adolph Kielblock, *The Stage Fright or How to Face an Audience* (Boston, 1891).

musical performance',[376] and it is certain that musicians of the past would have recognized at least some of these as issues. For example, Quantz (1752), in his advice to a flute player preparing for a public concert who is 'timorous, and as yet unaccustomed to playing in the presence of many people', suggests ignoring the audience, 'never turning his eyes to those present'.[377] Anxiety may also relate to the phenomenon of stuttering in public speaking, for which there is a very long historical record.[378]

SELECTING REPERTOIRE

Secular patrons, especially those with household musicians, such as Frederick the Great and the Princes Esterházy, were in a position to determine what was performed, or composed, for their court's entertainment.[379] Similarly, senior church dignitaries or officials could request or demand certain repertoire. Otherwise, the resident director of music would have been expected to select appropriate music and have it prepared in time. However, there could be limitations to this, as when the Sistine Chapel Choir in 1616 were given the right of refusal: 'it was resolved and decreed that the maestro di cappella for the time being may not cause any works to be sung in cappella unless they are first heard by the college of singers and they deem them to be good'.[380] Eight years later, the repertoire choices seemed to be allocated by rota, and choir librarian and alto Pietro Antonio Tamburini 'was responsible for choosing the week's music and the preparation of the music-books'.[381]

---

[376] Andrew Steptoe, 'Stress, Coping and Stage Fright in Professional Musicians', *Psychology of Music*, xvii/1 (1989), pp.3-11. See also Christopher Taborsky, 'Musical Performance Anxiety: A Review of Literature', *Update: Applications of Research in Music Education*, xxvi/1 (2007), pp.15-25 and Raluca Matei and Jane Ginsborg, 'Music performance anxiety in classical musicians – what we know about what works', *BJPsych International*, xiv/2 (May 2017), pp.33-35.

[377] Quantz (1966), p.199. Duirng the 19th century, newspaper reviews did sometimes mention performance nerves, as in a review of the singer Enrico Tamberlik, 6 April 1850: 'he was exceedingly frightened and nervous'. Richard Bethell, *Vocal Traditions in Conflict* (Hebden Bridge, 2019), p.190.

[378] Sibylle Brosch and Wolfgang Pirsig, 'Stuttering in history and culture', *International Journal of Pediatric Otorhinolaryngology*, lix/2 (14 June 2001), pp.81-87.

[379] For music at court in earlier periods, see Stevens (1979), ch.11.

[380] Lionnet (1987), p.12.

[381] Lionnet (1987), p.11.

SIGHT-READING

The ability to read music accurately at sight (*a prima vista*) is a very important rehearsal skill, and can greatly reduce the amount of time needed to learn a new work. Early writers thought that the basic skills could be taught very quickly: Odo of Cluny (d.942) asserted in his *Enchiridion musices* that boys can be taught to sight-sing 'without hesitation' in a few months by using the monochord; he also claimed that students could be taught to sing (it is not clear whether he means vocally, or using notation) in as little as three days.[382] A century later Guido of Arezzo (d.c.1050) was even more ambitious with his method, the *Epistola de ignoto cantu*, saying boys could be taught to sight-sing in two days.[383]

The skills extended into secular music traditions later: Edward, Lord Herbert of Cherbury, wrote in his Autobiography, 'During the time of living in the University or at home ... I attained also to sing my part at first sight in music,'[384] in 1664 Samuel Pepys reported that former Chapel Royal chorister Tom Edwards could 'sing anything at first sight',[385] while Francis North (Roger North's brother) 'sang any thing, at first sight, as one that reads a new book, which many, even singing masters, cannot do'.[386] Anton Stadler's 1800 'Musick Plan' notes that, after two years' training 'the student should be able to read most music at sight'.[387]

More complex music demanded a very much higher level of skill, and musicians like Handel and Mozart evidently had legendary sight-reading skills; the former (aged around 14) passed a fiendish test in the form of a chromatic cantata set for him by Bononcini, and 'treated this formidable composition as a mere trifle, not only executing it at sight, but with a degree of accuracy, truth, and expression hardly to be expected even from repeated practice' according to the anecdote in Mainwaring's *Memoirs of the Life of the late George Frederic Handel* (1760).[388] Similarly, in one of Mozart's letters of 1777 he mentions

---

382 Oliver Strunk, *Source Readings in Music History: I Antiquity and the Middle Ages* (London, 1981), pp.103 and 105.
383 Strunk (1981), i, p.124.
384 Harris (1938), p.131.
385 Mould (2007), p.130.
386 Wilson (1959), pp.35-36.
387 Poulin (1990), p.218.
388 John Mainwaring, *Memoirs of the Life of the late George Frederic Handel* (London, 1760), p.18. Thurston Dart, 'Bononcini sets Handel a Test', *The Musical Times*, cxii/1538 (April 1971), pp.324-325 suggests the work in question is Bononcini's *Era la notte*.

playing all the music in one Longotabarro's collection in Augsburg on 'a good clavichord by Stein', and accepting – on being told 'No one could tackle that' – with faux-modesty the challenge to play a difficult fugal sonata.[389] Interestingly, he provided in 1778 a description of the art of sight-reading, which included as one goal to play in a way that it sounded like 'the performer had composed it himself'.[390] Mozart evidently had a natural talent for this from a very early age, as in 1768 his father reported that people were unable to believe his skills; the following year he performed 'a very beautiful concerto' at sight.[391] What is missing from these descriptions is a sense of the actual accuracy of the result, but this comes in his description of Mlle Weber's clavier playing (1778): ' What surprises me most is her excellent sight-reading. Would you believe it, she played my difficult sonatas at sight, *slowly* but without missing a single note!'.[392] That same year, Mozart expressed concern about excessive speed when reading at sight: one Vogler played both too fast and too sketchily, for 'nothing is possible at that pace, for the eyes cannot see the music nor the hands perform it'.[393] In actual performance, matters could be quite different: from Vienna in August 1782 he wrote to his father that the finale of the Haffner Symphony K385 must be played 'as fast as possible'.[394]

Bach was also a legendary sight-reader, and is reported to have said that playing the organ was not difficult: all you had to do was 'hit the right note at the right time'.[395] A sight-reading anecdote in Forkel's 1802 biography was clearly derived from Bach family lore: at Weimar he told an acquaintance that he 'really believed he could play everything, without hesitating, at first sight'. Nemesis came when the friend deliberately supplied a score with an unplayable passage, to which Bach responded, after failing to negotiate it successfully: 'one cannot play everything at first sight; it is not possible'.[396]

Another instance of fluent reading being a professional skill likely to enhance a performer's reputation comes in a story about the Czech composer and harpsichordist Ernest Vanzhura (1750-1802) arriving in St Petersburg in 1779: very

---

389 Anderson (1989), pp.315 and 339.
390 Anderson (1989), p.449.
391 Anderson (1989), pp.81-82 and 101.
392 Anderson (1989), p.460. Burney even had a term for this, calling Madame Brillon in Paris an 'excellent sightswoman'; Burney (1974), p.19.
393 Anderson (1989), pp.448-449.
394 Anderson (1989), p.813.
395 Johann Friedrich Köhler; in David and Mendel (1998), p.412.
396 Forkel (1802), in David and Mendel (1998), p.435.

soon he 'became famous and popular here for his unusual skill playing the harpsichord. He plays not only everything from sight accurately and delicately, but also his tasteful fantasies and various very difficult concerts of his own composition, among which is one that he wrote for his own special fingering system and, surprisingly, performed with specially played passages at the octave. Balshau [Palschau], who heard him play, tried to play it as well, but had to admit that he couldn't have done it if he hadn't got a few days to rehearse'.[397]

While there has been considerable modern research on sight-reading skills,[398] references from the past suggest that high-level ability was sometimes regarded as an innate skill, rather than one that could be methodically taught. Nevertheless, as an advanced form of music notation comprehension, it was expected to some degree in certain societies, as the fictitious story of the shamed amateur gentleman that opens Thomas Morley's 1597 treatise *A Plain and Easy Introduction to Practical Music* shows: 'supper being ended, and Musicke bookes, according to the custome being brought to the table: the mistresse of the house presented mee with a part, earnestly requesting mee to sing. But when after manie excuses, I protested vnfainedly that I could not: euerie one began to wonder. Yea, some whispered to others, demaunding how I was brought vp: so that vpon shame of mine ignorance I go nowe to seeke out mine olde frinde master *Gnorimus*, to make my selfe his scholler'.[399] Henry Peacham's *The Compleat Gentleman* (1622) also asserts the necessity to 'sing your part sure, and at the first sight, withall, to play the same upon your viol'.[400] At this point these descriptions begin to sound more like social aspirations than educational or cultural obligations, and it is not possible from them to judge actual levels of musical literacy at the time.

There must have been many occasions, especially in church music, where good sight-reading was essential: Viadana (1602) speaks of 'when it is necessary to

---

397 Askold V. Smirnov, 'Johann Gottfried Wilhelm Palschau: reconstructing the composer's biography', *National Early Music Association Newsletter*, vi/1 (Spring 2022), pp.56-66 at 61.

398 See, for example, Justine Sergent, Eric Zuck, Sean Terriah and Brennan MacDonald, 'Distributed Neural Network Underlying Musical Sight-Reading and Keyboard', *Science*, New Series, xxlvii/5066 (3 July 1992), pp.106-109; Thomas W. Goolsby, 'Eye Movement in Music Reading: Effects of Reading Ability, Notational Complexity, and Encounters', *Music Perception*, xii/1 (Fall 1994), pp.77-96; Gary E. McPherson, 'Factors and Abilities Influencing Sightreading Skill in Music', *Journal of Research in Music Education*, xlii/3 (Autumn, 1994), pp.217-231; and Dneya Udtaisuk, *A Theoretical Model of Piano Sightplaying components*, PhD thesis (University of Missouri-Columbia, 2005).

399 Morley (1597), p.1. A modern version of the madrigal challenge appears in Kingsley Amis' 1954 comic novel *Lucky Jim*.

400 Woodfill (1953), p.217.

play concerted music on the spur of the moment', and recommends the organist take a 'preliminary look ... since he will always make his accompaniments better for understanding the music'.[401] While accepting that it could be and was done, William Byrd's preface to this *Psalmes, Songs, and Sonnets* of 1611 reminds readers that, 'the best song that ever was ... is seldom or never well performed at the first singing or playing'.[402] However, by the end of the 18th century, Dr Burney found Renaissance polyphonic notation (a Josquin mass in particular) impossible to conceive of being sight-read: 'these compositions must have been studied, and frequently rehearsed, before their performance; for though no rapidity of execution is required, yet, as there are no bars, and the value of the notes is frequently changed by position, as well as by the modal signs, upon very short notice, this, joined to the difficult solution of the canons, must have made it impossible for them to have been sung at sight, even by those who were accustomed to the notation'.[403]

It was the view of the 18th-century French that the Italians had more advanced reading skills. and François Raguenet (1702) makes positive comparison of Italian sight-singing to French practice: 'To sing at sight with them is no more than to read so with us ... our singers are forced to con it over and over before they can make themselves perfect'.[404]

One interesting view about the repetition process that is learning can be found in the preface to Dario Castello's *Sonate Concertante in Stil Moderne, Libro Primo* (1621), where performers were advised, with respect to his new-style sonatas, 'that although at first sight they may appear difficult, their spirit will not be destroyed by playing them more than once, and in so doing they will become practised and this will render them very easy, since nothing is difficult when pleasure is derived'. Castello may be hinting that sight-reading results in a form of spontaneity that actually learning a work might not.

Two letters from Monteverdi indicate the necessity of a work being 'looked over' (presumably, tried out) before a performance, in order to give it a fair hearing: in 1607 he instructs that a copy of his new ballo *Tirsi e Clori* is to be passed to musician Bassano Casola, 'so that he can rehearse it and get a firm grasp of the melody together with the other gentleman singers, because it is

---

401 Strunk (1981), iii, p.71; Donington (1989), p.369; Strunk (1981), iii, p.61.
402 William Byrd, *Psalmes, Songs, and Sonnets* (London, 1611).
403 Burney (1935), ii, p.739.
404 Oliver Strunk, *Source Readings in Music History: III The Baroque Era* (London, 1981), p.124.

very difficult for a singer to perform a part which he has not first practiced, and greatly damaging to the composition itself, as it is not completely understood on being sung the first time', while in 1615 he says, 'if you could let the singers and players see it for an hour before His Highness hears it, that would be a very good thing indeed'.[405] Gluck also complained that 'insufficient rehearsals and bad preparation' had harmed reception of his *Alceste* (1769), the performance thus being unfair to the work.[406] The composer was also unfortunate in this respect for his otherwise-successful *Clelia*, given at Bologna six years earlier, where even 17 full rehearsals were insufficient to produce the 'ensemble & precision' available in Vienna, according to Dittersdorf's account.[407]

Perhaps the most interesting historical sight-reading reference concerns choral rather than solo music-reading skills: in 1518 Henry VIII arranged a competition between his Chapel Royal and Cardinal Wolsey's choir, set as a sight-reading test, and the latter ensemble won, the piece being 'better and more surely handlydde'.[408]

In the 19th century, virtuoso sight-reading skills continued to impress audiences and listeners, as when Goethe heard Mendelssohn aged just 12: 'What this little man can do in extemporizing and playing at sight borders on the miraculous'. Ten years later the composer came to the conclusion that public improvisation, although demanded by his audiences, was too much of a circus act: 'it is abuse and nonsense simultaneously'.[409]

While expert sight-reading skills were obviously regarded with admiration, even awe, it is interesting that one literary reference finds Shakespeare turning it into a negative metaphor for female sexual incontinence: in *Troilus and Cressida* (c.1602), Ulysses says of Cressida. 'She will sing any man at first sight'.[410]

---

405 Arnold and Fortune (1985), pp.19 and 33.
406 Walls (2003), pp.111-112.
407 Parrott (2022), p.502.
408 Mould (2007), p.51; Harrison (1963), p.171. Interestingly, the narrator of Karen Heenan's historical novel *A Wider World* (2021) is the very chorister called Robin from Wolsey's choir who was handed over to the Chapel Royal as the 'prize' in this contest (p.31). There is even a contemporary description of Robin's skills, as he was praised by composer William Cornysh for his 'suer & clenly syngynge, but also for hys goodde & crafty descant'; Parrott (2022), p.378.
409 Dana Gooley, *Fantasies of Improvisation: Free Playing in Nineteenth-Century Music* (Oxford, 2018), pp.101 and 103.
410 William Shakespeare, *Troilus and Cressida* ((London, 1609), Act v, scene 2.

IMPROVISATION SKILLS

The ability to discant and improvise[411] was an essential part of ear training in some times and places: 'the technique of improvising polyphony on psalm tones and other liturgical chants *super librum* was practiced throughout the period 1475-1550, and possibly well before and after. All lesser vicars were expected to be skilled in this art, and it constituted a principal mode of performance at the canonical hours, at least on festal days of duplex rank'.[412] Such abilities would have assisted a singer who had lost their place,[413] and would have been fundamental to their understanding of both polyphony and performance: 'the art of discanting was in all likelihood taught and transmitted as a living practice, possibly without the use of a single treatise. What mattered was the practical skill of singing correct successions of consonant intervals: the rules were internalized, not by learning them from Latin manuals, but by applying them in lessons as well as in communal music making. At most, instruction would have involved books or slates with monophonic tunes, with the master singing the written melodies, and the pupils improvising (either by turns or together) counterpoints of increasing floridity'.[414] Similarly, fluency in solmization techniques (the *Ut, Re, Mi, Fa, Sol, La* hexachord system) would have been invaluable in creating an 'aural map' of a polyphonic work for a singer.[415] Thomas Morley noted that discanting was no longer common practice in 1597 Anglican England: 'As for singing vppon a plainsong, it hath byn in times past in England (as euery man knoweth) and is at this day in other places, the greatest part of the vsuall musicke which in any churches is sung'.[416] However, in 1564 'squares' (probably meaning a cantus-firmus-based composition) were still being sung liturgically, while at Ludlow Parish Church in 1581 and Norwich Cathedral

---

411 See Ernest Ferand, 'Improvised Vocal Counterpoint in the Late Renaissance and Early Baroque', *Annales Musicologiques*, iv (1956), pp.129-174, Wright (1978), Wegman (1996), Philippe Canguilhem, 'Improvisation as concept and musical practice in the fifteenth century', in Busse Berger and Rodin (2015), pp.149-163 and Massimiliano Guido (ed), *Studies in historical improvisation: from* Cantare super librum *to* Partimenti (London, 2019). Flynn (1995), p.188 describes how 'square-note' improvised singing could be part of an English singer's training.

412 Wright (1978), pp.313-314.

413 Gallus Dressler (1564) provides a method for singers needing to recover their place, advising listening 'to the words & points of imitation produced by the rest of the singers, & then in a soft voice try embarking on re-entries. If it is not possible to find one from the imitations & the words, someone who is reasonably familiar with the rules will eventually re-establish one quite easily at a cadence'; Parrott (2022), p.392.

414 Wegman (1996), p.416.

415 See Smith (2011), ch.3.

416 Morley (1597), 'The Annotations' [n.p.].

a decade earlier the weekday service was sung in 'plaine song' or to 'playne note',[417] likely using Merbecke's 1550 *Booke of Common Praier noted*.[418]

COMPOSITIONAL TIMETABLE PRESSURES

There are a number of instances in music history of works being composed at great speed, and this may well imply imminent performance, and thus serious constraints on rehearsal time. Richard Davy's 15-minute Eton Choirbook antiphon *O Domine coeli terraeque creator* of c.1490 was composed in just one day in Oxford (*hanc antiphonam composuit Ricardus Davy uno die Collegio Magdalenae Oxoniis*); while Mozart, finding himself short of music in Linz in Autumn 1783, wrote to his father on 31 October that 'On Tuesday, November 4th, I am giving a concert in the theatre here and, as I have not a single symphony with me, I am writing a new one [K425] at breakneck speed, which must be finished by that time'.[419] The most famous case of speed is found in an anecdote concerning *Don Giovanni*, for which Mozart wrote the overture during the night before the premiere in October 1787: 'The copyists were only just ready in time for the performance, and the opera orchestra, whose skill Mozart well knew, played it excellently *a prima vista*', according to the 1798 *Life of Mozart* by Franz Niemetschek.[420]

REHEARSAL AFTER A PERFORMANCE

Whether a (recent) successful performance obviated the need for further rehearsals to improve standards further is not known, but this is hinted at in a letter from Leopold Mozart in Salzburg in September 1777, with the story of a Michael Haydn horn concerto 'which has been performed once already': some players did not turn up before the concert and the angry composer said that 'the rehearsal was quite unnecessary and why should they wait for those Italian asses?'.[421] Mozart (1778) noted that Herr Ramm 'played for the fifth time my oboe concerto written for Ferlendis, which is making a great sensation here',[422] as if that number of performances was relatively high. In respect of rehearsal

---

417 Saunders (1997), p.25.
418 John Merbecke, *The Booke of Common Praier noted* (London, 1550).
419 Anderson (1989), p.859.
420 Eisen (1991), p.81.
421 Anderson (1989), p.275.
422 Anderson (1989), p.482.

of his own music, Mozart did not agree with Michael Haydn, and after some frustrating soloists' errors in the second performance of *Die Entführung aus dem Serail* in July 1782 he insisted on a 'short rehearsal for the singers' to put things right before the next outing.[423]

---

[423] Anderson (1989), pp.807-808.

CHAPTER 5
CONDUCTORS

THE ORIGINS OF CONDUCTING

The baton (either in the form of a military-type baton or more modern thin white stick) did not come into common usage until well into the 19th century,[424] but occasional references to such a device can be found from the Middle Ages onwards. In the early 14th century, a miniature from the Manesse Codex (1310-30), now in Heidelberg, appears to show Heinrich von Neissen with a baton as a conductor,[425] while Ercole Bottrigari, in *Il Desiderio* (Venice, 1594), describes the music of the San Vito convent in Ferrara, where the female conductor used 'a long, slender, and well-polished wand'.[426] The story of Lully's fatal long-baton stabbing is well known, but a recent re-examination of the evidence suggests that this often-misunderstood story may have referred to a rehearsal, not a performance, event.[427] The audible striking of a stick to keep time did nevertheless exist in French opera, as reported by François Raguenet in his *Parallèle des Italiens et des Français en ce qui regarde la musique et les opéras* (Paris, 1702): 'some years since the Master of the Musick in the opera at Paris had an elbow-chair and desk placed on the stage where, with the score in one hand and a stick in the other he beat time on a table put there for that purpose, so loud that he made a greater noise

---

424 See Holman (2020), ch.8. Modern baton conducting techniques were strongly influenced by Wagner's example, and reinforced in modern times by Toscanini; see Chris Walton, *Richard Wagner's Essays on Conducting: A new Translation with Critical Commentary* (Rochester, 2021), and Haynes (2007), p.98. For a collection of historical batons, see https://batuty.instrumenty.edu.pl/cn.
425 Reproduced in Ausoni (2009), p.221.
426 Stras (2018), p.235.
427 Holman (2020), p.20.

than the whole band on purpose to be heard by the performers. By degrees they removed this abuse from the stage to the music room [pit] where the composer beats time in the same manner and as loud as ever'.[428]

A further method of controlling the tempo of singers was through physical contact. Some early illustrations of choir directors sometimes show them with their hand in contact with a singer, and this tradition is described by Giorgio Vasari (1568) in respect of a marble relief carving, one of ten made by Luca della Robbia (c.1400-1482) for Florence Cathedral's *Cantoria* (singing gallery) in 1431-38. It shows a choir, with 'the musical director beating his hands on the shoulders of the younger singers', who are holding a bound book (illus.7),[429] while another panel illustrates three singers sharing from a scroll of music.[430] Recent research has shown that physical contact, or proximity, between performers does indeed aid synchronization, though collective breathing and heartbeat.[431]

In 1512 Venceslaus Philomathes complained about poor time-beating techniques, which suggests that such skills may well have been self-taught: 'There are those whose habit it is to lead songs with unsightly gestures, thinking that they know distinguished customs and a special manner of the singers. Some mark the tactus with both palms widely spaced, as if in the quarrel of the two of them one could not attack the other's hair with his nails, and the extended palm threatens lethal battle to its unarmed double'.[432]

---

428 François Raguenet, trans Johann Galliard, *A comparison between the French and Italian musick and opera's. Translated from the French; with some remarks. To which is added A critical discourse upon opera's in England, and a means proposed for their improvement* (London, 1709), p.x; this is discussed in Holman (2020) pp.36-37. For early references to time-beating, see Parrott (2022), pp.396-398.

429 Giorgio Vasari, trans Julia Conaway Bondanella and Peter Bondanella, *The Lives of the Artists* (Oxford, 1991), p.67.

430 Reproduced in Alberto Ausoni, trans Stephen Sartarelli, *Music in Art* (Los Angeles, 2009), p.209.

431 Elke B. Lange, Diana Omigie, Carlos Trenado, Viktor Müller, Melanie Wald-Fuhrmann and Julia Merrill, 'In touch: Cardiac and respiratory patterns synchronize during ensemble singing with physical contact', *Frontiers in Human Neuroscience*, 16:928563 (2022); Julia A. M. Delius and Viktor Müller, 'Interpersonal synchrony when singing in a choir', *Frontiers in Psychology*, 13:1087517 (2023).

432 Venceslaus Philomathes, *Musicorum libri quattuor* (Vienna, 1512), Book 3, ch.1; translation courtesy of Tim Braithwaite.

CHAPTER 5: CONDUCTORS

Illus. 7. Luca della Robbia, *Cantoria* relief carving (1431-38).

18th century practice in Britain (and indeed elsewhere) could involve the directing musician beating time with a roll of paper (as can be seen in a number of illustrations),[433] and Maurice Greene and William Boyce are both recorded as doing this at St Paul's Cathedral from the mid-1740s onwards. However, Peter Holman cautions that the musical director and the time-beater may not have been the same person.[434] A 'Handel' rehearsal etching from 1740 shows the composer apparently listening rather than actively directing or participating at that moment,[435] and Holman suggests that Handel's principle was to select the best musicians he could find, rehearse them carefully but give them freedom in actual performance, leading from the keyboard.[436] A comparison with Italy may be instructive, where a time-beater could be unnecessary if the players were good enough: the court orchestra of Turin, which included leading players such as Pugnani, Veracini, Somis (all violinists) and the Besozzis (oboe and bassoon), performed 'symphonic music' in the Chapel Royal every morning for an hour before noon, distributed between three galleries 'at some distance one from another. The understanding between them was so excellent that they had no need of anyone to beat time'.[437] By contrast, the two sides of the choir of Cambrai Cathedral evidently had some difficulty singing together, as a complaint made in December 1535 records: 'The vicars of the left side of the choir should be admonished to observe and be attentive to the harmony of the singers of the right side'.[438]

One further type of time-beater was the 'relay conductor' who helped keep dispersed groups of musicians together: in mid-16th century St Mark's, Venice, the beat of the *maestro di cappella* on the floor was relayed by the *maestro de' concerti* to the instrumentalists in the organ loft; in 1601 this was Giovanni Bassano.[439]

What a conductor with a full score at his disposal might have done is not known, as marked-up copies which include information as a reminder to himself (as is seen in modern practice, indicating for example entries, dynamics, tempo changes etc) do not exist at this early date. One might have expected the conductor to assist the performers by at least indicating entries, working as

---

433 Laetitia Hawkins called this a 'paper-truncheon'; Holman (2020), p.90.
434 Holman (2020), pp.89-90.
435 Holman (2020), p.138, with the etching on 139.
436 Holman (2020), p.140.
437 Romain Rolland, *Adelphi Collected Works of Romain Rolland* (2020), ebook.
438 Wright (1978), p.297.
439 Rosand (1993), p.78. See also Holman (2020), pp.6-10.

they were from parts, but Peter Holman suggests that written comments for the choristers like 'Lead away' in Boyce's performing material indicate they were left to their own initiative.[440] In late 18th-century Germany, however, Heinrich Christoph Koch reports that 'the *Kapellmeister* must have the score in front of him, partly in order to supervise the parts and keep them together, and especially in order to give the vocalists their cues by means of signs'.[441]

Burney, visiting the rather neglected Sistine Chapel in November 1770, took in the musician's gallery and noted 'only a large lectern or wooden desk for the score book of the maestro di capella and a marble bench at the back and sides'; he seems to assume a conductor directing from the copy, which may just be his assumption of actual practice, but the other details of his visit that day suggests he was shown round by an expert guide.[442] Earlier that same year, Burney's report from Milan suggests that choirbook practice had not changed much for nearly three centuries, although the nature of the description suggests that he thought the reader would need a precise explanation as to what a choirbook was and how it was laid out:

While at Milan in July 1770, the English traveler attended a service at the Duomo, and was shown a book printed in a very large note, on wood, in four parts, the cantus and tenor on the left side, and altus et bassus on the right, without bars. Out of this one book, after the tone was given by the organist [Jean Corbeli], the whole four parts were sung without the organ. There was one boy, and three castrati for the soprano and contr'alto, with two tenors and two bas[s]es, under the direction of Signor [Jean Andrè] Fioroni, who beat the time, and now and then sung. These services were composed about one hundred and fifty years ago [1619], by a Maestro di Capella of the Duomo, and are much in the stile [sic] of our services of that time, consisting of good harmony, ingenious points and contrivances, but no melody.[443]

The music is specified as ancient ('about one hundred and fifty years' old), and performed by eight singers, with a director who alternated time-beating with occasional singing (possibly to keep the parts accurate).

---

440 Holman (2020), pp.105-106.
441 Heinrich Christoph Koch, 'Kapellmeister', *Musikalisches Lexikon* (Frankfurt am Main, 1802).
442 Burney (1974), p.203. See also Holman (2020), p.90 in reference to 'a desk among the performers' mentioned by John Hawkins.
443 Cited by Jean-Paul C. Montagnier, 'Choirbooks and Musical Practice', in Jean-Paul C. Montagnier (ed), *The Polyphonic Mass in France, 1600–1780: The Evidence of the Printed Choirbooks* (Cambridge, 2017), pp.34-66 at 34.

Lastly, Coryat at San Rocco in Venice (1608) described the person who kept the 'sixteen or twenty men [singers] together' as 'their master or moderator to keepe them in order'.[444]

LEADERSHIP ROLES AND SOCIAL HIERARCHIES

Assignments of musical leadership have left a few archival traces, with a summary – sometimes more – of the duties and responsibilities of an appointee. This was sometimes drafted by a functionary with limited understanding of musical terminology and procedure: for example, under Henry VIII's New Foundation cathedral statutes, 'The Precentor was chosen from the Minor Canons, and was "handsomely to direct the singing men in the church and as a guide to lead them by his previous singing that they make no discords whilst they sing"'.[445] For a model musical director of the earlier Tudor period, a letter from the Dean of Cardinal College, Ipswich to Cardinal Wolsey of c.1529 praising one Lentall, Master of the Children at Wolsey's short-lived Ipswich institution, is indicative: 'but for Mr Lentall we cowde in a maner do nothing in oure quere. He taketh very great paynes and is always present at Mattens and all Masses w^t evyn song, and settith the quere in good ordre fro tyme to tyme and fayleth not at eny tyme. He is very sober and discrete, and bringeth up your Choresters very wele: assuring your Grace there shall be no better children in no place of England then we shall have here, and that in short tyme'.[446] This panegyric may need to be read with a pinch of salt, as the purpose of the Dean's letter was to reassure Wolsey that all was going well at his new institution.

Musicians themselves also recorded the abilities they understood as necessary, and these are sometime curious. Luigi Zenobi states that a director must be able to act as a safety-net for the individual performers; he must be able to 'anticipate in a certain way anyone about to lose his part rather than waiting for him to lose it'.[447] In reality, this must often have meant following the choristers' line (or that of the least experienced or able part) with them, in order to stop them straying.

---

444 Rosand (1993), p.83.
445 Harris (1938), p.118.
446 Henry Ellis (ed), *Original Letters, illustrative of English History* (London, 1824), i, p.189.
447 Smith (2011), pp.5-6.

In large-scale musical environments, divided responsibility was known (see above), and was even explained in practice, as at the Académie Royale de Musique (1713-14), where 'the *maître de musique* coached and supervised the singers and "stood in the wings with a [roll of] paper in his hand, ready to set the choruses in motion and keep them in time"; the *maître de ballet* was in charge of the dancers and the dances; and the *batteur de mesure* was "not only to beat time in both performances and rehearsals but also to supervise the members of the orchestra, ensuring that they present themselves for duty punctually and that they do not leave their places and instruments during the opera".'[448] Such assignment of specialist tasks raises the question of the way in which overall 'artistic direction' (in the modern sense) was undertaken; the Paris regulations give the composer of the work such a right, but how this might have been exercised effectually, given the three formal directors already present, is an interesting question.

Where an ensemble was unresponsive, or 'old and sleepy' in the words of Johann Friedrich Rochlitz (1769-1842), some energy could be inserted by the conductor in a rehearsal, as when Mozart found the 1789 Leipzig Gewandhaus orchestra 'dragged the *tempo* of an Allegro in his symphony, he called for more and more speed, and in urging them on stamped his foot so violently that his shoe lace broke'.[449] Burney had evidently seen many conductors attempting to rein in wayward orchestras, and describes 'the fury of the musical-general, or director, increasing with the disobedience and confusion of his troops, he becomes more violent, and his strokes and gesticulations more ridiculous, in proportion to their disorder'.[450]

Outside such rigid structures, past arrangements for musical control and decision-making had to take account of different layers of social hierarchy, and concepts of class, status, education and seniority may have affected the interactions of musicians in a way that they now do not. For example, Quantz (as the emperor's flute teacher) was the only one allowed to comment on his master's concert performances, and that with the word 'bravo' – which he could also withhold.[451] Given that the professional musicians of the past were by definition not drawn from the upper ranks of society (otherwise they would not have become musi-

---

448 Holman (2020), p.35.
449 Carse (1940), p.63.
450 Charles Burney, *An Account of the Musical Performances in Westminster Abbey and the Pantheon …in Commemoration of Handel* (London, 1785), Introduction, p.14.
451 Edward R. Reilly, 'Quantz and the Transverse Flute: Some Aspects of His Practice and Thought regarding the Instrument', *Early Music*, xxv/3 (August 1997), pp.428-438 at 433.

cians), but yet mixed personally and sometime intimately with kings, popes, bishops and lords, a refined understanding of the etiquette of cross-social interaction would have been necessary, as seen in the deferential form of address of Bach's concerto dedication to the Margrave of Brandenburg.[452]

APPOINTMENTS

Within musical institutions (principally ecclesiastical, but some at court and household level), appointments to leadership roles were often not made by musicians, but by church or aristocratic authorities. Such processes might lead to the appointment of those of distinguished reputation as musical organizers, performers or composers, as the desire to seek out musical talent to create or maintain local musical reputations was obvious. On the continent, diplomatic functionaries sometimes operated as talent scouts, looking to poach musicians (such as Josquin) with international reputations,[453] and these musicians therefore had real negotiating powers as regards salary, terms and conditions – at least until they were in post. Similarly, Handel toured Italy in search of opera soloists: 'New Singers must be sought, and could not be had any nearer than Italy. The business of chusing, and engaging them, could not be dispatched by a deputy ... After a short stay in Italy, he returned with STRADA, BERNACHI, FABRI, BERTOLDI, and others'.[454]

Traditional patronage processes operated everywhere in the early modern period, with appointments made as part of wider exchanges of favours between churchmen, royalty, aristocrats, court functionaries and others: as Iago says in Shakespeare's *Othello*, 'Preferment goes by letter and affection'.[455] In 17th-century English cathedral visitations, enquiry was made as to whether singing appointments were made on the basis of skill, or because of 'friendship, rewards, or money'.[456] This problem is one reason for Monteverdi's satisfaction with the artistic control given to him by his employment conditions at St Mark's, Venice, as expressed in a letter of 1620: 'no singer is accepted into the choir until they ask the opinion of the director of music'.[457] Such musically verified auditions were

---

452 David and Mendel (1998), pp.92-93.
453 See Lewis Lockwood, 'Strategies of music patronage in the fifteenth century: the *capella* of Ercole I d'Este', in Fenlon (1981), pp.227-248.
454 Mainwaring (1760), pp.112-113.
455 William Shakespeare, *Othello*, Act i, scene 1.
456 Woodfill (1953), p.151.
457 Arnold and Fortune (1985), p.44.

not unusual for obvious reasons; at Chichester Cathedral in 1610 it was decreed that, 'no Clerk, vicar or chorister be actually admitted to his place until he first make public trial of his voice and skill in the presence of the Dean and Chapter, together with the Master of the choristers or the Subchanter';[458] similar words were used at Worcester Cathedral in 1589, where incoming musicians were to be 'fit and sufficient both for voice and knowledge in song', and again in 1635.[459] However, clerical authorities sometimes sidelined their own musical experts even when making auditioned appointments, as in late medieval Paris.[460] The variable results of such systems may well be imagined: when in the early 15th century choristers were being directly appointed by the Dean of Newalke Collegiate Church in Leicester, some were described as 'totally unteachable'.[461]

Claudio Annibaldi provides a table of papal singers hired by audition or by 'motu proprio' (the personal decision of the pope) between 1600-1700, and the latter outnumber the former 88 to 49.[462] It is possible that this tendency fundamentally represented a move away from ordained singers to virtuoso soloists, but the records of increasing infractions clearly show the process was damaging to the discipline of the Sistine choir, with more 'negligent or irreverent behaviour during divine services, and the unprecedented number of singers involved in scandalous, and even criminal, activities'.[463]

Non-meritocratic promotions (and the modern concept of 'meritocracy' is not one that would have been understood at the time) must sometimes also have led to choirs and ensembles being placed under the control of those of inferior skill and ability. In one 1511 complaint in the Sainte-Chapelle of Paris, it was said that the previous Master of the Choirboys, Dreux Prieur, 'doesn't know how to read or sing and doesn't understand anything he says while reading'.[464] At King's College, Cambridge, from 1578 the choir was run for a time by a chaplain rather than a Master of the Choristers.[465] Conversely, the appointment of a

---

458 Brown (1969), p.34.
459 Saunders (1997), p.64; Woodfill (1953), p.151.
460 Wright (1981), pp.44-45.
461 Mould (2007), p.56.
462 Claudio Annibaldi, '"The singers of the said chapel are chaplains of the pope": some remarks on the papal chapel in early modern times', *Early Music*, xxxix/1 (February 2011), pp.15-24 at 16.
463 Annibaldi (2011), p.17.
464 Cited in Wegman (1996), p.429.
465 Bowers (2014), p.274.

person who was skilled in one particular area (for example, composition,[466] or keyboard performance) was no guarantee of their ability to recruit, train and manage singers.

---

[466] Although, as Roger Bowers notes of early modern England, 'nobody was employed specifically as a composer': 'Obligation, agency, and *laissez-faire*: the promotion of polyphonic composition for the Church in fifteenth-century England', in Fenlon (1981), pp.1-19, at 10. However, note that in Courtrai in 1559, Melchoir Haeghebaert was 'excused from attending the Office hours & the choir when he is occupied in composing music'; Parrott (2022), p.102.

CHAPTER 6
PERFORMANCE PRACTICE

Many of the practical decisions to be made about musical practice and interpretation come under the heading of what is now called 'performance practice'. Historically, these included local or national traditions which were well enough understood to need no explanation to the musicians, as well as specific components requiring previous or in-rehearsal decision, either collectively or by a director.

MUSICA FICTA

The addition of *Music ficta* (unwritten accidentals added for performance) is now the province of the editor or conductor, inserted as a result of harmonic analysis, but the historical process for doing this would have been different, and achieved by ear in the absence of a score. While some *ficta* (for example, sharpened leading notes at cadences) are straightforward,[467] there are two overall issues to address. First, are *ficta* additions intended to be consistent, as Karol Berger asks: should implied accidentals be considered part of the 'domain of the musical text (which, for any given work, had to remain invariable from one performance to another if the work was to retain its identity); or to the domain of performance (which might vary from one realization of the text to another without endangering the identity of the work)'?[468] That *ficta*

---

467 The use of different 'key signatures' in the lower and higher voices, with Bb in the bass part only being common, was likely also well understood in terms of its harmonic implications for the higher voices; see Harrison (1963), pp.325-326. Later Renaissance composers became very expert in arranging the voice-leading to suggest *ficta* (or sometimes, to deliberately make sure was it impossible).
468 Karol Berger, 'Musica Ficta', in Brown and Sadie (1989a), pp.107-125 at 107.

might have been a matter of difference between composer and performer is shown by a poem of 1504 attributed to William Cornysh and called *A Parable betwen Informacion and Musicke*. This is set as a debate between Information and Music, with the performer mentioning the 'many subtel semetunes most me[e]t for this song', and the composer responding that 'I kepe be rounde and he be square, / The one is bemole, and the other bequare'. However, the latter admits that 'the plain keyes . . . marred al my melody', and this story may portray a transitional moment in sound from modal towards tonal; the words 'subtle semitones' certainly imply a positive view of added *ficta*.[469] Thomas Morley also allowed individual taste to be an arbiter, at least at times: 'because I thought it better flat than sharp, I have set it flat. But if anie man like the other waie better, let him vse his discretion'.[470] Second, who decided which *ficta* were to be added,[471] the conductor or the individual singers, and in the latter case who had the authority to make a choice when there was more than one singer on a part? Both of these questions lie in the domain of rehearsal, not performance. When accidentals are added by ear rather than from examination of a score, which is now rather rarely done, the results can be grammatically curious but musically acceptable.[472]

TEXT UNDERLAY

Text underlay is another feature now under the control of an editor or conductor, where the original sources do not provide unambiguous alignment of musical notes and text syllables. In some cases, it is not even certain as to which 'phrases of text belong with which phrases of music, or even about the basic question of which voices should be sung with text'.[473] Modern performers need these decisions to be made, but it should not be assumed this was of equal concern in the past. From one particularly interesting later 15th century source of polyphony, where 'the copyist of the *Missa Ecce ancilla Domini* in Brussels 5557 was unusually painstaking in his precise placing of syllables under what

---

469 Bray (1970), p.31.

470 Morley (1597), p.88.

471 It might also be asked whether all the accidentals in a score – some of which were merely notated *musica ficta* – were regarded as inviolate by performers. Pietro Aaron (1523) notes that 'there are uncertainities & arguments about the *b molle* & the *diesis*' as to whether they are the responsibility of the composer or of the performer; Parrott (2022), p.267.

472 For a recorded example, see *The Eton Choirbook*, Huelgas Ensemble/Paul van Nevel, Deutsche Harmonia Mundi 88765408852 (2012).

473 Howard Mayer Brown, 'Introduction', in Howard Mayer Brown and Stanley Sadie (eds), *Performance Practice: Music before 1600* (Basingstoke, 1989a), pp.147-166 at 148.

he considered were the appropriate notes',[474] Gareth Curtis inferred seven rules of text underlay. Whether such rules were or could be taught to and internalized by singers to allow for consistent 'live' text underlay is an open question; in particular, the breaking of ligatures to accommodate syllables is not straightforward. In all this, the modern editorial assumption that text was to be performed in a uniform and aligned manner, and that all singers on each part – including a dozen or more choristers - would (or even could) lay out the syllables and melismas in exactly the same way and at exactly the same time, needs to be seriously called into question; neither composers nor performers of the time may have seen such consistency as necessary, or even possible. Multiple manuscripts from England show the different ways in which scribes variably interpreted text underlay: Peter Le Huray gives an example from Edmund Hooper's anthem *Behold it is Christ*, where the same four bars in just one voice appear in a dozen different ways in the sources.[475] Such variants might be explained by copyists expanding summary or partial texting (in some very syllabic canticle settings of the period, only the first word is given for the singers, for example), but singers aligning note and syllable live in performance are likely to have been even less consistent than were the copyists.

NUMBERS OF REHEARSALS

The number of times musicians met in order to prepare for a performance seems to have varied greatly, although the numbers three and four do seem the most common, at least for the 18th century. Elsewhere, rehearsals are sometimes defined as over a period (for opera, this would be several weeks), but regular practices outside church environments are rarely specified. One example is found in the London Waits' rules of c.1625, which determine that they were to assemble at 8 am every Monday morning 'to continue their practice upon several sorts of instruments until noon'; that the venue was not specified is implied by a provision that the city chamberlain would decide if they could not.[476] Although this sounds like a full weekly rehearsal, it might also have been a repertoire-selection gathering, or even a collective individual practice session of the type that so surprised Burney at the Conservatorio of S. Onofrio

---

474 Gareth R. K. Curtis, 'Brussels, Bibliothèque Royale MS. 5557, and the Texting of Dufay's "Ecce ancilla Domini" and "Ave regina celorum" Masses', *Acta Musicologica*, li/1 (January-June 1979), pp.73-86 at 75.

475 Le Huray (1967), p.106. Similarly, in Lucca in 1557 a room was assigned for the municipal wind players to rehearse two hours each Wednesday and Saturday, in the morning or afternoon depending on the time of year; Parrott (2022), p.394.

476 Woodfill (1953), p.44.

in Naples on his visit in October 1770, where each student worked on their own different pieces simultaneously, in the same room: 'Out of 30 or 40 boys who were practising I could discover but 2 that were playing the same piece ... The violoncellos are in another room and the wind instruments, such as flutes, hautbois etc in a 3rd. – The trumpets and horns either fag on the stairs or top of the house'.[477]

In August 1802 Prince Nicolaus II Esterházy instructed Haydn (still nominally in charge there as *Kapellmeister*) that 'the whole band – male and female singers, without exception – is to hold a weekly rehearsal; their superiors will decide on which day it is to be held'.[478] Later in the document both church and chamber music are mentioned, although the rehearsal stipulation is probably aimed at the former.

Sometimes a special event demanded a large number of rehearsals, as when Benvenuto Cellini joined an instrumental ensemble performing motets for the Pope's annual feast in Rome in 1524: 'for a week leading up to the August feast, we played together every day for two hours, so that on the festival we went to the Belvedere & while Pope Clement was dining we played those carefully rehearsed motets in such a way that the Pope admitted he had never heard music played more sweetly or with greater unanimity'.[479]

In 1631 the Rector of the Thomasschule in Leipzig complained that lessons were neglected as the boarders 'usually rehearse for weeks' for events such as St Gregory's Day; in 1733 a limit was placed on this rehearsal time, six to eight afternoons. These particular 'street singing' events were a valuable opportunity for the Leipzig students to collect money by singing around the town.[480] In 1723 Vivaldi had a formal agreement with his Venice employers at the Pietà to supply two concertos per month; when away, he would post them, and when he was present he would direct three or four rehearsals of the new works;[481] the same number is mentioned by Haydn in a detailed 1768 letter about the premiere of his *Applausus* cantata, to be prepared in his absence ('Since I cannot be present myself at this *Applaus* I have found it necessary to provide one or two explanations concerning its execution ... I hope for at least three or four rehearsals for the entire work'). Whether this number related to the length or difficulty

---

477 Burney (1974), p.135.
478 Robbins Landon (1959), p.207.
479 Parrott (2022), p.394.
480 Maul (2018), p.25.
481 Michael Talbot, *Vivaldi* (London, 1979), p.21.

of this work, or the quality of the performers, is uncertain, but three decades later Haydn sent a group of symphonies to Prince Oettingen von Wallerstein in October 1789 with an instruction that 'that these 3 Symphonies, because of their many particular effects, should be rehearsed at least once, carefully and with special concentration, before they are performed'.[482] The implication was that otherwise they would have been played at sight.

In England in the later 18th century, even for large-scale public events the number of rehearsals could be minimal, with Charles Burney implying that a full-scale choral and orchestral concert might have just one 'general rehearsal'. However, Stephen Storace's 'afterpiece' opera *Lodoiska* had a month of rehearsals in 1794, even though not all were music rehearsals.[483]

Mozart's letters sometimes mention the number of rehearsals, and there seems to have been a usual maximum of three: in Paris in March 1778, of the concerto for three keyboards K242, 'we had three rehearsals of the concerto and it went off very well'; while in Munich in December 1780, *Idomeneo*'s 'second rehearsal went off as well as the first. The orchestra and the whole audience discovered to their delight that the second act we actually more expressive and original than the first. Next Saturday both acts are to be rehearsed again'. For a concert of Mozart's Piano Concerto K466 on 22 March 1786 in Salzburg, with a rehearsal on the day, pianist Heinrich Marchand played 'from the score' (Haydn was page-turner), and 'We rehearsed it in the morning and had to practise the rondo three times before the orchestra could manage it, for Marchand took it rather quickly'.[484]

The length of a rehearsal was rarely documented at this date, although in a letter from May 1791 Haydn refers to a period of two-and-a-half hours ('a Rehearsal at the Opera House, which lasted from Two till Half-past Four on that Day') for a benefit concert in which he was taking part.[485]

---

482 Robbins Landon (1959), pp.9-10 and 89; he makes a similar point in November 1791 with regard to 'two new Symphonies' for Herr von Keess; Robbins Landon (1959), p.121.
483 Holman (2020), pp.156 and 290.
484 Anderson (1989), pp.517, 692 and 897.
485 Robbins Landon (1959), p.116.

REHEARSAL ETIQUETTE

While the social etiquette of the rehearsal process is rarely mentioned, Anton Stadler makes a point of noting this in his 'Musick Plan' of 1800, likely as a result of personal experience: instrumentalists should not 'publicly censure another musician's chance mistake, nor make him ridiculous', while conductors are told that players 'are not to be shouted at when they make a mistake, or made [to look] ridiculous, or treated with sarcasm, because then [they] lose their composure; their attentiveness is lost even more because their heart is put to shame or [they] become embittered'.[486] An example of a demanding opera conductor is given by Mattheson (1739), with respect to Johann Kusser: 'he knew how to reproach many a one for their errors in such a sharp manner that they often burst into tears. On the other hand, he calmed down again immediately and sought hard for an opportunity to bind the inflicted wounds, through exceptional courtliness. In this way he managed things so that nobody could have impugned him'.[487]

Like Stadler, Quantz (1752) also advocated a supportive approach, with individual players being coached into good habits: 'Should there be some among the ripienists whose execution differs from that of the others, the leader must undertake to rehearse them separately'.[488] Such uniformity begins to become more important with the rise of public concerts; Johann Adolph Schiebe's *Critische Musicus* (1745) notes that 'The conductor must see to it that all the violins use the same ornaments as their leader',[489] thus assigning both leadership and rehearsal responsibility to the director, rather than individual performers. Some sense of the social and musical tensions of rehearsals can be seen in the wording of the 'Petition' that his employer obliged Leopold Mozart resentfully to sign up to in September 1777, to 'conduct himself calmly and peaceably with the Kapellmeister and other persons appointed to the court orchestra'.[490]

Fear must often have been an incentive for younger musicians to meet the standards set by conductors, as described by Johann Friedrich Rochlitz, a former chorister at the Thomasschule in Leipzig: 'Already as a schoolboy (since 1782) I had to take part in performing Bach's eight-part motets ... Heaven knows that I only learned to sing them securely out of fear of severe punishment'.[491]

---

486 Poulin (1990), pp.220-222.
487 Parrott (2022), p.395.
488 Quantz (1966), p.210.
489 Donington (1989), p.193.
490 Anderson (1989), p.281.
491 Wilhelm Ehmann, 'Performance Practice of Bach's Motets', *American Choral Review*, xxix/3-4 (Summer and Fall 1987), pp.5-24 at 7.

PERFORMANCE STYLES

Instructions to musicians sometimes include brief information about performance styles, which can relate to consistency of tone, style, dynamics or other aspects: the 12th-century Bishop Ethelred complained about inconsistent plainchant singing, where 'one while the voyce is strained, anon it is remitted, now it is dashed, and then againe it is enlarged with a lowder sound';[492] the chantress at Syon Abbey in the early 16th century was to 'start the song smoothly and moderately, neither too high nor too low, but steadily and reverently after the due ceremony of the feast or day';[493] while a 1568 Sistine Chapel note says 'Remember that the Vespers of Epiphany should be intoned very softly'.[494] Elsewhere, the will of former St Omer chorister Robert le Fevre seems to specify the style of musical performance within a dramatic representation of the Annunciation, to be funded from his 1535 bequest: 'a little choirboy vested in an alb and dressed as an angel as one does on the day of the resurrection, instructed by the master of song to do this, is to sing with fine tone and at the same time in a natural manner all that follows in the said gospel by the said angel, and this at the left-hand side of the high altar and below.[495]

Mentions of excessive volume and lack of control of the voice suggest that conductors had limited ability to determine actual performing results, regardless of what was said in rehearsals: Giovanni de' Bardi (c.1580) describes singers who 'sing so loudly in the high register that they seem like criers auctioning off the pledges of the unfortunate',[496] while Luigi Zenobi (1601), as noted by Beverly Jerold, said that 'instrumentalists restrain their volume in chamber music for princes; but in church music and in large concerts, everyone plays as loudly as possible, which creates a great din and hides all the blunders and poor intonation'.[497] The confusion caused by excessive loudness is also commented on in Jean le Rond d'Alembert's *De la liberte de la musique* (1759), with a description of the Paris Opéra orchestra: 'The rage of our French musicians is to pile up parts upon parts. They make the effect consist of noise; their accompaniments cover and suffocate the voice ... So great is the lack of ensemble in our harmony that we think we are hearing twenty different books read at the same time.'[498]

---

492 Donington (1989), p.485.
493 Yardley (2008), p.55.
494 Sherr (1999), IV, p.92.
495 Cited in Kirkman (2020), p.52.
496 Oliver Strunk, *Source Readings in Music History: II The Renaissance* (London, 1981), p.109.
497 Jerold (2007), p.219.
498 Cited in Jerold (2003), pp.155-156.

While various early theorists, such as Nicola Vicentino (1555), by contrast wrote on the subtleties of expression, particularly mentioning the changes in dynamics and tempo used to reflect the meaning of texts, especially those in the vernacular,[499] such comments should be understood as applying only to the date, country, genre and musical style in question. The concept of 'expression' cannot have meant the same thing, or been the same musical goal, at all times and places, to judge by contemporary descriptions of performances.

NATIONAL STYLES

Travel made possible the exchange not only of music from different countries and traditions, but also of performing styles, and this could lead to problems. At Southwell Cathedral in 1484-86, one Thomas Cartwright, who 'does not conduct himself in a way becoming a priest especially in choir and singing', was also admonished because he did not 'observe the custom of the choir in psalmody and singing faburdon', but made 'great discord in singing having a foreign fashion not used among the choir'.[500] Some musicians had sufficient international knowledge to be able to describe these different international styles: 'The late fifteenth-century theorist Guillelmus Monachus, in his *De preceptis artis musicae*, presented an orderly account of the discant idioms of the English, the French, and "apud nos," probably the Italians'.[501]

Some references suggest that 17th and 18th century musicians also needed help across musical borders, as when Weckmann travelled to visit Froberger in the 1650s in order to learn in person how to play the latter's keyboard music, Corelli admitting he did not understand the French style,[502] or Couperin (1717) observing that certain performing information was notated in one style and not another: 'we write a thing differently from the way in which we execute it; and it is this which causes foreigners to play our music less well than we do theirs'.[503] Aside from such varying national and local traditions, there is also the matter of individual taste; Quantz pointed out that a diversity of musical taste

---

499 For example, Nicola Vicentino, trans Maria Rika Maniates, *Ancient Music adapted to Modern Practice* (New Haven, 1996), p.301. For a wider discussion, see Smith (2011), pp.102-109.

500 Harris (1938), p.117; Harrison (1963), pp.174-175; Wegman (1996), p.448. Note that 'foreign fashion' does not necessarily imply from another country, just that it was different.

501 Wegman (1996), p.421.

502 Mainwaring (1760), p.57.

503 François Couperin, trans and ed Anna Linde, *L'art de toucher le clavecin* (Wiesbaden, [1961]), p.23.

also depended on one's own temperament, and even a beginner flautist 'must acquaint himself with the pieces characteristic of different natures and provinces, and learn to play each in the style appropriate to it'.[504]

Finally, music from completely different cultures were usually be greeted with incomprehension: in 1481 Tinctoris heard Turkish prisoners-of-war at Naples consoling themselves with music, and considered their songs 'in truth so crude and absurd that it alone was quite sufficient to demonstrate their barbarity'.[505] Such cultural chasms worked both ways, as when the King of Siam thought the French Baroque opera airs he heard in 1687 not 'grave enough'.[506]

TUNING

Documentary references to tuning (many of which have been collected by Beverly Jerold and Andrew Parrott) tend to be of the critical type, and it is not possible to determine whether this means intonation elsewhere was either generally good, acceptable or poor (that Locatelli 'never was known to play one Note out Tune' shows such a thing as unusual, perhaps).[507] A number of these accounts make it clear that good tuning was part of the rehearsal process, and that it was the responsibility of the musical director or leader.

Comments praising tuning are relatively rare, but this does not mean it was exceptional, as in Bottrigari's 1594 mention of the 'sonorous and just intonation of the notes' of the San Vito convent ensemble in Ferrara.[508] The problem of non-standard pitch levels between instruments (see below) must have caused problems, regardless of the aural acuity of the actual performers,[509] and where tuning matters were inadequate, Stadler (1800) suggests events could be cancelled: 'often an out-of-tune instrument is the reason which prevents many from pleasure in entertaining or in studying, since one often has to perform … chamber and church music on out-of-tune instruments or even postpone the performance'.[510]

---

504 Quantz (1966), pp.298 and 115. See also Parrott (2022), pp.282-285.
505 Wegman (1995), p.306.
506 David R. M. Irving, 'Lully in Siam: music and diplomacy in French—Siamese cultural exchanges, 1680–1690', *Early Music*, xl/3 (August 2012), pp.393-420 at 420.
507 Parrott (2022), p.327; see also pp.411-413.
508 Stras (2018), p.236.
509 Jerold (2007), p.215.
510 Poulin (1990), p.218.

Reports of tuning problems refer either to individuals, ensembles or traditions. The former tend to be found later in the period, as in newspaper reports from 18th-century London, which could forcibly criticize performance deficiencies, naming individual instruments (or sometimes players) that had offended.[511] One story has a 'ridiculously out-of-tune' bassoon player being mocked by continuo player Muzio Clementi, who played the parts bitonally on the keyboard during a 1779 London opera rehearsal,[512] while the eminent violinist Ignaz Schuppanzigh (1776-1830), founder of the first professional string quartet, was described in print by Reichardt (1810) as able to 'play the most difficult passages clearly, although not always quite in tune'.[513]

General references to tuning difficulties include the 1553 John Stubs sermon mentioned above, where physical sanctions awaited offending choristers: 'Yf a scoler of the song scole syng out of tune, he is well wrong by the ears, or else well beatyn',[514] Pier Francesco Tosi's 1723 comment that 'I can in all truth say that (aside from a few singers) modern intonation is very poor',[515] Fux's belief (in his *Gradus ad Parnassum*, 1742) that instruments are needed to help keep choirs in tune – 'Intonation is difficult for the voices when they have no help, not even from other instruments'[516] – and there is also Alessandro Scarlatti's comment (made to Quantz in 1725), 'you are aware of my antipathy for wind instruments; they are never in tune'.[517] Charles Butler (1636) made a similar reference to string instrument tuning, noting that this could go awry in the middle of a piece: strings 'are often out of tun; (which soomtime happeneth in the mids of the Musik; when it is neither good to continue, not to correct the fault)'.[518] Georg Motz in 1703 was in despair over poor congregational singing: 'Here things often get wildly out of control; some sing quickly, some slowly, some go sharp, some flat. Some are out by a tone, others by a 4th, these by a 5th, those by an octave; each sings as he pleases…'.[519]

In terms of ensembles, a most surprising piece of previous bad practice in Italian opera houses – tuning *after* a work had begun! – was reported by Franc-

---

511 Holman (2020), p.277.
512 Holman (2020), p.274. Puccini used the same trick in the waltz from *Il Tabarro* (1918).
513 Strunk, *IV* (1981), p.160.
514 Harris (1938), p.119.
515 Jerold (2000), p.24.
516 Jerold (2000), p.23.
517 Rolland (2020).
518 Charles Butler, *The Principles of Musik* (London, 1636), p.103, cited in Parrott (2015), p.374.
519 Parrott (2022), p.481.

esco Maria Veracini in his manuscript *Trionfo della pratica musicale* (c.1760): 'Tuning the orchestra should be done *quickly, softly* and correctly before the beginning of the opera overture. We should abandon our predecessors' perfidious custom of beginning untuned and the making a continuous buzzing while a recitative is being sung'.[520] Perhaps this is what Haydn is satirizing in the comic Finale of his Symphony No.60 in C, '*Il distratto*', where the violins pause to audibly retune (ex.4).[521] Equally alarmingly, Daniel Gottlob Türk (*Wichtigste Pflichten*, 1787) tells of an orchestra where the organ and oboe were correctly in E♭, the violins were a semitone too high and the horns a semitone too low; as Jerold laconically notes, 'then someone noticed the blunder and one after the other retuned'.[522]

The issue of different instrument tuning systems was of concern to a number of writers: mixing fretted and keyboard instruments led to tuning problems due to temperament differences, a matter which Giovanni de' Bardi (c.1580) noted had previously 'gone unnoticed, or if noticed, unremedied'.[523] The issue of performing with tempered instruments is also mentioned by Johann Mattheson in his 1731 *Grosse General-Bass-Schule*, in the context of a cappella singing: 'Nowadays no one sings like the itinerant choirboys without instruments or accompaniment, for from that derives a much greater degree of poor intonation, out-of-tuneness and flattening of the voices than through all the false intervals in well-tempered instruments'.[524]

The ability of an ensemble to play well in tune will also have been dependent on the skill of those who tuned the instruments. Giovanni Maria Artusi, in *L'Artusi* (1600), gives eight rules necessary for an excellent ensemble, the last of which is that all the instruments (he mentions, strings, harps, lutes and keyboards) be 'tuned by the same person',[525] which seems impractical. As an alternative way of ensuring uniformity among the strings, violinist Giovanni Battista Farinelli (as reported by Mattheson in his 1739 *Volkommene Capellmeister*) took his correctly tuned open strings round to the other players, in turn and in silence.[526]

---

520 Jerold (2007), p.216.
521 The symphony derives from incidental music Haydn wrote for Jean-François Regnard's play *Le distrait*, so this passage may also have connotations of absent-mindedness.
522 Jerold (2007), p.218.
523 Jerold (2007), p.220.
524 Jerold (2000), p.24.
525 Giovanni Maria Artusi, *L'Artusi, overa delle imperfettioni della moderna musica* (Venice, 1600), cited in Stras (2018), p.316.
526 Jerold (2007), p.217.

Ex. 4. Joseph Haydn, Symphony No.60 in C, 'Il distratto', Finale, bars 1-16.

PITCH

Information about pitch standards up to 1800 exists in scattered and incomplete form, but it is possible to estimate and sometimes measure instrumental pitches, using surviving instruments and documents. The result shows great variation between country, century, tradition and instrument, although there do appear to have been instances where some form of standardization or partial standardization is evident, as indicated by both historical instruments (17th-century cornetts, for example)[534] and by consistent compositional compasses.[535] Other examples show great variety, including the seven relative keyboard pitches used by the Ruckers family,[536] the *chiavette* system for polyphony, the dual *chorton/kammerton* standard of Bach's Germany or the interchangeable *corps de rechanges* joints of a Quantz flute from 1740, ranging from about A387 to 414.[537]

With reference to rehearsal issues, the precise actual pitch now thought to be appropriate for any given repertoire by modern performers may be less significant than how such pitches were historically sounded, and especially how they were transferred between performers, and between spaces in venues.[538] There do exist examples of instructions for the giving of a relative pitch, such as the annotations (in Spanish) in the Paston lutebooks, which name a pitch for the singer to enter on by reference to the pitch given by the fret of a particular string,[539] but this is relative not absolute, as the precise sounding pitch of a historic gut-strung lute cannot be known.

---

534 Bruce Haynes, *A History of Performing Pitch: The Story of A* (Lanham ML and Oxford, 2002); see also Nicholas Mitchell, 'Choral and Instrumental Pitch in Church Music 1570-1620', *The Galpin Society Journal*, xlviii (March 1995), pp.13-32 and Parrott (2022), pp.401-406.

535 See the summary voice-range charts in Wulstan (1986), p.211-212. These can represent a considerable constraint on plausible modern options, as for example the very wide written choral compasses of nearly four octaves found in Tudor sacred music, or the nearly two-octave individual vocal ranges of Brumel's 12-part *Missa Et Ecca Terrae Motus*. Whether Eton College could ever have mustered 13 men each capable of singing the range of a 13th for Robert Wylkynson's canonic *Jesu autem transiens* in the Eton Choirbook is open to question; Harrison (1963), pp.413-415 suggests it was intended for Compline in Lent.

536 Grant O'Brien, *Ruckers: A harpsichord and virginal building tradition* (Cambridge, 1990).

537 Mary Oleskiewicz, 'The Flutes of Quantz: Their Construction and Performing Practice', *The Galpin Society Journal*, liii (April 2000), pp.201-220 at 217.

538 For a discussion of the issue of rehearsal pitches in practice, see Francis Knights and Pablo Padilla, 'The historical transmission of reference pitches in early music' (forthcoming).

539 Philip Brett, ed Joseph Kerman and Davitt Moroney, *William Byrd and his contemporaries: essays and a monograph* (Berkeley, 2007), ch.4. See also Caitlin Nolan, *Music of the Paston Household: Case Studies of Circulation and Adaptation in the Lutebook GB-Lbl Add. MS 29247*, PhD thesis (Newcastle University, 2023).

Early Tudor composers used a standard compass of F-g^2 for their church music, 23 notes when counted diatonically from the lowest man's note to the highest boy's. Carver, Sutton and others expanded the range by a tone in each direction, and Cornysh (Magnificat a5) even used low C. This gives a maximum written range of C-a^2, nearly four octaves, so the issue of standardized pitches becomes important, as there is little leeway for selecting a singable reference pitch before the parts become too high for the trebles and too low for the basses. Such problems are explicitly noted in the Évora Cathedral regulations of 1565, with a preference for the direction of error: 'After finishing the lesson, the cantor or the sub-cantor will begin the responsory, at such a pitch that everyone can sing it honestly, and it is better that the lowest note is not heard than the highest note sounds out of the choir's reach.'[540]

Where a rehearsal and a performance venue were not the same (a cathedral, and its song school, for example), some method of transferring a reference pitch between them must have been possible, and this is unlikely to have been simple human memory. The possible options for reference pitch sourcing, especially for unaccompanied vocal music, include: singers with perfect pitch;[541] the organ (which may not have been adjacent to the performers, and in any case required a physical organ-blower and a player) or other keyboard;[542] a small separate organ-type pipe functioning as a pitch pipe;[543] a suspended metal bar or tube functioning as a proto-tuning fork; a small bell or other pitched percussion

---

540 d'Alvarenga (2015), p.16.

541 The history of this ability is not well understood; for a modern medical study of the phenomenon, see Simon Leipold, Carina Klein and Lutz Jäncke, 'Musical Expertise Shapes Functional and Structural Brain Networks Independent of Absolute Pitch Ability', *The Journal of Neuroscience*, xli/11 (17 March 2021), pp.2496-2511.

542 A few institutions banned organs, such as Syon Abbey: 'organs schal theu never have none'; Harrison (1963), p.193. See also Parrott (2015), p.82 on the instability of organ pitch. At Lincoln Cathedral in 1570, Byrd was instructed by the increasingly Puritan authorities to just give the organ note for the choir; this seems to have been to avoid him playing complex organ preludes for this purpose, so may have a specific context; John Harley, *William Byrd: Gentleman of the Chapel Royal* (Aldershot, 1999), p.39.

543 During the English Civil War, individual organ pipes were mouth-blown when instruments were vandalized: at Exeter Cathedral, 'they brake down the organs, and taking two or three hundred pipes with them in a most scorneful and contemptuous manner, went up and downe the streets piping with them'; John Norman, *Box of Whistles: The History and Recent Development of Organ Case Design* (London, 2007), p.22. See also Parrott (2022), p.406 for a 1773 illustration of an organ-pipe pitch-pipe.

instrument;[544] a recorder or other suitable wind instrument;[545] a monochord (capable of holding stable pitch for many days, although itself needing tuning from a known pitch source in the first place); or a glass instrument.[546] Only the first and second of these are now usually considered as options,[547] although the lack of examples, descriptions or iconography by no means rules out other possibilities; this is unlikely to have been a process considered worth recording or describing at the time. In all these cases, the sounding object needs only to produce a sufficient clear pitched note at a volume that the choirmaster or other leading musician can hear, which can then be hummed or sung to the waiting ensemble. Usage could have varied hugely between country, date and institution. At València in 1683, for example, dulcian player Miguel Renart was instructed to 'enter the choir at the Gloria Patri of the first psalm of Sext to give the pitch for the *varillas*',[548] whereas in Manila in 1771 the *chantre* was to 'give the pitch of everything sung within the choir and in processions'.[549]

As well as the great variety of possible pitches in use across the period, there is also the issue of the level of accuracy required, or attainable, before the advent of technical pitch measurement systems such as those of Hertz. It is quite possible that a margin of error of as much as a semitone for fundamental pitch would have been considered acceptable, for example; and a drop in pitch during a twenty-minute unaccompanied Tudor votive antiphon might not even have been noticed.

---

544 Early bells are discussed by Hugh Willmott and Adam Daubney, 'Of saints, sows or smiths? Copper-brazed iron handbells in Early Medieval England', *Archaeological Journal*, clxxvii/1 (2019), pp.336-355. Sets of pitched bells were known at the Tudor court ('Hire of 17 dozen bells', 1511); Stevens (1979), p.274. For bells at one particular institution, see Kirkman (2020), ch.5.

545 Some brass instruments are also possible, but far less likely. A small recorder seems a suitable choice, as it could sound any note, was portable and sufficiently loud for all the musicians to hear.

546 Later developed into the glass harmonica and glasschord.

547 The pitched 'instrument' that actually led Pythagoras to his mathematical theory of harmonic relationships was the blacksmith's anvil, according to the *Manual of Harmonics* by Nicomachus of Gerasa (c.60-c.120); Nicholas Kenyon, *The Life of Music* (New Haven and London, 2021), p.18.

548 Royo (2021), pp.40-41.

549 Irving (2010), p.165; a *sochantre* (succentor) was to give the pitch for Psalms, introits and responsories, and all these regulations may have been following Spanish practice.

ORNAMENTATION

Extempore ornamentation was a very significant part of a number of historic music styles, although applied more in a solo than ensemble context, with the exception of standard ornaments such as Baroque cadential trills. The issues in rehearsal would have been: who was allowed or encouraged to ornament, and by whom? What sort of ornaments were thought to be appropriate, in which musical styles, and how often? Were these to be practiced in advance, or inserted spontaneously in performance? Finally, how were the composer's views on their own music (where known), or other performing traditions to be considered? (in 1727, Baron observed that custom dictated that for a performer, 'the piece belongs not to him alone but to others as well').[550]

As well as there being local traditions, personal preference appears to have been important, and that even differed between master and student (some of Bach's pupils seem to have used far more notated ornaments in their copies of Bach than he did). Three historic references cover the 'perform as written' tradition: 'When Josquin was living at Cambrai [sic] and someone wanted to apply ornaments in his music which he had not composed, he walked into the choir and sharply berated him in front of the others, saying: "You ass, why do you add ornamentation? If it had pleased me, I would have inserted it myself. If you wish to amend properly composed songs, make your own, but leave mine unornamented".'[551] John Hawkins said of Agostino Steffani that he 'would never admit of any divisions, or graces, even on the most simple and plain passages, except what he wrote himself',[552] while François Couperin absolutely insisted his music to be played as written: 'my pieces must be executed as I have marked them, and that they will never make an impression on those persons of real taste unless one observes to the letter all that I have marked without any additions or deletions'.[553]

However, many other musicians allowed performers much greater leeway, or even encouraged creativity, as in the story of Purcell and the young singer Jemmy Bowen: 'He, when practising a Song set by Mr. *Purcell*, some of the Music [the professional court musicians] told him to grace and run a Division in such a Place. *O let him alone*, said Mr. *Purcell; he will grace it more nat-*

---

550 Baron (2019), p.152.
551 Wegman (1999), p.322.
552 Donington (1989), p.156.
553 Translation from James R. Anthony, *French Baroque Music from Beaujoyeulx to Rameau* (New York, 2/1978), p.261. See also Parrott (2022), pp.388-390 on composers' intentions.

urally than you, or I, can teach him'.⁵⁵⁴ One particular argument in favour of such freedom is the difficulty of accurately writing out ornaments in normal rhythmic notation, as Roger North observed: 'It is the hardest task that can be to pen the manner of artificial Gracing the upper part. It hath bin attempted, and in print, but with Woeful Effect . . . the Spirit of the art is Incommunicable by wrighting'.⁵⁵⁵ For the same reason, performance subtleties like the *notes inégales* of the French Baroque seem to belong more to the rehearsal than the music notation process.⁵⁵⁶

TEMPO

Thanks to a century of recordings, and an omnipresent soundscape of pop music with a backbeat, regularity of tempo rarely seems to be a problem for modern classical musicians, who have internalized accurate pulsing. Some of the performers of the past, with no experience of any *precisely* regular movements (except perhaps for dripping water or a large clock's pendulum movement or tick),⁵⁵⁷ evidently found maintaining strict tempo a challenge: Giovanni de' Bardi (c.1580) warns of consort singers who 'disregard the time, so breaking and stretching it that they make it altogether impossible for their colleagues to sing properly',⁵⁵⁸ Henry Purcell (1696) noted that there is 'nothing more difficult in Musick then playing of true time',⁵⁵⁹ Quantz (1752) explained how to cope when a movement started at the wrong tempo,⁵⁶⁰ while Anton Stadler (1800) advised instrumentalists not to 'hold back or press forward the

---

554 Cited in Donington (1989), p.155.

555 Cited in Franklin B. Zimmerman, 'Performance Practices and Rehearsal Techniques', *College Music Symposium*, ix (Fall 1969), pp.101-111 at 101.

556 For an example of the very large literature on this contentious topic, see John Byrt, 'Inequality in Alessandro Scarlatti and Handel: a sequel', *Early Music*, xl/1 (February 2012), pp.91-110; a full-length study of the topic is Stephen Hefling, *Rhythmic Alteration in Seventeenth- and Eighteenth-Century Music* (New York, 1993).

557 Musical exceptions were clockwork instruments and automata, but these were very rare before the 19th century; see Arthur W. J. G. Ord-Hume, *Clockwork music: an illustrated history of mechanical musical instruments from the musical box to the pianola, from automaton lady virginal players to orchestrion* (London, 1973), David Fuller, 'An Introduction to Automatic Instruments', *Early Music*, xi/2 (April 1983), pp.164-166 and Beverly Jerold, 'A Re-Examination of Tempos Assigned to the Earl of Bute's Machine Organ', *Early Music*, xxx/4 (November 2002), pp.584-591.

558 Strunk (1981), ii, pp.108-109.

559 Donington (1989), p.410; these remarks were attributed to Purcell by the publisher.

560 Quantz (1966), p.198.

tempo'.⁵⁶¹ Leopold Mozart's very simple ear test (October 1777) for a potential pupil – who he suspected 'has no ear and therefore no sense of time' – was to be played just two bars of music to see if she knows the names of the notes and can 'imitate the time'.⁵⁶² Most concerned was the amateur writer Roger North, who said 'as to time, no practise is usefull, or will ever make a consortier, but in consort itself' and 'at hard places he will retard, and getting the better, goe too fast'⁵⁶³ – in other words, a solitary player was almost incapable of maintaining accurate tempo, in his experience. The same complaint ('frequent unsteadyness') was recorded of the otherwise admirable Philharmonic Orchestra in London as late as 1840.⁵⁶⁴

Where musicians did not have the skill to maintain time at all, the results could be very poor, as recorded by Sagudino (1515): 'Two musicians, who are also in his Majesty's service, played the organ, but very ill forsooth: they kept bad time, and their touch was feeble, neither was their execution good';⁵⁶⁵ while the young Geminiani in Naples was alleged to be 'so wild and unsteady' in tempo that he was relegated to the viola.⁵⁶⁶ Haydn, at a performance of William Shield's *The Woodman* at Covent Garden in December 1791, noted an unnamed opera tenor who was 'most unmusical … creates a new tempo for himself, now 3/4, now 2/4, makes cuts whenever it occurs to him'.⁵⁶⁷ Such 'singing actors' could be a trial to musicians, and Thomas Shaw's description of John Philip Kemble (1757-1823) failing at a duet in Grétry's *Richard Coeur de Lion* at Drury Lane in 1786 includes the dialogue between them, 'Mr. Kemble, Mr. Kemble, you are murdering the time, sir!' – 'Very well sir, and you are forever beating it!'⁵⁶⁸

Some performers evidently kept time physically with their feet, then as now regarded as poor practice, as noted by Quantz (1752).⁵⁶⁹ In 1512 Philomathes objected to many who were 'marking the tactus with a stamping foot, like a sated pack-horse who, playing in the green, stumbles in the grass and lust-

---

561 Poulin (1990), pp.220-221.
562 Anderson (1989), p.311.
563 Wilson (1959), p.98 and 257; he also speaks of 'sorry consortiers, who could not keep their time' (p.101) and notes 'that persons who delight much to play by themselves never keep with time in consort, but will either be too fast or too slow' (p.137).
564 *The Musical World* (27 February 1840), p.122; Carse (1948), p.248.
565 Giustinian (1854), vol.1, p.80.
566 Parrott (2022), p.415, Burney's account.
567 Hogwood (1980), p.49.
568 Cited in Holman (2020), p.287
569 Quantz (1966), p.198.

fully runs riot',[570] while Johann Samuel Petri (1782) describes town musicians keeping time 'with such ferocious stamping that we think ourselves in a paper mill or foundry'.[571] Even leading professional violinist Schuppanzigh had the 'accursed fashion, generally introduced here [Vienna], of beating time with his foot, even when there was no need for it' (Reichardt, 1810), although it is not clear whether audibly or silently.[572]

In matters of tempo precision, distinction needs be made between ensemble and solo music, between different styles of music, and between ordinary practitioners and experts, for as Thomas Mace (1676) said, 'when we come to be *Masters ...* we can *command all manner of Time*, at our *own Pleasures*; we Then *take Liberty* (and very often, for *Humour, and good Adornment-Sake*, in certain Places) to *Break Time*'.[573]

ACCENT AND DICTION

Regional accents would have been more pronounced in the past, with much less of a uniform sense of what an 'educated' or 'cultured' accent sounded like, in either English or Latin (compare 'BBC English' today).[574] This not only affected vowel sounds, but even the number of syllables in individual words: 'spirit' was pronounced with one or two syllables in the north and south of Elizabethan England respectively. Many choirs would have included singers trained (or never trained) differently in different places, and who approached both Latin and their vernacular in a variety of ways, so it seems unlikely that the high uniform level of present-day 'singers' vowels' would have been possible. However,

---

570 Philomathes (1512), Book 3, ch.1; translation courtesy of Tim Braithwaite.

571 Cited in Jerold (2005), p.81.

572 Strunk *IV* (1981), p.160.

573 Mace (1676), p.81.

574 McGee (1990), pp.58-59. See also Harold Copeman, *Singing in Latin: Or Pronunciation Explor'd* (Oxford, 2/1996), Alison Wray, 'The sound of Latin in England before and after the Reformation' and 'English pronunciation, c. 1500-c. 1625', in Morehen (1995), pp.74-89 and 90-108, Arthur Hughes, Peter Trudgill and Dominic Watt, *English accents and dialects: An introduction to social and regional varieties of English in the British Isles* (London, 5/2012) and Edward J. Marshall, *Do choirs have accents? A sociophonetic investigation of choral sound*, PhD thesis (University of Glasgow, 2023). For Tudor English pronunciation, see John Hart, *An Ortographie, conteyning the due order and reason, howe to write or paint thimage of mannes voice, most like to the life or nature* (London, 1569). The most recent study examines choral vowels during the 20th century: Edward J. Marshall, Jane Stuart-Smith, John Butt and Timothy Dean, 'Variation and change over time in British choral singing (1925–2019)', *Laboratory Phonology: Journal of the Association for Laboratory Phonology*, xv/1 (2024), pp.1-39.

Bathe's 'Rules' of 1600 (see above) do recommend that singers 'sunder the Vowels and Consonants, distinctly pronouncing them according to the manner of the place', suggesting some uniformity of usage could and should be achieved. This would presumably have been a matter for the director of music.

Diction was also a concern, and writers like Thomas Elyot, in *The Governor* (1531),[575] were concerned that upper class children were brought up to speak English that was 'clean, polite, perfectly and articulately pronounced, omitting no letter or syllable', and avoiding any rustic dialects that they might pick up from servants.[576]

In a rare instance of praise for singers' diction, Gregory Martin, who had lived in Rome in the late 1570s, particularly commented upon the clarity of texts sung by the city's choirs: 'this is singular and much to be noted, that they deliver every word and everie syllable so distinctly, so cleane, so commodiously, so fully, that the hearers may perceave al that is sung'.[577] Earlier in the century, an example of what could go wrong in performance survives from Paride de Grassis, the senior Master of Ceremonies in the papal chapel, who reported in 1510 that a polyphonic creed 'was sung in such a confused manner that many did not understand the words',[578] while at the Feast of San Lorenzo in 1673 'the music was chaos, a Babel of all the musicians in Venice, five organs, all the instruments, trumpets, trombones & everything there was in Venice, but there was nothing to enjoy except a constant murmuring, it being impossible to understand a word'.[579]

For the audience to understand the meaning of a text was equally important in opera, and Mozart (1778), having criticized the singer Meisner for his excessive vibrato, praised his rival Raaff for his 'excellent, clear diction'.[580]

---

575 Thomas Elyot, *The Book Named the Governor* (London, 1531).
576 Nicholas Orme, *Tudor Children* (New Haven and London, 2023), p.160.
577 Sherr (1999), XIV, p.607.
578 Sherr (1999), XI, p.255.
579 Parrott (2022), p.273.
580 Anderson (1989), p.552.

AMATEUR MUSIC-MAKING

The experience of rehearsal in an amateur environment may have been quite different, as the realities of both 'rehearsal' and 'performance' differed from professional practice. While standards may have still been high, the final level of expert polish may not have been regarded as necessary, as any listeners were there to enjoy the music rather than judge (or pay) the performers; and because the preparation goals were different, and perhaps less clear. For example, a domestic viol consort in Elizabethan England was likely made up of performers of varying ability and training, and probably also of different social classes (household servants could be drafted in). The play-through of a contrapuntal fantasia in a Long Gallery of an evening may have counted as a 'rehearsal', but a member of the family coming in to listen would have made it a sort of 'performance'; such boundaries were likely rather blurred. At the other end of the amateur spectrum, an affluent and musical family like the Sharps, who organized domestic, public and water-borne concerts in London and elsewhere from the 1750s to the 1780s, put on ambitious events with the support of an enormous circle of musical friends and professional supporters. An early instance in Durham from May 1754 was described in the local press as 'a Concert of vocal and instrumental Musick, by several Gentlemen, for their own Amusement'.[581]

Those estate owners wealthy or interested enough could retain a resident musician, as for example Edward Johnson and John Wilbye at Hengrave Hall, Richard Mico at Ingatestone Hall,[582] John Jenkins at West Dereham or even Handel at Cannons. Various illustrations show domestic musical activity, as in the mixed group of cittern, bandora and two sizes of violin in a mural at Gilling Castle in Yorkshire.[583] These resident musicians would have been responsible for teaching and training members of the family and their staff as required, sourcing music, keeping the instruments in good order and composing when asked.

Music lessons for the young could be quite demanding in terms of hours spent, but for the gentry were mostly left off when the children grew up (especially for girls), music being part of a cultured education rather than as professional preparation. In 1561 Sir Nicholas Bacon provided Sir William Cecil with his 'Articles devised for the bringing up ... of the Queenes Majesties Wards', which

---

581 Brian Crosby, 'Private Concerts on Land and Water: The Musical Activities of the Sharp family, c.1750-c.1790', *Royal Musical Association Research Chronicle*, xxxiv (2001), pp.1-118 at 12.

582 See Price (1981).

583 Reproduced in Price (1981), p.43.

involved lessons in Music from twelve to two and again from eight to nine in the evening, interspersed with other subjects.[584]

One particular form of domestic (in fact, literally sometimes 'underground') music-making in England was as part of the illegal Catholic services held by recusants in the later 16th century: for example, works by Byrd were performed as part of a forbidden mass with the Jesuit priests Henry Garnet (1555-1606) and Robert Southwell (1561-95) in the open air on the banks of the Thames in 1586.[585] One wonders who the musicians were taking such a potentially fatal risk, and what form of preparation they undertook – in situ rehearsal beforehand would have been impossible.

---

584 Harris (1938), p.131.
585 Jessie Childs, *God's Traitors: Terror & Faith in Elizabethan England* (London, 2014), p.136.

CHAPTER 6: PERFORMANCE PRACTICE

PART 2
ROMANTIC TO MODERN

CHAPTER 7
THE 19TH CENTURY

The continuing rise in general literacy, coupled with increasing middle-class affluence, musical literacy and education, and the availability of cheap performing materials, led to a significant increase in the numbers of those active in music from the 18th century onwards. One example in Britain was shown by the creation of numerous choral societies and music festivals during the 19th century (the Three Choirs Festival, founded in 1715, was an important model),[586] often including ensembles of a very large size. In Germany in this period, the comparable Sing-Akademie in Berlin had some 500 or so members, and 'met once a week, – a separate practice being held for the younger and less assured portion of its singers'.[587] Such weekly practices seem to have become (and remain) normal activity for many amateur music ensembles. More choirs meant more conductors, so instruction books started to appear (see below), in order to train the trainer.

The ensembles that performed most frequently, up until the 20th century, were the choirs of the major Anglican cathedrals: Lay Clerks' reminiscences of the legendary Norwich Cathedral organist Dr Zechariah Buck (1798-1879) record that choir sang twice daily on every day of the year but one; and although there were no full choir rehearsals, the men had no fewer than 229 separate rehearsals in 1869.[588] A short boys' rehearsal preceded each 10 am Matins, with a much longer one before Evensong at 4 pm. The size of the repertory and its level of difficulty at this period are not known, but experience in this environment has

---

586 Anthony Boden and Paul Hedley, *The Three Choirs Festival: A History* (Woodbridge, 2/2017).
587 Henry F. Chorley, *Music and Manners in France and Germany* (London, 1841), ii, p.226.
588 Francis Knights, 'Zechariah Buck of Norwich', *The Musical Times*, cxxxi/1764 (February 1990), pp.107-109.

shown that the more performances there are, the less rehearsals are needed overall, for example in Anglican chant.

Other significant changes from the early 19th century included affordable vocal scores (rather than the earlier single vocal parts)[589] and then scholarly editions, giving the musicians more confidence in the accuracy of their material – and assisting with both canon-formation and repertoire sacralization. Vocal scores enabled more convenient piano-accompanied rehearsals for choirs and for ballet, saving time in the full rehearsals, and led to the rise of the new role of repetiteur. Musical criticism, both in the national and local press, and in specialist publications such *The Musical Times*, provided (sometimes unwelcome) feedback, as well as a sense of national and even international standards of performance.[590] Elements of showmanship and musical gigantism crept in, with musical spectacles of an ever-grander nature, as in the extravaganzas of Louis-Antoine Jullien (1812-60);[591] new venues were also built on an epic, cathedral-like scale, such as the Royal Albert Hall in London (1871), which could seat over five thousand.

ENSEMBLE SIZE AND STANDARDS

Although large ensembles were known pre-1800 for particular special events, with 200 to 500 instrumentalists and singers (Rome, 1740; London, 1784; Berlin, 1786, for example), these were rarities. Nevertheless, ensemble sizes for court then professional orchestras typically grew from perhaps a dozen in the early 18th century to nearly a hundred by the mid-19th century.[592] The problem of widely-spaced performers was noted as far back as C. P. E. Bach, who advised in 1753, 'Because sound takes some time to travel, and cannot be heard so promptly from a distance as at close quarters, one must make use of one's eyes to look often at the leader, not only at the beginning of the piece, but also during the course of it, and in the event of any little disturbance.'[593]

---

589 Capdevila (2017).

590 See Carse (1940), ch.3.

591 Ateş Orga, *The Proms* (London, 1975), chs.4-5; Nicholas Slonimsky, *Nicholas Slonimsky's Book of Musical Anecdotes* (New York, R/2002), p.47

592 Carse (1940), pp. 46-47 and 18-27; Adam Carse, *The Orchestra from Beethoven to Berlioz* (Cambridge, [1948]), pp.46-63. See also Daniel J. Koury, *Orchestral Performance Practices in the Nineteenth Century: Size, Proportions, and Seating* (Rochester, NY, 1986) and Spitzer and Zaslaw (2004).

593 Carl Philip Emanuel Bach, *Versuch über die wahre Art das Clavier zu spielen* (Berlin, 1753), xvii, part vii, para 42.

The number of institutions and venues increased, in order to meet demand: in Paris in 1848 there were 25 theatres employing 636 players.[594] However, in the provinces both numbers and standards were almost always lower, and it is recorded that in America in 1829 there was only one oboe in the entire country – who lived in Baltimore. Even in a major musical centre like New York, orchestras could rarely muster two clarinets, and bassoons, trumpets and timpani could not be had.[595]

Despite the formulation of a nascent orchestral canon, the amount of new music performed in the early 19th century demonstrated a need for constant expansion of techniques and the increase in rehearsal for unknown works; a sample comparison of orchestral repertoire composed pre- and post-1800 in Paris, Leipzig and London during the 1830s made by Carse showed that 19th-century music comprised some 75% to 85% of the repertoire.[596]

Ambitious composers made full use of enhancements to musical instruments (keywork, valves and the like) from the end of the 18th century, from which point orchestras found themselves challenged by the new music. For example, the replacement overture to Beethoven's *Fidelio* (1805) 'was too difficult in the part of the wind instruments, which always executed their task to the great vexation of the composer. In the third overture which was substituted for the two former, too hard a task was imposed upon the string instruments, so that these also were found deficient in the requisite precision', as reported by Ignaz Moscheles.[597] Combinations of amateur and professional performers were common, with amateurs supplementing professionals for large events; and paid extras supporting what were essentially voluntary ensembles.[598]

THE IMPACT OF BEETHOVEN

The introduction of Beethoven's symphonies to Paris by François Antoine Habeneck (1781-1849) during the 1820s was a slow process, and the Third Symphony took a while to be appreciated, even if the Fifth went better with the musicians. In 1826 Habeneck tried the 'Eroica' again with an invited ensemble, and with an intense rehearsal. Rehearsals then continued for several years, and in March

---

594 Carse (1948), p.87.
595 *Harmonicon*, London (August 1829), p.192.
596 Carse (1948), p.8.
597 Anton Schindler, trans Ignaz Moscheles, *Life of Beethoven* (London, 1841), vol.i, pp.93-94.
598 Carse (1948), p.261.

1828 (a year after Beethoven's death) came the first concert of his music at the Paris Conservatoire. The *Société de Concerts* then took enthusiastically to his music, and in the next nine years their Beethoven symphony performances vastly outnumbered the works of all other composers combined. By 1859 they had given 280 performances of the nine symphonies, with Nos.5-7 being the firm favourites. This eventual appreciation was likely a combination of repeated exposure to the music, plus sufficient experience through rehearsal and performance to play it well – Wagner heard them play the Ninth with 'equable perfection'.[599] John Ella also heard this work in 1834, and identified the key to their diligence in rehearsal: '*Esprit de corps* incites them to do justice to the music, and to sustain the glory of the Institution, thereby securing to the *chef* any amount of study and practice'.[600] Habeneck also embedded the learning process: 'when the orchestra had thoroughly mastered a symphony, it was not played and put aside; it was played again at the next concert, and then again, and again'.[601]

Lesser orchestras in Paris suffered by comparison, such as Henri Valentino's (1785-1865) ensemble, which 'hurried the *tempo* in every movement, played every work in exactly the same way, and generally lacked enthusiasm', according to Anton Schindler. Provincial French theatre orchestras were even worse, as Castil-Blaze (1784-1857) reported, listing among their problems, 'the orchestra makes no effort to be any better because no one ever listens to it', most of the local players 'have never heard music well played', the pitch is 'about a semitone higher than in the Paris *Opéra*', 'old habits prevail … nothing good is expected, so mediocrity is tolerated' – and 'two rehearsals have to do for an opera which requires many, so the opera only gets going by about the tenth performance'. This latter point is a long-standing complaint regarding opera runs, where the rehearsal process bleeds into the performance cycle itself.[602] First nights were sometimes best avoided.

Matters might be no better in London ('the music of London is radically bad'), where François-Joseph Fétis (1784-1871) in 1829 wrote of the King's Theatre orchestra that it was too small, 'the rehearsals go badly, the playing is negligent', a result of the conductor being 'unable to apply any severity in exacting good service from the players, because if he did so he would expose himself at any moment to the risk of losing them, as they could always find employment elsewhere'.[603]

---

599 Carse (1948), pp.91-92 and 93-95.
600 John Ella, *Musical Sketches* (London, 1878), cited in Carse (1948), p.97.
601 Carse (1948), p.100.
602 Carse (1948), pp.100 and 105.
603 Carse (1948), p.183.

In Italy, Rossini's music partly fulfilled the same function as Beethoven's did in Austria, Germany and France in assisting with a rise in performing standards; nevertheless, an English magazine reported in 1837 that Italian orchestras were not up to playing German music – or 'any other music than that of their own country and time' – due to the use of difficult keys and 'the precision required in the performance of concerted music'.[604] At La Scala in Milan, Spohr found the orchestra for his opera *Alruna* was 'pure, vigorous, precise', but also noted errors due to their lack of sight-reading skills: 'the orchestra is accustomed to too many rehearsals to be able execute anything free from fault after one rehearsal only'. Worse, the audience was so noisy that one could hardly hear the performance.[605]

NUMBERS OF REHEARSALS

From about 1800 information, at least of an anecdotal kind, starts appearing that documents the number of rehearsals that took place (some of these figures may of course have been exaggerated, in either direction). While the Philharmonic Orchestra in London had a single Saturday rehearsal for a Monday concert in the 1830s, the Leipzig orchestra was 'so well trained in habits of attention by Mendelssohn and David, that two rehearsals sufficed to get up a long programme', according to Berlioz. Charles Lipinski in Dresden provided 'four long rehearsals … and the band itself would willingly have asked for a fifth if there had been time' for Berlioz's visit; Mendelssohn had eleven rehearsals for his *Midsummer Night's Dream* in Berlin; Weber in 1821 had twelve (four with orchestra) for his *Die Freischütz*; Nicolai had 13 for Beethoven's Ninth Symphony;[606] and Spontini in Berlin had 42 – and in one case as many as 80 – for an opera.[607] The Paris Opera was particularly generous in the matter of time for major productions, with about 30 rehearsals for some new works; Meyerbeer's *Robert le Diable* was in preparation for nine months, partly subsidized by the composer himself.

Italian opera houses worked at much greater speed, with a fortnight being common before a production opened; London seems to have been at least as fast – Berlioz unkindly called it 'the art of accelerated musical rehearsals'.[608]

---

604 *The Musical World* (4 August 1837), p.127.
605 Carse (1948), p.271.
606 Carse (1948), pp.124, 114, 466 and 369. For the Beethoven premiere, see Theodore Albrecht, *Beethoven's Ninth Symphony: Rehearsing and Performing its 1824 premiere* (Woodbridge, 2024).
607 Moritz Hauptmann, *Aus der Musikerwelt* (Berlin, 1875), p.90, cited in Carse (1948), p.345.
608 Carse (1948), pp.467-468.

While sectional rehearsals were not unknown, few composers could hope that the musicians would come to a rehearsal having already learnt their individual parts – assuming these had even been distributed beforehand (the initial read-through seems to be what Alma Mahler is referring to when she described 'reading-rehearsals').[609] It is unclear to what extent parts were available to performers in advance of a first rehearsal, or whether they actually made use of them when this was the case. Hans von Bülow (1830-94) was unusual in expecting players to be note-perfect in advance, in order to 'get right to work on the music itself'; this may be one of the many things (like making his Meiningen orchestra play standing) that created enmity from his musicians.[610] He himself wrote, 'My unpopularity in unbounded', taking it as a compliment to the success of his methods.[611]

That professional rehearsals were normally paid is seen by a reference to the Leipzig Gewandhaus orchestra, who (according to Rochlitz) willingly undertook additional unpaid rehearsals in order to manage the 'Eroica' symphony in 1807. At other times, additional rehearsals could be scheduled where the music required it, as when Mendelssohn premiered Schumann's first symphony in Leipzig in 1841 (some of this involved time needed for corrections to the composer's orchestral parts).[612]

For the *Spirituel-Concerte* in Vienna, an orchestra of around 50, including about a dozen paid wind professionals, performed symphonies and choral works (including Haydn, Mozart, Beethoven, Weber and Mendelssohn) with one or no rehearsals. In the 1820s their standard was so poor ('too little rehearsing and too many amateurs') that Schubert walked out of one of his own works.[613]

The efficiency of a permanent ensemble might also depend on a balance being struck between sufficient preparation time and being overworked: in the 1830s and 40s, while the Darmstadt orchestra (conducted by the Grand Duke himself, but with a subsidiary professional director) was required to perform standing every night for three or four hours ('no orchestra in the world is so harassed as this'), the admirable Rudolstadt court orchestra was only needed for the opera four to six weeks a year, and therefore had ample time for rehearsing and performing symphonic works the rest of the time.[614]

---

609 Mahler (1946), pp.61 and 80.
610 Lebrecht (2001), p.27.
611 Cited in Harold C. Schonberg, *The Great Conductors* (London, 1977), p.165.
612 Carse (1948), pp.219, 140, 124, 114, 133, 137-138.
613 Carse (1948), pp.261-262.
614 Carse (1948), pp.146-148 and 153.

Festivals offered some economies of scale, with musicians booked for a number of events over a short period of time, but much could then be expected: in the 20th century Henry Wood complained of a total of nine hours' rehearsal for six concerts at the Proms between the wars, meaning some repertoire repetition was necessary.[615]

PERFORMER BEHAVIOUR

References by Castil-Blaze, Berlioz, Wagner and many others paint a vivid picture of frequent orchestral inadequacy in the 19th century, with performers absent, asleep, making jokes – or refusing to play second to a colleague, with two or three doubling the first wind or brass part while leaving the second silent. Only in the best ensembles, such as those in Paris, Dresden, Munich or Berlin, were high standards demanded. What level of control over individual players a conductor had is uncertain, as with the first oboe in Wagner's Dresden orchestra, who had 'an irritating mania for trills and mordents', according to Berlioz.[616] Whether allowing such extempore additions to a score by this date was unenforceable, acceptable, or merely tolerated, is unknown, but Berlioz for one was clearly irritated by them. In Rome, Spohr (who wrote of their orchestral musicians, 'God help the composer whose work falls into such hands') directed particular ire at improvised additions: 'each individual makes just what ornamentation comes into his head and double strokes with almost every tone, so that the *ensemble* resembles more the noise of an orchestra tuning up than harmonious music'. Spohr (an advanced thinker in many respects) insisted no liberties should be taken with the written parts.[617]

In the London theatre orchestras of the 1830s, one performance a week could be a write-off, as Saturdays were hampered by orchestras having 'invariably' got drunk at pay-day: Adolphe Adam recorded extraordinary acts of misbehaviour from the players while the conductor and singers carried on 'as if nothing unusual was happening'.[618] All these issues seem to have been resolved by the increasing professionalism of 20th-century performers, but there are still references to orchestral musicians (such as the New Philharmonia in the 1970s, as noted by Lorin Maazel) reading books or playing chess during rehearsals, presumably at times when their part was silent.[619]

---

615 Orga (1975), p.70.
616 Carse (1948), p.124.
617 Louis Spohr, *Autobiography* (London, 1878), cited in Carse (1948), p.273; Carse (1948), p.53.
618 Adolphe Adam, *Souveniers d'un Musicien* (Paris, 1868), pp.54-47; Carse (1948), pp.193-194.
619 Stephen J. Pettitt, *Philharmonia Orchestra: A Record of Achievement* (London, 1985), p.167.

CONDUCTING MATERIALS

Until later in the 19th century, full scores were published after the parts, sometimes 20 years later, as for Beethoven's early symphonies,[620] so (following 18th century traditions) a conductor or violinist-conductor might have to manage without one. This must have severely affected their ability to correct errors during rehearsal, or give leads, without constantly coming over to check what was amiss with individual performers. Remarkably, Beethoven's large-scale 9th Symphony was rehearsed and performed in Leipzig without access to a score in 1828 (the Gewandhaus orchestra then employed a time-beater in addition to a director, for choral movements only). An intermediate notation was in use in France and Italy early in the 19th century – for example, at Paris in 1828 and Naples in 1829 – the leader directing from a special part 'written on two staves', presumably either Violin 1 and bass, or Violin 1 and the various cues; Berlioz called this a 'deplorable system'. A fuller version of this involved a four-stave manuscript score for the leader, with Violin 1, a reduction of other parts, the bass and a further stave with vocal material, such as recitatives; this system persisted at the Paris Opera until after the middle of the 19th century.[621]

The idea of a conductor working from a memorized score was introduced by Ferdinand Hiller,[622] the advantages and disadvantages of which remain unchanged in present-day practice – locating points for comment quickly in rehearsal is much easier with a score to hand, for example, while the conductor who never looks up from the score is not able to communicate with the players. Felix Weingartner took the view that the conductor should at least know the score 'so thoroughly that during the performance the score is merely a support for his memory'.[623] Some 20th-century conductors were famed for their memorized knowledge of the score, such as Guido Cantelli and Lorin Maazel, who knew the rehearsal letters and even the players' individual lines by heart.[624]

Full scores became more widely available from the start of the 19th century, although not that quickly (Mozart's *Marriage of Figaro*, 1819; Bach's *St Mat-*

---

620 The opera tradition was different, reflecting the different demand, and individual institutions made their own manuscript parts from a manuscript full score until the end of the 18th century; performances could also be controlled by publishers making material available for hire rather than for sale; Carse (1948), pp.425-426.
621 Carse (1948), pp.133, 135, 447, 317 and 446.
622 Ferdinand Hiller, 'Ueber das Auswendig-Dirigiren', in *Musikalisches und Persönliches* (Leipzig, 1876).
623 Felix Weingartner, trans Ernest Newman, *On Conducting* (London, 1906), p.40.
624 Pettitt (1985), pp.53 and 96.

thew Passion, 1830); their financial return was uncertain, and Schumann noted that 'orchestral scores are such costly and dangerous goods, that publishers will scarcely accept them as a present'.[625] Finding a source for printed material could also be difficult, as almost all publication took place only in London, Paris, Vienna and Germany, and there were few music shops. Piracy was a concern once copies were in circulation, and Beethoven worried about 'stolen copies' of *Fidelio* in 1814.[626] Sales of unauthorized piano or other arrangements might earn an unscrupulous publisher more than the original composer of a successful work did through royalties.

Errors in scores were a serious hindrance, hence Beethoven's irritation when Breitkopf & Härtel published some of his works without waiting for the composer's proof corrections, while Wagner marvelled that serious errors in the parts for *Figaro* were repeatedly performed without correction. The impact on rehearsal efficiency was acidly noted by Thomas Busby in 1825: 'Out of a dozen rehearsals, *twelve* are attended with delays and inconveniences, owing to mistakes in some of the principal or subordinate parts', making clear that when such mistakes were made, the whole movement would have to start at the beginning.[627] 'Starting again from the beginning' was likely standard rehearsal practice for centuries, but this a rare mention of it as such.

The traditional rehearsal-letter (or number) system developed in the 19th century turned into something more precise for modern music, especially chamber music. Bartók made particular use of this in his works, and his String Quartet No.5 (1934) includes not only rehearsal numbers and bar numbers, but minutes-and-seconds timings for individual sections; the sixth quartet (1939) abandons regular bar-numbering (normal previous practice was either bar numbers at the start of each line, or attached to each bar in multiples of five or ten) for irregularly spaced and large bar numbers at significant points, placed above and in the centre of a bar (ex.5). The system was likely intended to speed location of difficulties in more challenging works, and to allow smaller sections to be repeated – the 'letter' system of the 19th century inefficiently results in a relatively small number of set choices for rehearsal starting points.

---

625 Robert Schumann, trans Fanny Raymond Ritter, *Music and Musicians* (London, 1891), vol. ii, p.40.
626 Alexander Wheelock Thayer, *Life of Beethoven* (New York, 1921), vol.ii, p.284.
627 Busby (1825), vol.ii, p.134.

Ex. 5. Béla Bartók, String Quartet No.6 (London, 1941), score, p.29

THE CONDUCTOR

The 'dual system' – a violinist-leader plus the director at the keyboard – was proving inadequate even at the end of the 18th century, and a 1796 *Jahrbuch der Tonkunst* article noted that the latter sometimes needed to beat time to steady matters – 'it would be a good thing if they studied the piece together and came to some agreement about the *tempo*'.[628] In 1820 Spohr described the English system as 'having two conductors, but neither really functions', a later London critic adding, 'either a conductor is useless, or a leader is useless'.[629] The transition from this joint method to a single baton conductor (described as an 'ancient quarrel' in early 19th century France)[630] nevertheless took half a century to complete, and eventually the demands made by larger ensembles, bigger venues and more difficult repertoire made the process inevitable.[631]

Where there was still no baton conductor, the audible beating of time did not die out: Rousseau had claimed that ensemble at the *Academie Royale* could only be maintained by audible beating, and Berlioz complained at Naples of the opera's violinist-director tapping his bow on the desk to keep to keep the players together, an act also recorded there by visitor William Gardner in 1846: 'I was much annoyed by the leader tapping a tin candlestick all night with his bow, to beat the time, when he had better have been playing'. And not only the bow was used: Rochlitz in Vienna said that he rarely heard a *forte* or *fortissimo* without a good deal of foot-stomping by the leader, and the 'merciless *stamping of feet*' also occurred in London. Even baton conductors were known to 'pound the score' audibly – Bernard Anselm Weber in Berlin was described as 'too noisy', and even wore a deep hole in his conducting stand at Prague.[632]

The orchestral piano (and sometimes still harpsichord) remained in Italy up to the time of Rossini, having already died out in Germany, but it now served rather as a safety-net for the director sitting at it, figuring 'as a sort of non-combatant [as] the conductor's desk, where it may serve at need to bring back an errant vocalist to the sense of musical propriety', in the words of H. Suther-

---

628 Cited in Carse (1948), p.295. At a Sacred Harmonic Society concert in 1840, divided direction resulted in the choir and orchestra being a bar out; *Musical World* (16 April 1840), p.242.
629 E. Speyer, *Wilhelm Speyer, der Liedercomponist, 1790-1878* (Munich, 1925), p.51, cited in Carse (1948), p.320; *Musical World* (25 April 1844), p.141.
630 *The Harmonicon* (June 1825), p.103.
631 See Holman (2020).
632 Carse (1948), pp.310-311, 272, 307, 336, 297 and 337.

land Edwards.[633] Direction 'from the pianoforte' (and occasionally the organ) survived in England to at least the late 1830s, and the pit piano itself until the time of Michael Costa (1808-84) in the 1850s.[634] Interestingly, the violin also served as a tool for some conductors, where having an instrument to hand in a rehearsal meant that the correct execution of a passage could be demonstrated rather than just described: Charles Hanssens of the Brussels Opera (1840) is shown with his violin available and ready on a shelf below the conducting desk (illus.8). François Antoine Habeneck (1781-1849) in 1840 conducted with his bow, but with the violin to hand 'in case of need'.[635] The voice was also a tool; Wagner believed that Mozart, when rehearsing his operas, was able by singing his themes to 'communicate the proper expression to the players'.[636]

What power newly-empowered conductors had over their performers seemed to result from a combination of how well paid and well treated the performers were; and of the leadership skills of the conductor. Nevertheless, it is not always certain that the rehearsal process enabled a director to achieve higher technical standards from individual players; for example, ensemble tuning seems to be referred to by most commentators (including leading composers and conductors) as something innate, rather than a standard that could be achieved through painstaking rehearsal. In 1842 Berlioz offered rare praise regarding intonation of the Kärtnerthor Orchestra in Vienna – 'selected, drilled, and led by Nicolai' – that had an 'exquisite sonorousness, owing doubtless to the accurate way in which the instruments play together, as much as to the perfect manner in which they play in tune'.[637] Carl Maria von Weber developed a high reputation in Prague when conducting his *Silvania* there in 1810, as reported by Carl Friedrich Moritz Paul von Bruhl (*Intendant* at Berlin): 'in a short time he raised the rather mediocre orchestra at Prague to a remarkable state of efficiency ... whereas most conductors would have required six or seven rehearsals to prepare the difficult music, Weber did it in three rehearsals'.[638] A more specific description survives from his time at Dresden: 'He had eyes and ears for everything; a wrong note from the remotest corner of the orchestra brought the offending player a sharp glance; tirelessly would he stop the playing in order to repeat a passage; now he was in the orchestra; now on stage putting a singer

---

633 H. Sutherland Edwards, *Life of Rossini* (London, 1869), p.158.
634 Carse (1948), pp.318, 327 and 332.
635 *Musical World* (26 March 1840), p.195. For Habaneck, see Schonberg (1977), pp.99-106.
636 Richard Wagner, trans Edward Dannreuther, *On Conducting* (London, 1897).
637 Hector Berlioz, trans Rachel Scott Russell Holes Holmes, *Memoirs of Hector Berlioz* (London, 1884), vol.ii, p.185.
638 Julius Kapp, *Geschichte der Staatsoper Berlin* (Berlin, 1937), p.29

Illus. 8. Charles Hanssens conducting at the Brussels Opera (1840).

or supernumerary right, giving directions to the scene-shifters, simultaneously doing the work of stage-manager and conductor, and giving his orders with such precision that there could be no delay in carrying them out'.[639] A similarly glowing report of Gaspare Spontini (1774-1851) at the Berlin Opera made by one of the professional violinists there dates from the same time, including a reference to what seems like an improbably large number of rehearsals: 'Berlin possessed a jewel such as no other place in the world could produce. It is impossible to describe how perfectly, elegantly and gloriously these operas were put on stage. Spontini's *piano*, played by the whole mass, sounded like the *pianissimo* of a string quartet, and his *forte* surpassed the loudest thunder. Between the extremes were his inimitable *crescendo* and *decrescendo*. He bestowed the greatest care on the light and shade. By means of numerous rehearsals, sometimes as many as eighty, everyone who took part in them became completely familiar with the operas. As a result of constant rehearsal the ensemble was impeccable'.[640]

Personality was often a major factor in the successful management of ensembles, and descriptions such as those of George Smart (1776-1867), a leading conductor in London and of provincial festivals, outline what some thought as the proper approach: 'He seemed able, as if by intuition, to detect in an instant if anything were wrong among the several members of his orchestra, and at set it right by a pleasantry which put everyone in good humour. He never wearied his forces by constant fault-finding'. This is the conductor as 'gentleman', rather than tyrant, perhaps an English ideal.[641] Arthur Nikisch (1855-1922) knew the names of his players by heart, so could refer to them directly rather than impersonally as 'first horn' or 'second oboe', while Adrian Boult (1889-1983) described his own rehearsal style as 'leisurely', avoiding making the musicians feel they were under pressure.[642]

Something of the process of improvement that could be made by an incoming conductor is seen in the career of the very influential Michael Costa in London; arriving from Italy to work as a singer, he then became a keyboard player (called *Maestro al Cembalo* at the King's Theatre, a rather old-fashioned designation for 1830) and afterwards conductor there. Taking over at the

---

639 Max von Weber, *C. M. von Weber, ein Lebensbild* (Leipzig, 1864), vol.ii, p.59.
640 Hauptmann (1875), p.90, from Carse (1948), p.345. The Berlin orchestra, being used to Spontini's firm discipline, were somewhat unruly to his successor Mendelssohn; Carse (1948), p.351 and Schonberg (1977), p.121.
641 [John Edmund Cox], *Musical Recollections* (London, 1872), vol.i, p.204.
642 Norman Lebrecht, *The Maestro Myth* (New York, 2/2001), pp.33 and 41. See also Schonberg (1977), pp.204-215.

London Philharmonic Society in 1846 – and on condition that he was given 'entire control' over the orchestra – he wielded stick rather than carrot. When previously at Covent Garden he had abolished the (ineffectual) fining system for absenteeism, announcing quietly but firmly to the orchestra that instead any unauthorized rehearsal absences would lead to forfeiting the engagement. According to John Ella, 'the complete band attended at all future rehearsals ... The six or eight rehearsals were gradually reduced to two or three, and finally the choir and band were so thoroughly well drilled, that the revival of any opera never required more than *one* patient rehearsal'.[643]

It was thought to be part of the skill of an expert rehearser in the early part of the 19th century to be able to set a work going, then leave it for the musicians to proceed safely on their own: Weber at Dresden needed only to beat through the first four bars of his *Die Freischütz* allegro – 'Musicians may well be proud when they see their chief fold his arms on such occasions', thought Berlioz.[644] Schumann noted the same thing of Mendelssohn in Leipzig: 'often enough, in the course of the performance, he would lay down the baton on the desk and leave it there for some time, while the orchestra played on without any further guidance'.[645] This was only possible where effective and efficient rehearsing was the norm. Remarkably, Habaneck was known to cease conducting in order to take snuff, leading to disaster during an 1837 performance of Berlioz's *Requiem*.[646]

Not everyone responded well to the rising 'tyranny of the baton', as noted by one of Spohr's violinists at Kassel: 'the cursed little white stick always did annoy me, and when I see it domineering over the whole orchestra, music departs from me; it is as if the whole opera exists merely for the sake of beating time to it'.[647] Audiences could also find it distracting, as is recorded in a press report of conductor Hieronymus Payer beating time with a baton in Amsterdam in 1826: 'Nothing could be more unseemly, or better calculated to destroy the quiet and

---

643 Carse (1948), pp.382-387, Ella (1878), pp.246-248. See also Marten Noorduin, 'The Rehearsal Practices of the London Philharmonic in the Early to Mid-Nineteenth Century', in Claire Holden, Eric F. Clarke and Cayenna Ponchione-Bailey (eds), *Practice in Context: Historically Informed Practices in Nineteenth-Century Instrumental Music* (Oxford, 2025), pp.66-83.

644 Berlioz (1884), vol.ii, p.71.

645 Alfred Dörffel, *Geschichte der Gewandhaus Concerte zu Leipzig* (Leipzig, 1884), p.85, cited in Carse (1948), p.302. See also David Milsom, 'Mendelssohn and the Orchestra', in Siegwart Reichwald (ed), *Mendelssohn in Performance* (Bloomington, 2008), pp.85–100.

646 Carse (1948), p.371.

647 Moritz Hauptmann, *Briefe von Moritz Hauptmann an Franz Hauser* (Leipzig, 1871), vol.i, p.196, cited in Carse (1948), p.304. For Mendelsohn as conductor, see pp.349-351.

pleasurable feelings of an audience'.[648] Even Schumann had reservations about musical dictatorship in concert music, where 'the orchestra should stand like a republic in a symphony, refusing to acknowledge a superior'.[649]

Looking back on a century's practice in 1895, Joseph Bennett described 'well remembering the time when orchestras played great works without any conductor at all, quite to the satisfaction of the public. But, having determined the tempo of an overture or symphonic movement, he kept to it, unless the composer had otherwise directed, marching along with the regular step of a regiment on parade. That also was an easy and comfortable process. For the rest, he strove to keep his men in hand, to observe the *p*'s and *f*'s, as regards which, however, vague and various conceptions existed, and generally to follow the letter of the composition with reasonable exactness. This method was favoured by much of the music played – music which had, as a rule, broad and obvious significance was clear and simple in construction and not guilty of meaning one thing when it appeared to say another. As for 'readings,' in the present sense of that word, the primitive conductor did not dream of them. There was the text, with the composer's indications for its rendering; why should he travel out of, or attempt to fill in, the record? Not that the conductor put this question to himself; the idea simply never occurred to him'. By the turn of the century, however, 'Eminent conductors are being played off one against another in the field of enterprising interpretations. This became inevitable as soon as the *chef d'orchestre* lifted himself, or was forced up by others, from the position of a student-translator, hidden as much as possible behind the work interpreted, into the position, almost, of a creative artist'.[650] That word 'almost' was to give way to something much more decisive in the age that was to come.

THE COMPOSER AS CONDUCTOR

The success of a composer as conductor depended on having a high level of skill in both, as for Mendelssohn. Where this was lacking, it was often more a result of personality issues: for example, Robert Schumann is described by Adam Carse in these terms: 'Excepting his musical gift, which was ample, Schumann appears to have lacked all the necessary qualities of a good conductor'. An eye-witness account of a rehearsal of Schumann's *Faust* in Dresden in 1849 by Ludwig

---

648 *Harmonicon*, London (February 1826), p.40.
649 Schumann (1891), vol.i, p.37.
650 Joseph Bennett, 'The Conductor in Music', *The Musical Times and Singing Class Circular*, xxxvi/629 (1 July 1895), pp.437-440 at 437-439.

Meinardus referred to the composer's 'peculiar' manner and deep absorption in the score, where 'Inattention on the part of the players often brought about confusion or even chaos, and constant but inevitable repetition served only to increase the despair of all who were present'. Schumann remained 'polite and friendly' even as the orchestra were in a state of 'amazement'.[651]

The desire of a composer to conduct often arose out of necessity, as where a flawed performance of *Harold in Italy* under Narcisse Girard led Berlioz to take up the baton again seriously (an earlier 'defeat' at the *Théâtre Italien* had led him to give up): 'I resolved in future to conduct myself, and not allow anyone else to communicate my ideas to the performers'.[652] Fortunately he met with great success, being variously described as 'one of the greatest and most intelligent of conductors' who took 'endless trouble to get everything right', and (by Charles Hallé in 1837) 'the most perfect conductor that I ever set eyes upon'.[653]

One further use of first performances and rehearsals was for composers to have sufficient opportunity to hear and revise a work before it was presented in a fixed form through publication. For example, Brahms's Symphony No.4 was given from manuscript parts from around November 1885 to May 1886 before being publihsed in October 1886: 'Brahms apparently used these performances as "Proben," both tests and rehearsals, to try out the piece and make revisions as needed prior to the permanent version'.[654]

WAGNER AS CONDUCTOR

Richard Wagner's followers and critics left a number of anecdotal or descriptive reports about his approach to conducting, which are best read in conjunction with his influential 1869 book on the subject – where (like Mozart) he turns out not to be a very generous commentator on his contemporaries, and was particularly hostile to Mendelssohn.[655] Joseph Bennett summarized it thus: 'In his unspeakably venomous and vituperative, yet always clever and often rea-

---

651 Hermann Erler, *Robert Schumanns Leben* (Berlin, 1887), vol.ii, p.96, cited in Carse (1948), p.363.
652 Berlioz (1884), vol.i, p.282.
653 Carse (1948), p.375.
654 Marcia J. Citron, 'Gender, Professionalism and the Musical Canon', *The Journal of Musicology*, viii/1 (Winter 1990), pp.102-117 at 107n.
655 Carse (1948), pp.352-361; Wagner (1897). See also Walton (2021) and Schonberg (1977), pp.128-143.

sonable essay on "Conducting," the Bayreuth musician showed to his contemporaries and successors a way safe enough for himself, perhaps, but extremely dangerous for most of them'.[656]

Wagner's conception was one of flexibility and metrical freedom; Berlioz called it 'free style', and it was described by Wagner's friend Ferdinand Praeger: 'Wagner did not beat in the old-fashioned automato-metronomic manner. He leaves off beating at times – then resumes again – to lead the orchestra up to a climax, or to let them soften down to a *pianissimo*, as if a thousand invisible threads tied them to his baton'.[657] Other commentators mention his 'iron energy', 'spirit and fire' and 'revolutionary spirit'. Anton Seidl, a true Wagner enthusiast ('none could resist the power of this wonderful man'), nevertheless left a rehearsal account which shows that orchestras needing winning over to this new style of working: 'At first the rehearsals went badly, because the master was impatient and expected everything to be perfect at once; the strange and significant movements of his long baton bewildered the players, and put them out until they began to understand that it was not the time-beat that ruled here, but the phrase, or the melody or the expression. But his look soon chained them, the magnetic fluid engulfed them, and the master had them all in the hollow of his hand'.[658] This marks a separation of the 'ensemble' conductor from the new 'interpretative' conductor, a dichotomy that remains to this day. Wagner's rehearsal technique was also described by Praeger as 'unrelenting', with many sectional rehearsals, and he also marked up the orchestral parts himself.[659]

Where Wagner did not speak the local language, or have time to work on interpretative detail, things were less successful, as with his disastrous 1855 season with the London Philharmonic Society. Most of the London critics were very hostile indeed (Wagner was 'not a musician at all', 'ultra-sentimental', 'a sorry figure'), which Adam Carse puts down to his differences from their beloved Mendelssohn, whose reputation in Britain long survived him.[660]

---

656 Bennett (1895), p.439.
657 Ferdinand Praeger, *Wagner as I knew him* (London, 1892), p.235.
658 Cited in Carse (1948), p.354.
659 Praeger (1892), p.141.
660 *The Musical World* (17 March 1855), p.171 and (31 March 1855), p.203.

CHAMBER MUSIC

Small-ensemble rehearsal was inevitably a more private matter than that for an orchestra, and accordingly the documentary record is much more limited. However, as with the symphonic repertoire, more challenging repertoire needed much greater preparation, and records from the early 19th century show that 'There is the best authority for stating that [the quartet] did not think six or eight rehearsals, previous to the production of a work in public, too much trouble, or time and application thrown away, or even unnecessarily bestowed. The success of their undertakings has been commensurate with the pains which they underwent to secure it'.[661] George Duborg is here writing about Beethoven's late quartets in the 1830s; in 1845 *The Times* noted seven or eight rehearsals as normal in such circumstances.[662]

CATHEDRAL MUSIC

Church music retained more of its historical practices than did other genres, simply because its traditions were dictated by relatively stable liturgies, venues and employment; for example, conducting Anglican cathedral choirs did not become universal until well after the Second World War, the previous system of having the organist at their instrument accompanying the choir using discreet 'beaters' across the sides having proved sufficient until church music became too difficult for this to be viable,[663] with new repertoire by Howells, Leighton and others. Catholic traditions persisted in the same way in many places, and a choir singing plainchant in the late 19th century would have looked (although it might have sounded) little different from such an ensemble three hundred years earlier. An 1876 rehearsal illustration by Gustave Doré (illus.9) illustrates the point, with choristers working from not one but two four-sided lecterns in the quire of Burgos Cathedral, under the direction of a chapelmaster.[664] As they are seated, this must be a rehearsal; the men (one is visible) seem to be placed on the other side of the lecterns. An interesting feature here is that the choirbooks (possibly polyphonic, more probably chant) are duplicated for the choristers, and possibly also for the men; the latest copying date for a surviving Toledo manuscript chant book of this kind is 1892.[665]

---

661 George Duborg, *The Violin: Some Account of that Leading Instrument and its most Eminent Professors* (London, 4/1852), p.301, cited in Bashford (1996), vol.i, p.120.

662 Bashford (1996), i, p.182.

663 For the history of this, see Holman (2020), pp.52-57.

664 Jean Charles Davillier, *L'Espagne* (Paris, 1874).

665 Michael Noone and Graeme Skinner, 'Toledo Cathedral's Collection of Manuscript Plainsong Choirbooks: A Preliminary Report and Checklist', *Notes*, Second Series, lxiii/2 (December 2006), pp.289-328 at 293, 313 and 327.

Illus. 9. Gustave Doré, engraving of 'Le choeur de la Cathédrale de Burgos', from Jean Charles Davillier, *L'Espagne* (Paris, 1874)

MILITARY MUSIC

One very under-studied environment is that of the military musician (the 'musical warrior'), and surviving British archives from the Napoleonic Wars provide evidence that 'Officers' concern for musical education went hand in hand with their insistence on continual practice, an ambition made possible by the full-time nature of service in the professional forces. Standing orders stipulated that musical warriors attend rehearsals regularly and, in most cases, daily, with additional practices scheduled for beginners. Ample evidence suggests that these assiduous rehearsal schedules were widely observed'.[666] Contemporary diaries and letters provide complaints from onlookers as to the duration and volume of these practices (one Scottish farmer claimed sixteen drummers practicing caused the death of his cow),[667] and beginning drummers might be expected to spend four to six hours daily at their instruments. The value of this effort was noted, and extended practice time 'was critical to the military's dissemination of musical skills, as contemporaries fully understood. Recalling his past membership in a sacred music society, a contributor to *The Atlas* [1829] contrasted the easy-going ineptitude of the civilian amateurs with the simultaneous progress made by a militia band rehearsing in a neighbour's garden. Although the dozen raw performers initially made the "most insufferable brattling and belching with their horns and trombones", they became a polished ensemble through "regular practice" under a capable instructor'.[668]

---

666 Eamonn O'Keeffe, *Musical Warriors: British Military Music and Musicians during the French Revolutionary and Napoleonic Wars*, DPhil thesis (University of Oxford, 2022), p.191. See also Trevor Herbert and Helen Barlow, *Music and the British Military in the Long Nineteenth Century* (New York, 2013).

667 Eamonn O'Keeffe, 'Military music and society during the French wars, 1793–1815', *Historical Research*, xcvii (2024), pp.108–128 at 124.

668 O'Keeffe (2022), pp.192-193.

CHAPTER 8
REHEARSAL IN THE 20TH CENTURY

The institutional and musical practices related to rehearsal and established by the end of the 19th century continued into the 20th largely unchanged, the critical difference being in the arrival of commercial sound recording and radio in the 1920s. Composers, performers and listeners had the opportunity to become acquainted with a much wider repertoire, and to get to know such music well through frequent repetition. In particular, performers now had feedback as to what they – and their contemporaries further afield – actually sounded like, and this inevitably introduced more direct forms of technical competition, with a consequent rise in standards, the rehearsal process feeding into this.[669]

THE 'STAR' CONDUCTOR

The arrival of the professional baton conductor meant that such musicians had to justify their existence (and ever-increasing salaries) in terms not only of their skills as an orchestral trainer, but as a musical *interpreter*. Joseph Bennett, writing in 1895, saw the latter component beginning to predominate: 'The tendency to extremes inevitably operates, and we now find that the medium who, conveying to us a composer's ideas, must needs give also a part of himself, is giving us all himself and only a part of the composer. To that, broadly speaking, have

---

669 See Philip (2004).

we come, and for it the evolution of the conductor is mainly accountable'.[670] Increasing ease of travel, followed by the invention of broadcasting and recording, led to the best-known exponents working all over the world, sometimes simultaneously running ensembles in different countries, or even on different continents. The creation of hierarchies of Principal Conductor, Assistant Conductor, Guest Conductor and so on made such peripatetic careers ever more possible, sometimes at the expense of individual orchestras' 'house' style.

Success brought with it many new constrictions: the more expensive an individual concert or opera was, the more concerned or risk-averse an institution's management could become. As well as audiences voting with their feet, repertoire choices often became constrained by the introduction of repertoire committees (for orchestras, opera houses and recording companies alike), seen by some as a necessary bulwark against conductors with unrealistic financial expectations for their musical choices.[671] Subsidies (private or state) enabled some support for new commissions or lesser-known works, while successful tours could be a rehearsal-efficient way of repeating programmes. Nevertheless, once audiences normalized the technical standards possible on LP and CD, pressure on ensembles to produce such levels of precision live became a particular challenge. The end of the CD boom after about 2000 meant that recordings were less able to subsidize live performance, although major orchestras were able to shift their subsidy income into areas such as recording film scores.[672]

While the extraordinary levels of power that some star conductors were accorded – or demanded – became legendary, other famous conductors still retained a modicum of humility: Hans Richter (1843-1916) took personal responsibility for the breakdown in a Tchaikovsky work, announcing to a Leeds audience that they should not 'blame the orchestra for that mistake. It was my mistake and mine only'. But when Toscanini apologized after a concert, it was directly to the musicians, afterwards and in private.[673]

---

670 Bennett (1895), pp.437-440 at 437. He adds: 'The need of an interpreter between composers and the public is sometimes made an occasion of remarks unfavourable to music as compared with the sister arts. We are told, and the assertion, of course, cannot be questioned, that poetry, painting, sculpture, and architecture make a direct appeal to observers, with no possibility of misrepresentation and no chance of failure save in so far as the public are incapable of appreciating what is addressed to them' (p.438).

671 Pettitt (1985), p.113.

672 Felix Richter, 'The Rise and Fall of the Compact Disc' (17 August 2022), https://www.statista.com/chart/12950/cd-sales-in-the-us.

673 Lebrecht (2001), pp.38 and 78.

A further consequence of high-profile conductor roles was the devising of specific conductor training courses (usually at conservatoires), and the related writing and publication of tutors for these. The conductor could also be co-opted into corporate and business education, with musicians such as Raphael von Hoensbroech giving workshops on conducting as 'Leadership', seeking analogies between the consensual dictatorship of the conductor and the top-down control of a company Chief Executive Officer.[674] A major change came in the rise of women conductors – following on from the rise of women orchestral musicians, and accelerating in the 21st century – but not one with any apparent effect on rehearsal techniques as such.

The measure of a conductor's success in the post-war era might be measured in the number of recordings made, or prizes and honours awarded; for Karajan, this metric could also be counted in riches, as he died in 1989 worth about $163 million.[675]

CONDUCTORLESS ORCHESTRAS

As was seen in the 19th century, the rise of the all-powerful conductor was resented by some musicians, and alternatives models were experimented with, by analogy with large chamber ensembles, a number of which (such as the Orpheus Chamber Orchestra) still exist. The issues there are exactly as for the early Romantic period, with a practical limit on the number of musicians that could be directed in performance by a leader who was seated rather than standing, and the necessity for someone to efficiently control the progress of a rehearsal, This historical model also suited the newly-founded early music orchestras using period instruments, such as the Academy of Ancient Music, the English Concert and the Orchestra of the Age of Enlightenment, which variously used joint direction, leader direction, or direction from the keyboard.[676]

One other form of conductorless orchestra owed its existence to Marxist theory, in particular the notion of equality of status among the performers (the musical 'proletariat'), such as the Russian First Symphonic Orchestra, founded

---

674 See Yaakov Atik, 'The conductor and the orchestra: Interactive aspects of the leadership process', *Leadership & Organization Development Journal*, xv/1 (1994), pp.22–28.
675 Lebrecht (2001), p.120. For comparative concert fees and conductors' salaries since the 1880s, see pp.320–321.
676 See Lebrecht (2001), ch.14, Helen Wallace, *Spirit of the orchestra* (London, 2006) and Richard Bratby, *Refiner's Fire: The Academy of Ancient Music and the Historical Performance Revolution* (London, 2023).

in 1922 but defunct six years later, partly due to the intrinsic rehearsal inefficiency of leaderlessness.[677]

PREPARATION OF MATERIALS

The level of uniformity required in the post-war era led to an increasing workload for orchestral librarians and section principals alike in the pencil marking-up of parts before rehearsals, an effort that would be partly alleviated by the arrival of cheap photocopying. All such preparation work could save significant rehearsal time. Some conductors were more concerned about issues such as string bowings - or at least, their own personal opinions as to any bowing already marked in the parts - than were others. Karajan and Furtwängler fell into the latter category, whereas Guido Cantelli often brought pre-marked parts borrowed from the NBC Symphony Orchestra to his Philharmonia rehearsals.[678] Raymond Leppard (1927-2019) described his process thus: 'The best solution is to possess your own set of parts for everything. You can mark them up to a point, and then ideally you should have the Leader alone for an hour to do the bowings. Alas, this is not always possible'.[679]

REHEARSAL AND RECORDING

The growth in recording activity from the 1950s meant that some leading orchestras found themselves under serious pressure in terms of activity: the Philharmonia in London had about 30 concerts booked for the 1956-57 season, but no fewer than 309 recording sessions, often three a day.[680] Some ensembles were able to cross-subsidize concert preparation by combining rehearsal work for recordings: Walter Legge at the Philharmonia disliked the principle of relying on the musicians' sightreading ability to schedule only one rehearsal per concert, so chose where possible to combine concert and recording activity, from the 1940s.[681] Concerts might therefore become part of the recording preparation process, as still happens today.

---

677 Slonimsky (2002), pp.20-21.
678 Pettitt (1985), p.48.
679 Raymond Leppard, 'Music and the conductor', *Journal of the Royal Society of Arts*, cxxi/5207 (October 1973), pp.707-716 at 715.
680 Pettitt (1985), p.87.
681 Pettitt (1985), p.33.

A further development was the studio 'rehearse-record' process, where individual passages could be 'played, and assessed as it is being rehearsed, and then immediately "performed" - in other words recorded and preserved', as composer Arthur Butterworth described it, adding, 'Of course, there must always be the consideration that repeated concert performances of a work ensure a familiarity to the performers that a "rehearse-record" situation cannot quite bring about. However, we live in a world not just of artistic idealism but of practical economics, and we must take account of this'.[682] Raymond Leppard agreed with this last point: 'I don't think there is a public concert in the world now that pays for itself. Because of the expense, great pressure is put on conductors and orchestras to prepare concerts in the shortest possible time'.[683]

However, there were still occasions when sufficient time was allowed for concert rehearsal, which was so important for new works: Butterworth described the 'thorough and adequate preparation' for the Cheltenham Festivals of the 1950s, where Sir John Barbirolli and the Hallé Orchestra 'spent a week each July in presenting new works. This was preceded by a whole week of rehearsals in Manchester before the orchestra travelled to Cheltenham. It was a great privilege for me to have my own First Symphony given its first performance there in 1957. I find it hardly credible now to reflect on the fact that the Symphony had no less than a total of nineteen hours of rehearsal! This included the first hour of reading through it, which I conducted myself in the Royal Hall, Harrogate, while Barbirolli listened; followed by sectional rehearsals in Manchester the following week and a final rehearsal at Cheltenham on the morning of the performance. The enormous prestige and finesse of those Hallé performances at Cheltenham in the halcyon days of the 1950s were due to the meticulous, detailed rehearsals which Barbirolli demanded, and it paid off handsomely. I have conducted this First Symphony a few times since, but the most rehearsal it has been allowed has been around three hours in total, sharing time with having to rehearse other - more routine and familiar - things in the programme'.[684]

A further cost-saving but potentially high-risk process devised in the CD era was the live recording – itself partly a reaction against 'over-perfect' studio recordings – which might take only one rather than the usual three days of studio time. These were marketed as having a special level of 'live' spontaneity, but were very pressured for the musicians to make, as the level of tuning, ensemble

---

[682] Arthur Butterworth, 'Rehearsing and Recording' (2009), http://www.musicweb-international.com/classrev/2009/Apr09/Rehearsing_Butterworth.htm.
[683] Leppard (1973), p.713.
[684] Butterworth (2009).

and so on expected by listeners was little different from that of a multi-take studio recording. Sometimes the previous rehearsal was recorded, so that sections were available to patch-in should there be any mishaps in the actual performance – in these cases, the rehearsal could (as in the 18th century) function as a kind of 'pre-performance'.

One outcome of increased time in the recording studio was the documentation of the rehearsal process, either intentionally or by accident.[685] From the 1960s onwards an additional resource for the study of rehearsal practice comes in the form of visual recordings. Some of these can be found in television and film documentaries as part of the exploration of particular works and conductors, and there are also examples to be found on YouTube. However, there are relatively few substantial rehearsal films,[686] although examples from Karajan and Boulez are discussed below.[687]

GUSTAV MAHLER

Four key figures for whom there is good documentation are discussed individually below, covering between them the period from the very end of the 19th century to the end of the 20th, in Germany, Britain, France and the US.

The first of these is Gustav Mahler (1860-1911), a controversial figure as a conductor, and one who can be seen as having emerged from the Wagnerian tradition - as he also did as a composer. Evidently a self-confident prodigy, early in his career he was interviewed at Kassel by the opera director and asked whether he could conduct *Martha* without a rehearsal in order to fill an urgent vacancy that evening. Mahler claimed to know the work and, having 'learned the whole score by heart' that afternoon 'conducted so brilliantly at night that he was

---

685 Examples include *Sir Thomas Beecham in Rehearsal*, HMV Haydn Box SLS 846, disc 7 and Adrian Boult rehearsing Vaughan Williams, *The Pilgrim's Progress*, EMI LP SLS 959; both can be found on YouTube.

686 Those that do exist are sometimes rather uninformative: for example, Jeremy Siepmann notes of the 1969 Schubert 'Trout' documentary featuring Barenboim, Perlman, Zuckerman, du Pré and Mehta (Teldec VHS 2292-46239-3) that the rehearsal discussions are 'scarcely revelatory'; Michael Scott Rohan (ed), *The Classical Video Guide* (London, 1994), pp.309-310. There are examples of Rattle, Dudamel and others on YouTube, while the 'Charles Barber Conductors on Film' collection at Stanford University includes more than 300 conductors from 1879-2003; see https://searchworks.stanford.edu/view/10401369.

687 For a specifically pedagogical recording, see *Conducting lessons of Professor Musin* (St Petersburg, 2006).

engaged on the spot'.[688] Of his time at Olmütz in 1883, Jacques Manheit noted 'he hardly knew a single opera, learning them all as he went along'.[689]

Alfred Sendrey vividly described Mahler as treating his musicians 'as a liontamer his animals'. Sometimes the impossible could be achieved, as with the New York Philharmonic – with whom he had a troubled relationship – at the very end of his life: 'He never could get enough volume out of us to play the first movement of Beethoven's Fifth', noted bassoonist Benjamin Kohon, 'He always wanted more and more, like a cataclysm, a volcanic eruption. He wanted something we really couldn't give him. Well, one day he finally got what he wanted. And he was really delighted'.[690] Once in 1906 Mahler was 'plaguing the orchestra so unmercifully over the three opening notes of Beethoven's Fifth Symphony that some jumped up to go and some sat in stubborn fury, resolved not to play another note. Mahler seeing this shouted out: "Gentlemen, keep your fury for the performance, then *at last* we shall have the opening played as it should be"'. His strictness with Mengelberg's 'undisciplined' orchestra in Rome in 1910 caused them to walk out, while an argument with the troubled pianist Josef Weiss (1864-1945) caused a 1910 rehearsal to be abandoned, so the actual performance of the Schumann concerto was given unrehearsed by an inadequate substitute, so badly that 'Mahler from anger and shame could scarcely go on conducting'.[691]

Composer Wilhelm Kienzl wrote, 'the orchestral players feared him because in artistic matters he made no concessions whatever and, in his unwearying diligence at rehearsal, was as reckless with his musicians as he was with himself. He would not suffer sloppiness, nor let the slightest fault pass'. Writer Stefan Zweig vividly described him in rehearsal: 'angry, twitching, screaming, irritated, suffering at all the inadequacies as if in physical pain' (see illus.10 for a drawing by Arpad Schmidhammer). The musicians tolerated this (where they did) because his purpose was the music, not his ego. Czech soprano Ernestine Schumann-Heink, who was not sympathetic to Mahler, wrote that always 'sought endlessly for perfection ... he forgot that when the orchestra was before him it was only eighty or a hundred men who were not geniuses like himself, but simply good workers. They often irritated him so terribly that he couldn't bear it; then he became a musical tyrant'. Another soprano, Selma Kurz, took an alto-

---

688 Mahler (1946), p.90.
689 Norman Lebrecht, *Mahler Remembered* (London, 1987), p.31. See also Schonberg (1977), pp.223-235.
690 Lebrecht (1987), pp.124 and 294.
691 Mahler (1946), pp.81, 143 and 139.

gether more positive view: 'Working with Mahler in rehearsal was marvellous. By means of will-power and enthusiasm, he forced everyone to give of their best and their last gasp, and he too was totally exhausted and wrung dry after every rehearsal'. Singer Marie Gutheil-Schoder reported on Mahler's preparation approach in Vienna, where he 'never came to rehearsal with a finished, worked-out directorial concept'. Every scene was rehearsed 'as often as required. For that Mahler always had time. He would reorganize a scene as many as twenty times, making changes even at the final orchestral rehearsal ... that is what made his rehearsals so interesting and every performance a step upwards'. This 'workshop' approach to rehearsal was also described by Klaus Pringsheim with regard to the composer's own music: 'Often it was a testing rather than simply a rehearsing in the conventional sense. Until the last rehearsal before a premiere performance he used to change, correct, try over and over again'; subtle and unmarked changes were made in the interests of tone colour and balance, such as dropping out individual desks of strings. When premiering his Symphony No.7 he made alterations to the proofs even at the final rehearsal.[692]

Rehearsal issues appear quite frequently in the documentation of Mahler's conducting career. For example, in Munich in 1888 a concert of Beethoven and Berlioz included only the Andante from Mahler's Symphony No.2, as there was not enough rehearsal time to prepare more;[693] while on a later occasion he was prepared to ride roughshod over the timetable in order to get everything covered: when Rachmaninov was due to rehearse his third piano concerto with Mahler in Carnegie Hall in 1910, the booked rehearsal slot was 10.00-12.30 so the pianist arrived at 11.00, but he did not get to start until midday. Mahler then over-ran until 1.30 and no-one was allowed to leave until he was done.[694] In a 1908 letter Mahler refers to a proposed performance of Mozart's *Marriage of Figaro* on 19 December where the entire period of 30 November to 17 December would be piano rehearsals, 'with which a whole cast is extremely difficult and tedious', and not leave enough time for 'the producer's rehearsals and the orchestra rehearsals';[695] in a letter two years earlier he reported that the Amsterdam Royal Concertgebouw Orchestra were 'all brilliantly rehearsed in advance. Result magnificent' - the work in question may have been his Symphony No.5,[696] and it is

---

692 Lebrecht (1987), pp. 60, 305, 187, 114, 115-116, 191 and 267; Mahler (1946), p.120.
693 Lebrecht (1987), p.187.
694 Dolly Rutherford (trans), *Rachmaninov's recollections, told to Oskar von Reisemann* (London, 1934), pp.158-160.
695 Mahler (1946), p.217.
696 See https://mahlerfoundation.org/mahler/locations/netherlands/amsterdam/gustav-mahler-himself-in-amsterdam.

Illus. 10. Arpad Schmidhammer (1857-1921), 'Gustav Mahler conducting', published in the magazine *Jugend* (c.1900).

uncertain whether the work had been rehearsed by someone else in preparation for his arrival, or whether he was referring to private practice by members of the orchestra. In addition, it is clear that the 18th-century practice of individuals attending rehearsals was now very dependent on receiving the appropriate permission: in 1909, jeweller Louis Comfort Tiffany (1848-1933) had asked to attend Mahler's rehearsals 'in concealment owing to his shyness'. That December in Europe Mahler enthusiast Arnold Schoenberg had asked permission of the Concert Club to attend the final rehearsal of Mahler's seventh symphony; he 'received no reply, although there were critics present', raising the question of who controlled access – Schoenberg had already been known to the composer for about five years (Mahler wrote of him, 'Schönberg, who for all his wrong-headedness is a very original fellow … the world will talk of him before long').[697]

There are several other first-hand descriptions of Mahler's actual rehearsal and conducting technique: conductor Willibald Kähler hearing the third

---

697 Mahler (1946), pp. 194, 135, 223 and 66.

symphony in 1904 reported that 'Mahler's stick technique in the rehearsals had been somewhat violent and often excessively vivacious, in the performance the great moderation of his gestures was surprising'; he also noted that Mahler did not use his left hand in conducting.[698] London music critic Hermann Klein described Mahler working on *Tristan* in London in 1892; despite his 'very little English', he rehearsed the orchestra first in sections, and 'they soon understood him without difficulty'.[699] He took trouble with individual musicians, as when in 1904 he persuaded an oboist to play a passage in his third symphony bell-upwards, or coached a particular brass player in Act 3 of Wagner's *Die Walküre*.[700]

THOMAS BEECHAM

Sir Thomas Beecham (1879-1961) was a very different character from the neurotic perfectionist that was Mahler. Described by critic Neville Cardus as 'Falstaff, Puck and Malvolio all mixed up', his own descriptions of his conducting practice show some of the self-deprecating humour of an Edwardian gentleman, making interpretation of his actual thoughts difficult. Fortunately, as well as an audio recording of Beecham in rehearsal, numerous anecdotes survive from colleagues, composers and performers to get a sense of his philosophy of rehearsal. Beecham had an interesting and idiosyncratic attitude to concert preparation, holding that excessive rehearsal spoiled spontaneity. At his 80th birthday lunch he summed up his conducting philosophy: 'I just get the best players and let them play … at rehearsal they play the piece through; any mistakes they know about as well as I do, so we play it through again; then they know it. And *I* know what they are going to do … *They don't know what I am going to do* … so that at the performance everyone is on his toes, and we get a fine performance'. Another time he put it even more strongly: 'After a very long experience I have discovered that the only way to have a really living and vital performance is not to rehearse it. Everyone will be listening hard to the music and that makes a great tension'.[701] This attitude was by no means new: Nikisch likewise believed

---

698 Lebrecht (1987), p.166.
699 Hermann Klein, *Thirty Years of Musical Life in London (1870-1900)* (London, 1903), p.365 and Hermann Klein, *The Golden Age of Opera* (London, 1933), pp.163-164.
700 Lebrecht (1987), pp.166 and 262.
701 Harold Atkins and Archie Newman, *Beecham Stories* (London, 1979), pp.86 and 19. This volume collects anecdotes from the standard Beecham literature, including Neville Cardus, *Sir Thomas Beecham* (London, 1961), Humphrey Proctor-Gregg, *Beecham Remembered* (London, 1976) and Charles Reid, *Thomas Beecham* (London, 1961). See also Schonberg (1977), pp.289-299.

that the purpose of preparation was to enable spontaneity, saying 'My interpretation changes almost with every performance according to the powers of feeling aroused within me'.[702] Yet another approach was that of Constantin Silvestri, who deliberately used more extreme changes of tempo in rehearsal than in the performance, which 'gave him exactly the natural flexibility he wanted'.[703] An extreme example comes from Leonard Bernstein conducting his second symphony 'at about half the speed we had rehearsed it' on 22 November 1998, according to pianist Krystian Zimerman – the composer felt depressed, having noted that day was the 25th anniversary of Kennedy's assassination.[704]

Beecham also believed in the orchestra taking responsibility: rehearsing Sibelius's *Lemminkainen*, he advised the orchestra, 'you may find it a matter of some difficulty to keep your places. I think you might do well to imagine yourselves disporting in some form of locomotion such as Brooklands, or a switchback railway. My advice to you is merely: hold tight and do not let yourselves fall off. I cannot guarantee to help you on again'. The rehearsal process was intended to develop in an organic way: 'When you rehearse a work, let the orchestra play it to you. Learn from the orchestra then you can make your suggestions'. Composer Richard Arnell noted that, 'Beecham didn't stop the orchestra if it made a mistake. But the second time round he did so and began to interpret the work. The third time round it was better than anyone else could do it'. With recordings he took especial care: the first four minutes of Rossini's *William Tell Overture* took a full three-hour recording session before Beecham was satisfied.[705]

Beecham had strong opinions on many composers, including Bach ('too much counterpoint'), Brahms ('that old bore'), Wagner ('too often excessively theatrical and emotional'), Stravinsky ('no continuous personality') and Schoenberg ('unintelligible'), although he was warm in praise of Mozart, Beethoven, Delius, Britten and some others. Vaughan Williams he did not care for much, and rehearsing one of the symphonies, Beecham carried on beating time in an absent-minded manner even after the movement had ended, and on being told by the leader that it had finished, answered, 'So it is. Thank God!'. Critically, Beecham needed listeners, performance being for him a very different matter from rehearsal: a former player of the London Philharmonic Orchestra described him in rehearsal as going through a work 'with an apparent lack of

---

702 Lebrecht (2001), p.31.
703 Christopher Seaman, *Inside Conducting* (Rochester, NY, 2013), p.54.
704 Cited in Lebrecht (2001), p.188.
705 Atkins and Newman (1979), pp.25, 30, 20 and 50.

enthusiasm, sometimes in a haphazard fashion; but place *one* listener in the body of the hall, and the atmosphere changes at once. The rehearsal suddenly becomes interesting, subtle effects are obtained and the sparkle of his wit flashes like electricity'.[706]

Other contemporary performers did however enjoy rehearsing: Henry Wood wrote, 'The pleasure of conducting does not lie in the actual performance but in the preparation of the performance – the pulling together of the whole thing. This is the conductor's view of the situation: the player's opinion is the opposite. It is a peculiarity of choruses and instrumentalists that they don't like rehearsals'.[707]

HERBERT VON KARAJAN

Austrian conductor Herbert von Karajan (1908-1989) was for many years the highest-profile and most financially successful classical musician of the post-war era.[708] Principal conductor of the Berlin Philharmonic for 34 years, Karajan's career conveniently aligned with the trajectory of the developing recording industry so closely that he was able to record some major works numerous times, from shellac to stereo to LP to CD to Laserdisc to DVD; he is thought to have sold as many as 200 million records.[709] Such repetition – in concert and on disc – had the danger of performances becoming routine, something to be fought against, and Riccardo Chailly mischievously described Karajan's fourth Beethoven symphony cycle as 'rehearsed for accuracy and sparkle'.[710]

As a practical manager of musicians, Karajan was aware of their needs, and his players appreciated not being overworked: a Philharmonia rehearsal or recording session under Karajan in the 1940s 'rarely ended later than five minutes before the official finishing time', while principals having difficulty found a different section was rehearsed while they recovered themselves. He was also 'impervious to tantrums, by singers and players alike, so they simply did not bother'.[711]

---

706 Atkins and Newman (1979), pp.49-53 and 15.
707 Orga (1975), p.71.
708 See Roger Vaughan, *Herbert von Karajan: A Biographical Portrait* (New York, 1985) and Richard Osborne, *Herbert von Karajan: A Life in Music* (Boston, 2000).
709 For a recordings list, see John Hunt, *Philharmonic autocrat: the discography of Herbert von Karajan (1908-1989)* (London, 4/2016).
710 Lebrecht (2001), p.126.
711 Pettitt (1985), pp.53-54.

An important documentary record of Karajan rehearsing survives from the mid-1960s, including the only visual record of him doing a complete work.[712] This was made as part of a 13-episode broadcast series, using a sequence of different works to make different points about musical performance; in a short interview, the conductor explained that he wanted to 'show how much work and concentration' goes into a performance, something a concert-goer never sees. The main work is Schumann's 4th symphony, to which an hour is devoted, half of which is on the first movement alone (the first note is worked on in considerable detail, for example). This was the last rehearsal before the studio recording the following day, so much of the effort involved reinforcement of previous comments, and further refinements. The Vienna Symphony Orchestra is highly responsive, and clearly used to working with the conductor: there are many quick stops, a lot of ground is covered and immediate improvements are evident. Karajan concentrates on the main passages which are important for the 'atmosphere of the piece', and everything is strongly characterized. As well as general points ('too much rhythm and too little expression'), he emphasizes the importance of precise dynamics and articulation, continuing when happy ('very nice', 'much better' or 'this is all going wonderfully'). Metaphors are used to explain musical points, and some individual parts (especially the upper strings) are singled out for special treatment, Karajan mentioning bowing a great deal, and demonstrating arm movements with gestures, as well as singing the lines. There is a great deal about tone, phrasing, structure and form, and particular care is taken with transitions. A score is to hand, for occasional reference to rehearsal and bar numbers. There is relatively little discussion of accompanying parts, Karajan being very thematically focused.

The second item is from a year later, in 1966, and comprises part of the second movement of Beethoven's 5th, with the strings of the Berlin Philharmonic Orchestra. In the 16-minute sequence, Karajan works with an unnamed student conductor, who is reduced mostly to listening, as Karajan asks and answers all own questions – the effect is like an enthusiastic lecture with live music examples, and is very analytical (for example, the orchestra is made to play the main theme against its later variation) and informative; he also demonstrates passages on the piano from memory. The student is advised to 'create the sound quality' like a sculptor selecting marble.

---

712 *Herbert von Karajan in Rehearsal and Performance*, DVD Euroarts Unitel 2072118 (2006), in black-and-white. The subtitle translations from the German are by Janet and Michael Berridge.

The two 'live' studio performances of the complete symphonies show the results of the rehearsal process; Karajan now works entirely through the baton, with his eyes seemingly closed; there is a good sense of what has come from previous preparation and what emerges in the performance event itself.

PIERRE BOULEZ

The work of composer and conductor Pierre Boulez (1925-2016) can be examined both through recordings and his own words. A 1996 interview with Robert Ponsonby asks many pertinent questions, including about his start in the profession: 'I founded the Concerts of the Domaine Musicale, which were exclusively dedicated to contemporary music, and I was the least expensive conductor in my organization, so therefore I began to conduct the works'.[713] One interesting comment mentions the way in which familiarity has led to rising standards since those early days: '*Le Marteau sans maitre*, my own work, was first performed 30 years ago with Rosbaud as conductor and I think he had something like 50 rehearsals because, especially with the percussion instruments, there was a lot of difficulty, and also for the viola, and for every instrument there was some technical difficulties. Now when I do it with my group in Paris, the Ensemble Intercontemporain, I need half a rehearsal. So that is proof that things which are possible can be mastered much quicker now than they were 30 years'. The impact of recordings is also noted: 'that notion of accuracy also relates to the standards of our period: if now you hear a recording, even only twenty times, you cannot stand a chord which is not together twenty times - hence all the editing. We must not forget that editing came rather late in the recording industry - I mean tape - and now of course our listening habits have changed completely, and also the dynamics'.[714]

In terms of planning rehearsals, he notes, 'At the beginning I was more careful than I am now. Now you know more or less what you want to do, it's more instinctive, because I know the difficulties of the score, especially when I have conducted it a couple of times. I know where the difficulties are and I read the score with the orchestra. Even with all the disasters of the first reading, sight reading, they have an idea of the continuity. I have done, for instance, *L'Heure Espagnole*, which is not very difficult music, but it constantly changes tempo, so you must here sub-divide, here not sub-divide, here you stop, here you conduct

---

713 Robert Ponsonby, 'The Art of the Conductor: Pierre Boulez in Conversation', *Tempo*, lxii/243 (January 2008), pp.2-15 at 3.
714 Ponsonby (2008), pp.12 and 10.

this way, here you conduct another way, and it's like that every two or three bars. With this piece no sight-reading is possible because everybody would be lost. So there are cases where you can really not do this sight-reading. But generally you can do the sight-reading and, afterwards, you take immediately the places which are difficult. I'm not the first one to do that: Stokowski was famous for choosing the places which were difficult and which would not improve without rehearsing. He also said there were places which do improve without rehearsing, partly because they are not that difficult and even if a musician has made a mistake, he will not do it the next time'.[715]

The visual record of Boulez at work, with the Vienna Philharmonic Orchestra, was made in 1998, and is a short programme (under a hour) including rehearsal of Berg's *Three Pieces*, Op.6 (1913-14) and the conductor's own *Notations I-IV* (1945).[716] It is a great pity the actual performances were not included on the DVD, in order to see the effects of the rehearsal on the concert. Intercut with the music sequences (in German, with subtitles) there is an interview with Boulez in English about the music. In many ways this is more like filmed excerpts than a documented rehearsal, with restless mobile multi-cameras likely set up for a subsequent broadcast.

Boulez is a polite ('Can we do it again?'), watchful but unsmiling communicator, and the orchestra seems rather disengaged, although everyone seems to concentrate a little harder when his own music is being worked on. The rehearsal process is analytical: balance, rhythms and tuning are carefully checked, while individual instruments are extracted for comment (one of the trumpets is singled out), often by family. The result is efficient, helpful - he explains the niceties of his own beating - and relatively unpressured, with Boulez repeating each short exercise until he is happy ('very good'). He has a particular concern with clarity in the lower parts, and with the polyphonic relationship between the musical lines, but (unlike Karajan) says nothing about character of the music.

Helpfully, his process on the podium exactly matches his interview descriptions from two years earlier: 'I remember with the B.B.C. Symphony Orchestra … I did sometimes find in some Webern pieces, when I wanted to draw attention to this intonation problem, I took some chords, very clear and very exposed, and I constructed the chords. For instance, I took out of the chords the fifth, or the fourth, or the third, and then I built the chord progressively and the musi-

---

715 Ponsonby (2008), pp.7-8.

716 *Pierre Boulez with The Vienna Philharmonic Orchestra, in Rehearsal*, DVD Arthaus Musik 100 290 (1998).

cians, without me saying anything, were aware how the chord could be properly adjusted to the tuning. Once you have done that with a couple of chords then everybody is alert and everybody is aware that the sonority will change completely'. Similarly with comments on balance: 'Mahler ... knows very well the dynamic balance of everything, the relationship of the instruments between one another; and also Stravinsky - with Stravinsky you have absolutely no problems rehearsing a piece, because he's very practical. But with Berg - and it's nothing to do with the quality of the music - with Opus 6, for instance, you have to change the dynamic because, if you want to have the main voices and the secondary voices in the right proportion, then he was not as experienced as Mahler, and therefore you have to readjust'.[717]

STUDIES OF CONDUCTING PEDAGOGY

The study of conductor training has recently become a topic, including discussion based on the work of particular conductors, as in Luke Dollman's comparison of Ilya Musin and Jorma Panula,[718] while Anu Konttinen has researched the general education of conductors in Finland.[719]

CONDUCTING TUTORS

Despite the views of some musicians like Boulez, who said, 'There is almost nothing to teach or to learn about conducting,[720] the first half of the 20th century saw a number of concise and modestly-priced practical tutors, written by professional experts but aimed principally at amateur musicians wanting or needing to acquire new skills, such as A. Madeley Richardson's *Choir Training based on Voice Production* (1899), Herbert Antcliffe's *The Chorusmaster* (1926), Henry Coleman's *The Amateur Choir Trainer* (1932), Harvey Grace's *Choral Training and Conducting* (1938), Leslie Woodgate's *The Chorusmaster*

---

717 Ponsonby (2008), pp.9 and 13.

718 Luke Dollman, 'A gulf of difference: conducting pedagogues Ilya Musin and Jorma Panula', *The Musical Times*, clvii/1936 (Autumn 2016), pp.63-74.

719 Anu Konttinen, 'Conductor education in Finland', *Finnish Musical Quarterly*, iii (2006), and *Conducting gestures: institutional and educational construction of conductorship in Finland, 1973–1993*, dissertation (University of Helsinki, 2008).

720 Ponsonby (2008), p.2.

(1944), and Joseph Lewis's *Conducting without fears* (1945).[721] Similar books were also published after the war, such as Gordon Reynolds' *The Choirmaster in action* (1972).[722] For a few shillings, a new newcomer could discover how to organize a choir, beat time, accompany, choose repertoire and plan programmes. Rehearsal is always mentioned, but usually briefly and often rather vaguely; Grace is unusual in devoting six pages to 'The Weekly Practice', even if only skimming the surface of the topic with his sensible practice advice. Even the longest of these books – Coleman, with 143 pages – does not offer a specific chapter on the subject. Although it is not clear from their titles, the guides written by cathedral organists (Coleman at Peterborough, Richardson at Southwark) have a particular focus on male choirs and the problems of training boys' voices, and make reference to the post-Victorian decline of that voice.

The conversational tone of Imogen Holst's *Conducting a Choir: A Guide for Amateurs* (1973)[723] is rather different, and the book is illustrated with numerous musical examples and a number of photographs. The length (161 pages) is now sufficient to cover many more topics, including editions, arranging concerts, taking part in festivals, and performance nerves, while repertoire and publisher lists emphasize practical utility. About six pages are devoted to rehearsal, principally issues around administration and behaviour – very little is said about how a rehearsal is actually to be managed, although two earlier sections cover 'Correcting the faults' and 'Aiming at a better sound'.

A further recent class of writings are multi-author historical or scholarly surveys that include broad discussion of conducting and rehearsal, as in Colin Lawson's *The Cambridge Companion to the Orchestra* and André de Quadros' *The Cambridge Companion to Choral Music*.[724] The latter includes two short chapters on rehearsing by Ann Howard Jones and Simon Carrington;[725] both are personal narratives that mirror practical advice from earlier traditions.

---

721 A. Madeley Richardson, *Choir Training based on Voice Production* (London, [1899]), Herbert Antcliffe, *The Chorusmaster* (London, [1926]), Henry Coleman, *The Amateur Choir Trainer* (London, 1932), Harvey Grace, *Choral Training and Conducting* (London, [1938]), Leslie Woodgate, *The Chorusmaster* (London, 1944), Joseph Lewis, *Conducting without fears* (London, 1945).

722 Gordon Reynolds, *The Choirmaster in action* (London, 1972).

723 Imogen Holst, *Conducting a Choir: A Guide for Amateurs* (London, 1973).

724 Colin Lawson (ed), *The Cambridge Companion to the Orchestra* (Cambridge, 2003) and André de Quadros (ed), *The Cambridge Companion to Choral Music* Cambridge, 2012).

725 Ann Howard Jones, 'A point of departure for rehearsal preparation and planning' and Simon Carrington, 'Small ensemble rehearsal techniques for choirs of all sizes', in Quadros (2003), pp.272-280 and 281-291.

There are also a number of separate essays, such as Kyle J. Hanson's 'A Rehearsal Refresher', where the main components are categorized as musical, vocal production and intellectual/spiritual. These are organized into a tabled hierarchy, with these components organized into 'Establishing the Sound'; 'Expressing the Sound'; and 'Securing the Sound'.[726]

PROFESSIONAL GUIDES

As well as introductory texts, a number of more substantial books appeared, with detailed coverage of technical and other issues. Many were intended for conservatoire-level students, so focused on the orchestra as the medium. One important and different example covering choral society conducting was Henry Coward's 1914 guide *Choral Technique and Interpretation*, published in Novello's 'Handbooks for Musicians' series and more than 330 pages in length. This unusually begins with a detailed section on the whys and hows of rehearsal, and lists three methods of taking rehearsals: the 'Conventional Generalizing'; the 'Critical Particularizing'; and the 'Compartmental Specializing'. Each is built around a structured form of repetition, and Coward makes a point of satirizing how each of his methods might be done badly. However, when all the methods are efficiently combined, and all goes well, the conductor 'will go home delighted, and refreshed in spirit though perhaps tired in body'.[727]

Orchestra-focused guides necessarily have a large amount of additional material about instruments, stick technique, tuning and balance, as with Michael Bowles's 1961 *The Conductor: His Artistry and Craftsmanship*, the title of which (if not the content) dates it somewhat.[728] It covers all the ground clearly and in detail – the contents derive from the author's university teaching courses in the United States – and the section on rehearsal is nearly 30 pages in length. Very practical in its approach, it discusses the logistical, musical and psychological aspects of the process, built around the idea that 'the primary aim of rehearsal is to eliminate the possibility of faulty response to the conductor during a concert'.[729] The advice about dealing with correcting faults is sensible and avoids extremes, and account is also taken of the longer-term structuring of a series of rehearsals. John Lumley and Nigel Stringthorpe's *The Art of Con-*

---

726 Kyle J. Hanson, 'A Rehearsal Refresher', *The Choral Journal*, lviii/10 (May 2018), pp.49-58.
727 Henry Coward, *Choral Technique and Interpretation* (London, 1914), pp.8-18.
728 Michael Bowles, *The Conductor: His Artistry and Craftsmanship* (London, 1961).
729 Bowles (1961), p.149.

ducting (1989),[730] offers a shorter chapter on rehearsal, which opens with the useful reminder that, 'Rehearsals are for the benefit of the performers, and not the conductor'. The 14 pages that follow are among the most helpful found in such books, covering various different genres and ensembles, and with views as to (for example) the importance of keeping to a schedule, not wearing out the performers and understanding the function of a dress rehearsal.

Some conducting texts are written by teachers, and others by performers; Christopher Seaman's detailed *Inside Conducting* (2013) belongs to the latter category, and has no fewer than 51 sections in nine groups.[731] The format is very original, beginning with 'The Conductor's Mind' and moving through his 'skills' and 'hands', then taking into account the score, instruments, audience, the profession and so on. Although the nine-page section on rehearsal seems brief, much additional relevant information is referenced to be found elsewhere in the book, while useful anecdotes include advice from an experienced player to the author, who talked too much when he started out: 'It's either too loud, too quiet, too long, too short, too sharp, or too flat. Don't tell me why, and don't give me any clever stuff'. Seaman concludes, 'Orchestras don't want to be lectured, but they sometimes need a *short* explanation so they can do what you want with more conviction'.

As well as the volumes mentioned here, there are numerous other texts on conducting published in the past hundred years, by Adrian Boult, James Jordan, Ilya Musin, Hideo Saito, Herman Scherchen, Markand Thakar, Henry Wood and others.[732]

---

730 John Lumley and Nigel Stringthorpe, *The Art of Conducting* (London, 1989).
731 Seaman (2013).
732 Adrian Boult, *A Handbook on the Technique of Conducting* (Oxford, 1921), Herman Scherchen, trans Michel D. Calvocoressi, *Handbook of Conducting* (London, 1934), Henry Wood, *About Conducting* (London, 1945), Hideo Saito, ed Wayne J. Troews, *The Saito conducting method* (Tokyo, 1988), James Jordan, *The Choral Rehearsal: Technique and Procedures*, vol.1, Evoking Sound (Chicago, 2008), Ilya Musin, trans Oleg Proskurnya, *The technique of conducting* (Lewiston, 2014) and Markand Thakar, *On the Principles and Practice of Conducting* (Rochester, NY, 2016). Seaman (2013) has an extensive bibliography of books about conducting and conductors, including memoirs.

CHAPTER 9
THE IMPACT OF TECHNOLOGY IN THE 21ST CENTURY

Technology has significantly changed some of the ways in which musicians rehearse, since the advent of commercial recordings in the early 20th century, from digital metronomes and tuning apps on mobile phones to pdf scores read from a tablet. In a similar way, technology has made also made possible the study of different aspects of performance; this includes the exploration of the causes and implications of the historical transformations involving 'the size and nature of the orchestra and the rise of the modern conductor'.[733]

The impact of technology on rehearsal has also transformed the way many musicians prepare and collaborate. This includes the use of digital tools that facilitate practice and communication, with apps and software to record rehearsals, thus allowing players to review performances and identify areas for improvement. This capability not only has the potential to enhance individual practice, but can also favour a more informed and constructive group rehearsal environment. Online platforms also enable real-time virtual collaboration, making it easier for musicians to work together regardless of loca-

---

[733] Cayenna Ponchione-Bailey and Eric F. Clarke, 'Digital Methods for the Study of the Nineteenth-Century Orchestra', *Nineteenth-Century Music Review*, xviii (2021), pp.19-50 at 19. See also Cayenna Ponchione-Bailey and Eric F. Clarke, 'Technologies for investigating large ensemble performance', in Renee Timmers, Freya Bailes and Helena Daffern (eds), *Together in music* (Oxford, 2022), pp.119-128.

tion. Video conferencing tools mean that musicians can connect and create despite physical distance, but they also open opportunities for hybrid rehearsal formats (combining in-person and online elements) and the ability to collaborate on projects that would have been logistically impossible in the past.

The integration of such tools into music education has enhanced rehearsal preparation and productivity, with metronomes, tuners and even Artificial Intelligence (AI)-driven practice assistants providing musicians with immediate feedback on aspects of their performance. This can help young musicians develop their skills more efficiently, and encourage a more disciplined approach to practice. AI and Machine Learning technologies are beginning to influence music rehearsal through tools that can analyze performances, suggest improvements or even generate an accompaniment.

MUSIC MINUS ONE

The history of technological support for rehearsal and preparation dates back to well before the digital age. Concerto and solo repertoire preparation has always been a challenge, most of the work having to be done with an accompanist using a piano reduction before players were able to rehearse with a full orchestra. The Music minus One series (illus.11), started in 1950 and still active, originally provided the solo part plus an LP orchestral backing recording to work with, the disadvantage being that the recorded part was fixed, but with the advantage that selected passages could be repeated for practice. This idea has been revived in the digital age, with piano accompaniment apps such Piano-Accompaniments.com, youraccompanist.com and Appcompanist, which are either adaptable or use feedback systems to 'follow' the soloist, thus providing a more musical accompaniment.[734]

COLLABORATIVE DIGITAL REHEARSAL AND VIRTUAL ENSEMBLES

Video-conferencing platforms like Zoom and Microsoft Teams, originally designed for remote business meetings, were repurposed for music particularly during the 2021 Covid-19 pandemic, allowing for remote rehearsals by

---

[734] See Adriana Olmos, Nicolas Bouillot, Trevor Knight, Nordhal Mabire, Josh Redel and Jeremy R. Cooperstock, 'A High-Fidelity Orchestra Simulator for Individual Musicians' Practice', *Computer Music Journal*, xxxvi/2 (Summer 2012), pp.55-73 for the Open Orchestra system.

Illus. 11. 'Music Minus One' LP of Telemann, Pergolesi and Gluck, MMO 110 (1968).

chamber ensembles, and even orchestras and choirs. This enabled ensembles like amateur and school choirs to continue to function socially, although the latency (delay) issue could be problematic even if wide bandwith and high-quality equipment were available.[735] One descriptive educational study concluded

---

735 Janet Galván and Matthew Clauhs, 'The virtual choir as collaboration', *The Choral Journal*, lxi/3 (October 2020), pp.8-19 at 15.

that 'Although the online rehearsal situation is not ideal, we found value in the significant amount of student engagement during our online meetings'.[736]

Such technology also made possible 'virtual vocal ensembles' like Eric Whitacre's Virtual Choir,[737] a method described by music education scholar Christopher Cayari as 'a video containing multiple audio-visual tracks layered together through a technique called multitracking. In this performance practice, a virtual vocal ensemble creator records and combines multiple tracks to make a choir of clones or works with others in collaborative or collective ways'.[738] The process could be broken down to allow individual training, as outlined by Janet Galván and Matthew Clauhs: 'During rehearsals, students sang as the conductor played their parts or the accompaniment, and all singers had their microphones muted while they sang. The group would sing small sections and then take time for questions or clarifications. I would answer verbally or with a vocal demonstration. Before moving on to the next section, I would check on the singers' comfort level with the part of the composition just rehearsed. Occasionally, one person would demonstrate an idea of pronunciation, articulation, or phrasing. Specific vowel formation was also addressed. Students chanted text with microphones on so that vowels could be unified. Also, as a regular part of each rehearsal, the group members spent time giving a brief statement of how things were going as people signed on. Each rehearsal had a dedicated time for anyone to discuss news or concerns'.[739]

Video platforms are also now used for individual remote music teaching; this can either be done live, or the student can upload a performance for online assessment by a teacher; the feedback process is therefore the discussion of a recording. A number of examining boards also allow or require certified video performances for music performance exams.

---

[736] Matthew Swanson, Eva Floyd and David Kirkendall, 'Choral Rehearsals During COVID: Examining Singer Engagement', *The Choral Journal*, lxi/9 (April 2021), pp.75-79 at 78.

[737] ericwhitacre.com/music-catalog/sing-gently.

[738] Christopher Cayari, *Virtual Vocal Ensembles and the Mediation of Performance on YouTube*, PhD disssertation (University of Illinois at Urbana-Champaign, 2016), p.ii.

[739] Galván and Clauhs (2020), pp.10-11.

DIGITAL WORKSTATIONS, DIGITAL ORCHESTRAS AND COLLABORATION PLATFORMS

Digital Audio Workstations (DAWs) like Ableton Live, Pro Tools and Logic Pro enable musicians to record, edit and produce music digitally. Such tools enable the layering of parts, experimentation with arrangements and orchestrations, creating backing tracks for rehearsals, and producing high-quality output recordings. This editing flexibility can be used to refine music as part of rehearsal processes.

A new system developed by Shelley Katz and called the Symphonova Instrument is a conductable digital orchestra, meaning that performance elements necessary for expressive performance can be incorporated live.[740] It can be used to supplement live instruments, and enables conductors to rehearse both familiar and new scores in a way that saves valuable preparatory time. Similarly, composers can refine their music before hearing it from a live orchestra for the first time.

Remote collaboration platforms like Soundtrap and BandLab allow musicians to work together on projects remotely, including recording and mixing tracks together online, and also in real time. Individual musicians have become experienced in multitracking complete performances using click-tracks, as with the recorder player James Howard Young.[741] The 'rehearsal' process for this involves checking the ensemble and tuning accuracy of each added track before moving on to the next.

LEARNING RESOURCES FOR PERFORMERS, CLOUD STORAGE AND FILE SHARING

Before virtual ensembles became possible, aspects of technology were already being used for preparation and feedback: in 2009 Philip Copeland described the ways in which email and other communication technologies could be used for choir logistics, rehearsal feedback communication and the sharing of sources.[742] This preparatory sharing of sheet music, practice materials and recordings via Google Drive, Dropbox, OneDrive and other cloud services improves com-

---

740 https://symphonova.com.
741 https://www.jnote.com.
742 Philip Copeland, 'Technology for the 21st-Century Choir', *The Choral Journal*, l/5 (December 2009), pp.22-30.

munication between conductors, administrators and musicians, potentially saving time in advance of live rehearsals. Scrolling scores have been created for a number of works on platforms like YouTube and Vimeo, which can help with repertoire learning, and also musical notation learning. There are in addition services which provide digital readings of individual vocal parts, to assist with learning for those less fluent in reading musical notation.[743]

MUSIC NOTATION SOFTWARE, MOBILE APPS AND RECORDING TECHNOLOGY

Music notation software, which provides digital versions of scores, including a playback facility (of variable sonic quality) is widely available, and such tools (for example, Sibelius, Dorico and MuseScore) allow composers and arrangers to create, edit and share sheet music digitally. The music can also be easily edited in order to provide individual performing parts. Feedback for composers via an electronic score enables earlier assessment of results, but there is a danger that technical issues and levels of difficulty may not be sufficiently taken into account: most digital playback not only sounds 'inhuman' in terms of its lack of flexibility and nuance, but can be made inhumanly accurate or fast relative to human performers.

A wide range of mobile applications now provide musicians with useful tools for practice and rehearsal, including tuners, metronomes and backing tracks. Apps like SmartMusic and Yousician offer interactive practice environments, providing immediate feedback and helping musicians improve their skills more effectively without a teacher. The advent of portable recording devices and high-quality microphones has also made it easier for musicians to document their rehearsals, both allowing for critical self-evaluation and providing a way of tracking progress over time.

---

743 See, for example, https://choirguides.com.

CHAPTER 10
RESEARCH INTO REHEARSAL

Present-day academic research into rehearsal has taken two principal paths, the managerial and the perceptual, with a strong pedagogical bias, resulting in a general neglect of the important area of professional skill analysis (see below). The exploration of rehearsal management at school or college level[744] – where it is outlined how rehearsal technique can be *taught* – has focused on aspects of performance technique,[745] the use of music analysis in rehearsal preparation,[746] ideas around leadership,[747] moving beyond

---

[744] See Arthur L. Williams, 'Planning an Instrumental Rehearsal', *Music Supervisors' Journal*, xviii/2 (December 1931), pp.23-25 and David L. Brunner, 'Carefully Crafting the Choral Rehearsal', *Music Educators Journal*, lxxxiii/3 (November 1996), pp.37-39; Brian Gorelick, 'Planning the Perfect Choral Rehearsal', *Music Educators Journal*, lxxxviii/3 (November 2001), pp.28-33 and 60 outlines a rather inflexible micromanagement system.

[745] Paul Broomhead, 'A Study of Instructional Strategies for Teaching Expressive Performance in the Choral Rehearsal', *Bulletin of the Council for Research in Music Education*, No.167 (Winter 2006), pp.7-20, Joy Hirokawa, 'Teaching Vocal Technique in the Choral Rehearsal', *The Choral Journal*, lvi/4 (November 2015), pp.73-77 and Atik (1994).

[746] Gordon (2006), pp.62-64; James L. Byo, 'Applying Score Analysis to a Rehearsal Pedagogy of Expressive Performance', *Music Educators Journal*, ci/2 (December 2014), pp.76-82.

[747] Niina Koivunen and Grete Wennes, '"Show us the sound!" Aesthetic leadership of symphony orchestra conductors', *Leadership*, vii/1 (2011), pp.51-71.

notation,[748] the observation or proposal of effective rehearsal techniques,[749] the effect of directed observations on the development of performer taste,[750] or particular engagement techniques.[751] Some of these resonate with historical practice, in relation to fundamental ideas about training and education, especially with respect to observational apprenticeship models.

TEACHING AND LEARNING

Technology has made practice-based study more possible in recent years, although precise assessment of such material can be challenging. In one study of time use in instrumental rehearsals by 30 different band directors of varying levels of experience, 60 videos of American Middle School band rehearsals were recorded and subject to analysis using many different temporal variables, from arrival to warm-up to rehearsal to the end of the session; generally, experienced teachers talked less and rehearsed more.[752]

In another video-based rehearsal study, this time of seven examples of choral repertoire performed by a university ensemble under a single conductor, ten categories of both student and teacher behaviour were assessed by scaled marking, including time use, musicianship, accuracy of presentation, student attentiveness, student performance quality, enthusiasm, intensity, pacing, personality, and overall effectiveness.[753] The optimal ('high-magnitude') teacher was

---

748 Zimmerman (1969).

749 Kenneth C. Murray, 'Effective Rehearsal Time: What Research Has to Offer', *The Choral Journal*, xx/5 (January 1980), pp.11-13; Val Hicks, 'Attention, Effort and Motivation in Rehearsal and Performance', *The Choral Journal*, xxvi/10 (May 1986), pp.11-16; Thomas W. Goolsby, 'Time use in instrumental rehearsals: A comparison of experienced, novice, and student teachers', *Journal of Research in Music Education*, 44 (1996), pp.286-303; Daniel Taddie, 'Achieving Peak Performance: Rehearsal, Performance Attitudes, and Pre-Concert Routines, *The Choral Journal*, xli/9 (April 2001), p.41; Charles R. Chaffin, 'Perceptions of Instrumental Music Teachers regarding the Development of Effective Rehearsal Techniques', *Bulletin of the Council for Research in Music Education*, No.181 (Summer 2009), pp.21-36; and Cavitt (2003).

750 Kevin L. Droe, 'The Effect of Teacher Approval and Disapproval of Music Performed in a Rehearsal Setting on Music Preferences', *Journal of Research in Music Education*, lvi/3 (October 2008), pp.267-278.

751 Karen L. Bruno, 'Creativity and Artistry in the Children's Choir Rehearsal', *The Choral Journal*, lvi/8 (March 2016), pp.34-42; Kathryn Emerson, *The social organisation of the choir rehearsal: How interaction between conductor and choir is used to shape the choir's singing*, PhD thesis (University of Sheffield, 2018).

752 Goolsby (1996).

753 Cornelia Yarbrough and Katia Madsen, 'The Evaluation of Teaching in Choral Rehearsals', *Journal of Research in Music Education*, xliv/4 (1998), pp.469-481.

defined as 'one who maintained eye contact with the group or individuals, who approached and departed the group often during rehearsal, who used expressive conducting gestures, who maintained a rapid and exciting rehearsal pace, and whose speech was characterized by varying speeds, pitches, and volume'; the 'low-magnitude' teacher was essentially the opposite. The resultant marks (on a scale of 1 to 10), averaged lowest/highest numbers as 5.52 and 8.06 for the seven music excerpts, not particularly extreme, but this conceals the fact that there were often examples where the conductor seemed good at one thing and less good at another: the mean range was therefore only from 6.49 to 7.6. The data showed that the highest-scoring rehearsal example revealed the conductor as more focused, faster paced, more positive and more varied. The challenge would be to turn such analytical data into feedback for conductors.

In the second category of studies, perceptual work covers the effect of rehearsal on the effective 'visual field' of a score (skill differences disappear after a large number of rehearsals),[754] the importance of pattern-matching skills for sightreading,[755] the effect of conductor personality types,[756] the concept of 'attentional shifts'[757] and the development of memory skills.[758] In terms of this last skill, Hans Phaf and Gezinus Wolters distinguish between *maintenance* and *elaborative* rehearsal: 'Rehearsal of items has two effects. First, it serves to maintain information in a temporarily active state. Second, it plays a role in the creation of more permanent memory representations'.[759] Both of these are obviously important in practical performing environments, on the one hand for a 'reminder rehearsal' of a previously-performed work, and on the other for quick assimilation of a new work.

---

754 Douglas D. Burman and James R. Booth, 'Music Rehearsal Increases the Perceptual Span for Notation', *Music Perception*, xxvi/4 (April 2009), pp.303-320.

755 Andrew J. Waters, Geoffrey Underwood and John M. Findlay, 'Studying expertise in music reading: Use of a pattern-matching paradigm', *Perception and Psychophysics*, lix (1997), pp.477-488.

756 Barbara Pollack and Harriet Simons, 'The Psychologist and the Conductor: Solving Rehearsal Problems Using Awareness of Personality Types', *The Choral Journal*, xxxvi/10 (May 1996), pp.9-16.

757 R. Hans Phaf and Gezinus Wolters, 'Attentional Shifts in Maintenance Rehearsal', *The American Journal of Psychology*, cvi/3 (Autumn 1993), pp.353-382.

758 Veronica J. Dark and Geoffrey R. Loftus, 'The role of rehearsal in long-term memory performance', *Journal of Verbal Learning & Verbal Behavior*, xv/4 (1976), pp.479–490.

759 Phaf and Wolters (1993), p.353.

Another pair of experiments looked at sight-reading skills using 30 newly-composed melodies read by three groups of musicians of standards from Associated Board Grade 2 to 8; and for a second example used undergraduate-age (musician and non-musician) readers.[760] More experienced musicians were able to do better, using fewer and shorter glances between the melodies, and could more rapidly perceive notes or groups of notes in the score; this confirms that pattern-matching is part of music reading skills.

THE PROFESSIONAL REHEARSAL

There has been relatively little examination of the actual processes of professional rehearsal, but a ethnographic (specifically 'fieldwork') study by Amanda Bayley explores one modern string quartet (the Kreutzer Quartet's rehearsal of Michael Finnissy's Second String Quartet in 2007), and asks (but does not quite answer) the question, 'How might a conceptual model for a rehearsal process be constructed for a potential audience of both scholars and performers?'.[761] Bayley makes the interesting observation as to the balance between verbal communication and actual playing in rehearsal: 'Talking and playing often merge in rehearsal such that separating the two for the purpose of analysis can often prove difficult'. Five criteria (originally devised by Jane Davidson and James Good) are assigned to categorize rehearsal interactions: Social conversation; Nonverbal social interaction; Musical conversations; Nonverbal musical interactions; and Musical interactions.[762]

The Kreutzer Quartet results indicate that, of the total rehearsal time, 41% is spent playing, 18% is about co-ordination, and 18% is related to sound quality (the remaining fifth is made up of much smaller elements such as humour, content and notation); crucially, the 'sound quality' issues were a main focus of the composer himself, when present. Of the total session time, 'in the absence of a full score, during the first 14 minutes of the rehearsal (prior to Finnissy's arrival) the players initially attempted to understand each other's parts'. This

---

760 Waters, Underwood and Findlay (1997).

761 Amanda Bayley, 'Ethnographic Research into Contemporary String Quartet Rehearsal', *Ethnomusicology Forum*, xx/3 (December 2011), pp.385-411 at 393. See also Ananay Aguilar, 'People in the studio: performers and producers observed', Art of Record Production conference (29 April 2013), Ponchione-Bailey and Clarke (2021) and Ponchione-Bailey and Clarke (2022).

762 Jane W. Davidson and James Good, 'Social and Musical Co-ordination Between Members of a String Quartet: An Exploratory Study', *Psychology of Music*, xxx (2002), pp.186-201.

reinforces (as was the case in early 19th century conducting), that access to the score can resolve many queries efficiently.

Bayley concludes that, even with the relatively detailed notation provided in a modern work, 'Without input from the composer, a rehearsal will be based on the musicians' combined complementary or even conflicting historical knowledge and experience about the composer and his/her musical style, and the limited information supplied in the notation. Notation and its historical perspective thus plays a large part in determining the musical interaction among players who generally identify their goal as the most appropriate or "correct" interpretation'. There is also a 'constant intersection between technical and interpretative choice'.[763] By comparison, the interpretation of music from three or four centuries ago, with its less-prescriptive notation, is in some ways far more challenging, despite the performance practice hints provided by the then-theorists and writers – working directly with a living composer is a modern performer's privilege.

---

[763] Bayley (2011), pp.396, 389 and 390. In respect of composer/performer collaboration in such environments, see Sam Hayden and Luke Windsor. 'Collaboration and the Composer: Case Studies from the End of the 20th Century', *Tempo*, lxi:240 (2007), pp.28-39.

CHAPTER 11
REHEARSAL IN THE PERFORMING ARTS

Surviving historical evidence of the preparatory material for the various creative arts before the 18th century varies greatly from discipline to discipline. While there are a considerable number of preliminary drawings and sketches for Renaissance and Baroque art-works, and some early drafts of literary creations, the situation for the performing arts generally is far worse, with very little evidence of rehearsal processes for dance, theatre or music. When the performance itself is a temporary activity, written documentation for the preparation of it is unlikely either to have been created, or retained.[764]

All these arts require preparation of material, and the crucial difference between music (except opera) and the other performance arts is the need for memorization of the content. Such memorization is an individual rather than a collective act, and is therefore undertaken previously and in private, except (for example) where taught to a group of choristers in a class; the rehearsal process therefore involves creating the artistic whole from the memorized parts, whether of speech or movement. In other words, sight-reading, that great musical safety-net, is not an available option when on stage.

---

764 Other forms of 'performance' not related to the performing arts but involving similar aspects of repetition by way of preparation for a specific high-level outcome include, glassblowing, forging metal, military marching, gymnastics and other sports, and circus routines.

DRAMA

For Ancient Greek drama, a single 30-line Roman papyrus fragment from Euripides' *Alcestis* is the only hint of the nature of a rehearsal process,[765] while even for the Elizabethan period thousands of years later few documents survive. Nevertheless, evidence from the latter suggests that 'three weeks seems to have been the usual length of time for preparing a play, there is no evidence to suggest that more than the traditional single group rehearsal was held within that period, as private learning ("study"), often with a teacher, was the most important part of preparation. For superior players this teacher was sometimes the playwright; major players instructed lesser players. "Study" seems to have involved teaching a part by imitation…', and textural variants appear to have emerged even during performing conditions: 'performances were "rehearsals"'.[766] In an earlier period, where companies of players were more peripatetic, 'strolling players seem generally to have studied new plays at their patron's house just before Christmas'. Actors in the London playhouses (illus.12) could have very large repertoires indeed: the Admiral's Company gave 38 plays in 1594-95, and the following year did fourteen in one month alone.[767] New works were constantly added, although those numbers diminished in the early 17th century. Individual actors could end up with very large numbers of roles in their repertoire: between 1594 and 1597 Edward Alleyn 'had to secure and retain command of about seventy-one different roles, of which number fifty-two or fifty-three were newly learned'.[768]

As has been observed with respect to 18th-century opera, runs of performances led to attendance decline: the (now-lost) anonymous Elizabethan play *Galiaso* was performed at the Rose Theatre in London nine times between 26 June and 25 October 1594, with gaps of a fortnight or longer between performances, and manager Philip Henslowe's recorded takings fell from £4 3s to £2 6s to £1

---

[765] C. W. Marshall, '"Alcestis" and the Ancient Rehearsal Process ("P. Oxy." 4546)', *Arion*, Third Series, xi/3 (Winter 2004), pp.27-45. Irene Plant, *Ancient Drama: Stagecraft and Signcraft*, PhD thesis (King's College, London, 1999), argues that 'the rehearsal teaching of texts was almost without doubt on an oral basis' (p.32).

[766] Tiffany Stern, 'Rehearsal in Shakespeare's Theatre', in Tiffany Stern (ed), *Rehearsal from Shakespeare to Sheridan* (Oxford, 2007), pp.46-123 at 121. See also John C. Meagher, *Pursuing Shakespeare's Dramaturgy: Some Contexts, Resources, and Strategies in His Playmaking* (Madison and Teaneck, NJ, 2003) and Evelyn Tribble, 'Distributing Cognition in the Globe', *Shakespeare Quarterly*, lvi/2 (Summer 2005), pp.135-155.

[767] Stern (2007), pp.47 and 53. One special class of actors from the period (some of whom were also musically trained, as choristers) should be remembered: the Elizabethan and Jacobean boy performers; see Mould (2007), p.117, Harry R. McCarthy, *Boy actors in early modern England: skill and stagecraft in the theatre* (Cambridge, 2022) and Orme (2023), pp.206-216.

[768] Bernard Beckerman, *Shakespeare at the Globe* (New York, 1962), p.9.

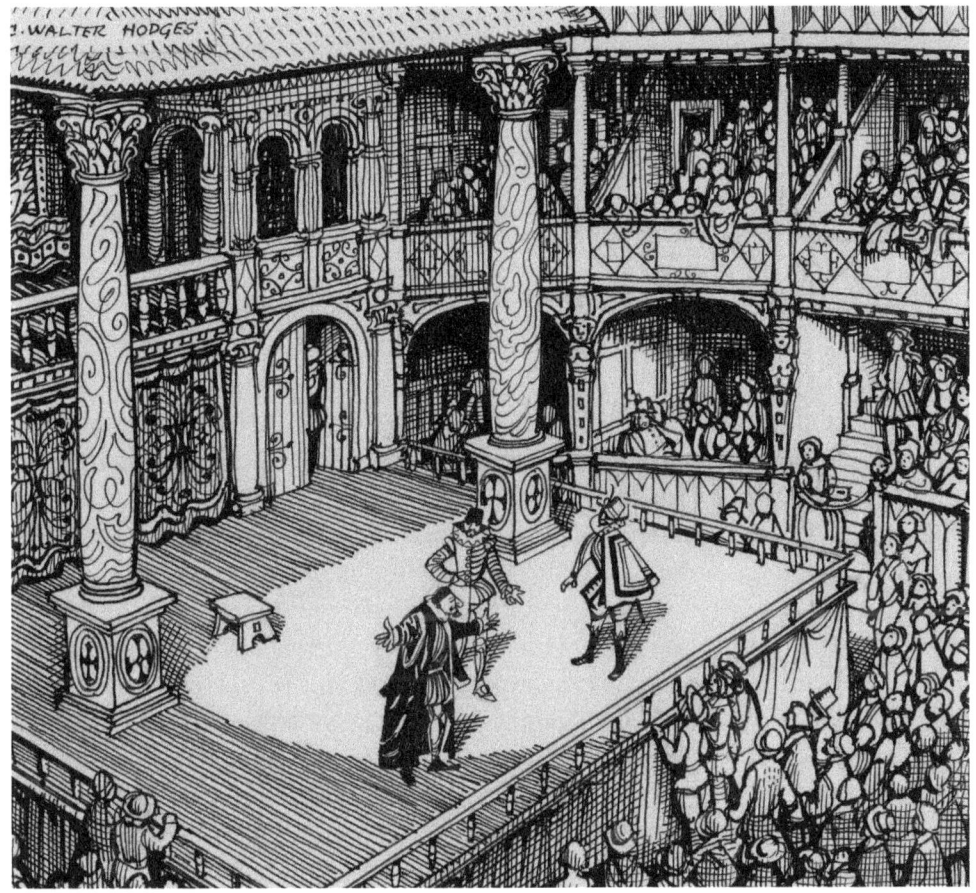

Illus. 12. Reconstruction of Shakespeare's *Merchant of Venice* (Act 1, scene 3), from C. Walter Hodges, *The Globe Restored: a study of the Elizabethan theatre* (London, 1953). (Folger Shakespeare Library ART Box H688 no.3.1/Creative Commons).

11s to just 11s over this period of four months: there was clearly a 'premiere premium' at work.[769]

After the Restoration, George Villiers' satirical play *The Rehearsal* (1672) mocks Dryden's bombastic style, but does not convey any actual information about the theatre rehearsal process, despite its setting; neither does Catherine Clive's play *The rehearsal: or, bays in petticoats* (1753). For later 18th century English drama, 'Collective evidence clearly indicates that rehearsals for stock

---

[769] Ruth Goodman, *How to be a Tudor* (London, 2016), p.224.

pieces were few in number and routine in nature. As long as a group of actors continued to play their regular characters in the stock plays, there was little need for rehearsal'.[770]

Memorization skills must have been at a premium in the early theatre, with the expectation that works could be learnt (or revived) at great speed. This constraint would have placed significant interpretative autonomy in the hands of individual actors rather than being given to any overarching director. A key factor in the preparation timeline for drama was the need not only for individual performers to memorize their own parts, but also the actual sequence of such speeches, cues, movements, music and the like.[771] As well as textual refinements arising during the rehearsal process, mis-memorization or minor extemporization by individuals likely accounts for a number of textual variants in the eventual printed copies, some of which appear to have been later written down by or from the actors.[772] One further major difference was that performers normally spoke in dialogue sequence, not in ensemble (as in music), resulting in different requirements for coordination, and hence for rehearsal.[773] Note that 'reading in' (a substitute performer, holding a script on stage) was a possibility where an actor became indisposed just before a performance, as noted by Haydn on his second visit to London in 1791.[774] This could even happen in an oratorio: when Susannah Cibber was taken ill just before Handel's *Hercules* was performed at the King's Theatre in January 1745, a weak substitute 'was obliged to read a few lines here and there of recitatif to carry on the sense of the Drama … This produced a little laughter and a faint Hiss from the Audience', according to the Earl of Shaftesbury.[775]

---

770 David G. Schaal, 'The English Background of American Rehearsal-Direction Practices in the Eighteenth Century', *Educational Theatre Journal*, xii/4 (December 1960), pp.262-269 at 264. For an exploration of modern practices, see Robert Marsden, *Inside the Rehearsal Room: Process, Collaboration and Decision-making* (London, 2022) and Nancy Meckler, *Notes from the Rehearsal Room* (London, 2023).

771 Simon Palfrey and Tiffany Stern have studied theatre cue texts in their *Shakespeare in Parts* (Oxford, 2010).

772 For practical examinations of Shakespeare texts through modern rehearsal, see David Richman, 'The King Lear Quarto In Rehearsal and Performance', *Shakespeare Quarterly*, xxxvii/3 (Autumn 1986), pp.374-382 and Nora J. Williams, 'Writing the Collaborative Process: Measure (Still) for Measure, Shakespeare, and Rape Culture', *PARtake: The Journal of Performance as Research*, ii/1 (2018). See also Laurie E. Maguire, *Shakespearean suspect texts: The 'bad' quartos and their contexts* (Cambridge, 1996).

773 For the history of the Greek chorus in drama, see Magdalena Zira, *The Problem of the Chorus in Contemporary Revivals of Greek Tragedy and Directorial Solutions in the Last Forty Years*, PhD thesis (King's College London, 2019).

774 Hogwood (1980), p.49.

775 Burrows et al. (2020), p.261.

Another form of rehearsal assistance available in the theatre was through the author's own demonstration: Baldinucci (1682) reports that playwright-actor – and, more famously, architect – Gian Lorenzo Bernini (1598-1680) would demonstrate all the parts himself to the actors.[776]

ART AND DANCE

The idea of 'rehearsal' as preparation for a final version is found in public speaking (for example, the recitation of poetry) and also in the preliminary studies of artists, from Raphael to Picasso. A story from China illustrates performative practice in the fine arts: an emperor commissioned a painting of a rooster, but the artist said it would take him three years to complete. The painter practiced all this time, and at the end produced the desired painting live in front of the emperor in just three minutes. In response to the emperor's complaint about the long wait, the artist showed him a house full of sketches and said, 'Without those three years of labour how could I possibly have produced that perfect rooster for you in less than three minutes?'.[777] However, it is in dance that the closest rehearsal/performance analogies can be found to music and the theatre. While the systematic notation of choreography was not developed until the 18th century,[778] as a format it has some of the same limitations as musical notation, functioning variously as a medium for creation, a set of performance instructions and a rehearsal *aide-memoire*.

CEREMONIES AND SPECIAL EVENTS

As an equivalent of early modern theatrical processes, the rituals of clergy activity in major liturgical events – presided over by a form of Master of Ceremonies, as in the well-documented Sistine Chapel practices of the 17th century[779] – required planning and rehearsal or testing before a public 'performance'. The same must have been true (in respect of planning, if not rehearsal) with elaborate civic ceremonies such as processions, the idea of which dated back to the

---

776 Cited in Roger Savage and Matteo Sansone, '*Il Corago* and the staging of early opera: four chapters from an anonymous treatise *circa* 1630', *Early Music*, xvii/4 (November 1989), pp.495-511 at 509. See also Robert Fahrner and William Kleb, 'The Theatrical Activity of Gianlorenzo Bernini', *Educational Theatre Journal*, xxv/1 (March 1973), pp.5-14.

777 https://www.envisage-arch.com/single-post/2017/11/22/the-tale-of-the-rooster.

778 See Ken Pierce, 'Choreographic Structure in Baroque Dance', in Jennifer Nevile (ed), *Dance, Spectacle and the Body Politick, 1250-1750* (Bloomington, 2008), pp.182-208.

779 See Sherr (1999).

Triumphs of the Roman emperors. One remarkable 1588 Florentine account details the protracted, complex and difficult genesis of a play-with-music for a Medici wedding celebration;[780] Lully's vexations bringing *Atys* to stage in 1676 are also recorded;[781] while Monteverdi mentioned in a 1628 letter the rehearsal preparations for a grand 'tourney' to which he had contributed the music.[782]

REHEARSAL AS DRAMA

A final example uses the only new medium represented here, that of film. An entire drama on the theme of musical rehearsal was created by Federico Fellini in 1978 for Italian television, and entitled *Prova d'orchestra*, or *Orchestra Rehearsal*.[783] The actors included Baldiun Baas (as the conductor), Clara Colosimo, Elizabeth Labi, Ronaldo Bonacchi and Ferdinando Villella, with the score was by Nino Rota.[784] This is a fairly unsubtle political allegory where an autocratic conductor has to deal with a quarrelling orchestra going on strike in the presence of a documentary television crew, ending with the symbolic destruction of the venue. It was later made into an opera by Giorgio Battistelli (1995).[785]

---

780 Jennifer Nevile, "'I had to fight with the painters, master carpenters, actors, musicians and the dancers": rehearsals, performance problems and audience reaction in Renaissance spectacles', *National Early Music Association Newsletter*, vi/1 (Spring 2022), pp.7-25.

781 Parrott (2022), p.394.

782 Arnold and Fortune (1985), p.81.

783 *Orchestra Rehearsal*, Infinity Arthouse DVD INF211 (2006).

784 See Dinko Fabris and Michela Grossi (eds), *Prove d'orchestra - Nino Rota e la sua musica da concerto* (Barletta, 2025).

785 There are a number of other recent fictional and fictionalized films about conductors, including *Young Toscanini* (1988), *Taking Sides* (2001), *The Concert* (2009), *Antonia, the conductor* (2018), *Crescendo* (2021), *Tár* (2022), *Divertimento* (2023) and *Maestro* (2023), some of which incorporate rehearsal sequences.

CHAPTER 12
CONCLUSIONS

REHEARSAL GOALS

Modern rehearsal techniques aim at efficiently preparing works for performance to the highest standard achievable in the limited time available. Artistic or practical goals need to be defined in order for this to be achieved, as in the eleven-step process devised by Arthur Williams a century ago: 'The first necessity is to determine the purposes for holding the rehearsal. They may be many and varied, but the important point is that SOME purpose MUST be determined. Without this, a rehearsal cannot be properly planned'.[786] Wilhelm Furtwängler (for one) was not an analytical rehearser of this kind, and his orchestral players in pre-war London noted that he would move on to another passage, having failed to sort the problem in a previous one.[787]

Attitudes likely varied considerably in different times and places in the past, and there is rather little evidence as to what defined rehearsal outcomes might have been before the 19th century, other than 'getting through' the piece more or less complete. The notion of performance quality may have been secondary in some circumstances, and it is possible to imagine circumstances in church where an objectively bad performance that included vocalization of the complete text (the crucial element, from a religious point of view) may have been acceptable liturgically, even if not musically: for example, one post-Civil War Fellow of Eton said that 'God was as well pleased with being served in tune, as out of tune'.[788]

---

786 Williams (1931), p.23.
787 Lebrecht (2001), p.85.
788 Cited in Saunders (1997), p.48.

COMPOSITIONAL STRUCTURES FOR REHEARSAL

From an analytical point of view, it is easy to now regard those composers who included 'hidden' structures that could not have been perceived by their hearers, as in John Dunstable, or applied balanced mathematical layouts, as Robert Fayrfax's *Regali* mass or John Taverner's *Playn Song* and *Western Wind* masses,[789] as using devices from *Musica Speculativa* for primarily structural or intellectual reasons. However, composers were also aware of their listeners (human or divine) as regards reception of their works, and also of actual or potential musicians in terms of performability. Thus, some of what appear to be sub-structural components may have had a further practical purpose: for rehearsal. This could have included formal features such as *da capo* arias, rondos, or binary repeat structures: early Haydn symphonies of a substantial twenty-five minutes' length comprising four binary movements with no separate first-time or second-time bars could not only be composed in a mere two dozen pages of score, but (if necessary) be concisely rehearsed in half the time they took to perform in concert.[790]

More complex early examples are found in the Eton Choirbook repertoire, such as John Browne's eight-voice antiphon *O Maria Salvator Mater*: the structural diagram Frank Harrison made of that piece lays out the sections in terms of scoring, alternating reduced-voice sections in black with shaded full choir sections.[791] Some of these sections are demarcated by single barlines in the Eton manuscript (transcribed as double barlines in modern editions) and therefore represent potential start and stop portions for rehearsal; as with the Haydn symphony example, they may be regarded as defined 'Rehearsal Units'. Although of differing lengths, and sometimes including both full and reduced sections, in this antiphon they include five main divisions – plus a further possible subset of five – within a 231-bar piece of around 15 minutes' duration (in modern transcription and performance). Few sections are longer two minutes in length, meaning that even repeating one of these from the beginning each time would represent a reasonably efficient method for sectional rehearsal of a difficult multi-voice work. It would also have been possible to rehearse the reduced-voice sections using solo voices (as is usually understood by the red-colour text underlay in Eton) separately and previously.

---

789 Benham (1977), pp.43 and 44-45. Proportional and length relationships are discussed on pp.43-47.

790 However, note that a letter of Susan Burney describing an initial opera rehearsal in London in May 1780 has one of the soloists apologizing that there would be 'a great many Da Capos which will tire you!', implying rehearsal of the full content; Holman (2020), pp.273-274.

791 Harrison (1963), p.316.

It is also worth asking whether the success of some stylistic changes in music over time might sometimes have been aided by their practical utility in rehearsal, and therefore performance. For example, pervasive imitation in mid-16th-century music is actually very useful to performers working from original partbooks, as it is easy to hear repeated melodic material in the other voices,[792] which is both placed at predictable rhythmic distances and limited to defined pitch areas. This would also have helped create a clearer 'aural map' structure within which a performer who got lost could recover themselves, unlike in most 15th century polyphony.

For individual performers too, what look like purely compositional decisions may also have had a practice component: for example, some of Bach's longest organ fugues include very substantial episodes for manuals alone, with the pedals inactive for a third or even half of the piece.[793] Given the practical difficulties of organ practice at that time (unheated churches, poor lighting, one or more additional people needed to blow the organ), making portions of the work accessible for domestic manuals-only practice would have made good sense.

ENSEMBLE INTERPRETATION

In view of the limited historical record of ensemble rehearsal, and the questionable control likely exercisable by musical directors working with performers of mixed ability using imperfect source material, it is worth asking whether the baton-led nuanced interpretational styles familiar from all-powerful orchestral conductors from the end of the 19th century has any place in earlier music.[794] Reichardt (1791) certainly had low expectations of conductorial powers: 'The present director has only to beat time. These compositions [...] are of such dignity and power that they make a great effect, even with the most wretched execution imaginable. With their mostly miserable voices, worn-out castrati and some old clerics completely chop up this noble, majestic composition ... One might weep when hearing masterworks bungled so wretchedly, yet one still experiences the great power and majesty'.[795] While soloists and chamber musi-

---

792 See Francis Knights, Pablo Padilla and Mateo Rodríguez, 'O Splendor gloriae: Taverner or Tye?', Early Music, xlix/4 (November 2021), pp.565-578 at 568-569 for a discussion of the difference between structured and loose imitation.
793 See Francis Knights, 'Bach's Orgelbüchlein as a keyboard tutor', National Early Music Association Newsletter, vii/1 (Spring 2023), pp.21-34.
794 See Walls (2003), ch.6 and Haynes (2007), pp.96-101.
795 Jerold (2006), p.79.

cians would have been able to achieve any level of refinement they chose, it is not so certain that the idea of 'interpretation' in the modern sense, as opposed to straight performance, was conceptually part of earlier ensemble music-making.[796] If so, it has left little documentary trace.

CREATIVE MISTAKES

While most rehearsal effort would have been directed at correctly reproducing the pitches provided by the composer, there must have been many error-laden occasions among musicians, of the kind satirized by Mozart in his *Musical Joke* of 1787. In particular, the sound of bitonal natural horns he notates (bars 17-19, ex.6), and 'cracked' brass notes, must have been familiar in rehearsals of the late 18th century. The most extreme example of such humour is found in the chaotically polytonal section of the *Battalia* a10 of 1673 by Biber, a work appropriately 'dedicated to Bacchus'. On other occasions, however, ambiguities in the notated musical content may have led to creative inspiration, as when an unfigured bass part was simultaneously realized slightly differently by a number of basso continuo players, giving rise to unusual chords. There are certainly instances in the composed music of Monteverdi,[797] Kapsberger, Purcell and others from the 17th century (and even as late as Beethoven)[798] which sound as if a rehearsal error has led to actual compositional inspiration, especially where technical rules are deliberately breached for apparently artistic ends.

ABANDONED OR SUBSTITUTED REPERTOIRE

There being comparatively few records dating from before the early 18th century of specific works on music lists for performance,[799] it is tempting to see the surviving manuscript and printed sources themselves as representing a perfor-

---

[796] Nir Cohen-Shalit also discusses the idea of 'Interpretation-free' performance, in 'The Romantic Conductor-Scholar: What I Learned from the Archives', in Bruno Forment (ed), *Performing by the Book? Musical Negotiations between Text and Act* (Leuven, 2024), pp.143-161 at 158.

[797] For an analytical exploration of some of Monteverdi's harmonic excursions, see Youyoung Kang, 'Monteverdi's Early Seventeenth-Century "Harmonic Progressions"', *Music Analysis*, xxx/2-3 (July-October 2011), pp.186-217.

[798] For example, the opening of the finale of the Symphony No.9.

[799] For some examples, see Crosby (1980) and Thomas Tudway, *A Collection of all the Anthems daily used in Divine Service, throughout the year, in King's College Chapel in Cambridge* (Cambridge, 1706).

Ex. 6. Mozart, *Ein musikalischer Spaß*, K522 (1787), Minuet, bars 1-26.

mance (or potential performance) repertoire. However, before the period of public concerts and operas, where works and performers were announced in advance, few audiences or congregations would have known exactly what they might be about to hear when attending a musical or liturgical event, and it is seems uncertain that many would (unlike now) have made their choice to go or not on the basis of the actual repertoire on offer. This meant that performers were in a position to offer last-minute 'backup' repertoire, should a rehearsal not go well; all experienced ensembles would have had pieces that were well known to them and could be immediately substituted.[800] For Latin liturgical repertoire, a plainchant version of the text would always have presented an acceptable alternative. From this point of view, the congregation attending Eton College Chapel during the early 16th century might sometimes have heard a plainchant (or *super librum*) *Salve Regina* replacing the failed rehearsal of a polyphonic work,[801] or one where complex music could not be performed that day due to absence or illness among the singers. While the Eton statutes required a polyphonic antiphon every evening – as did those of King's College, Cambridge – this can hardly have been enforced, in such circumstances.[802] To what extent the Eton Choirbook collection even represents a 'performed' repertoire as a whole is open to question: of the fifteen polyphonic *Salve Regina*s and twenty-four Magnificats originally in the source, the choir might only have known and used a small number that were suitable for regular performance to a good standard. With all early sources, it must be remembered that some pieces that were copied, printed or circulated were likely never learned or performed at all, and this may even include a number of Bach's keyboard works.[803]

PERFORMANCE PRACTICE AND REHEARSAL

There are numerous records from before 1800 of rehearsals having occurred, and a great deal of associated evidence about some of these events, including where it happened, who was present, what the music was, what materials it was performed from, and for how long, but there is relatively that says what actually took place *during* any such rehearsal, or what the precise goal or outcome of it was. Nevertheless, examination of the circumstances surrounding all-important performance preparation processes can give insights into some aspects of why and how certain repertoire was composed, what the expectations of listeners might have been and what practical challenges the musicians of the past

---

800 Whether or not the weekly cycle of seven polyphonic lady-masses by Nicholas Ludford of c.1520-30 was part of a wider repertoire for this particular liturgy, they would likely soon have become familiar to the singers if performed many times each year, or even each week; see Harrison (1963), pp.285-287.

801 What was done when a work broke down, or too many performers got lost for it to continue, must have varied depending on circumstance and tradition; the issue of a 'completed' liturgical text must have been a concern in sacred music.

802 Harrison (1963), p.162.

803 See Francis Knights, 'J. S. Bach's keyboard works: from performance to research', *Muzikologija*, xxxi (2021), pp.161-180.

learned to overcome in their performing repertoire.[804] The more detailed and extensive information available in the modern era, such as video recordings, still awaits fuller investigation, and rehearsal history and technique remains a subject with enormous potential.

---

[804] See, for example, Clive Brown, *Classical and Romantic Performing Practice 1750–1900* (Oxford, 1999) and 'Performing 19th Century Chamber Music: The Yawning Chasm between Contemporary Practice and Historical Evidence', *Early Music*, xxxviii/3 (2010), pp.476–480.

BIBLIOGRAPHY

Adolphe Adam, *Souveniers d'un Musicien* (Paris, 1868).

Gillian Adler and Paul Strohm, *Alle Thyng hath Tyme: Time and medieval life* (London, 2023).

Ananay Aguilar, 'People in the studio: performers and producers observed', Art of Record Production conference (29 April 2013).

Theodore Albrecht, *Beethoven's Ninth Symphony: Rehearsing and Performing its 1824 premiere* (Woodbridge, 2024).

Johann Georg Albrechtsberger, ed Ignaz von Seyfried, trans Sabilla Novello, *J. G. Albrechtsberger's Collected Writings on Thorough-Bass, Harmony, and Composition, for Self-Instruction* [Vienna, 1826] (London, 1855).

Emily Anderson (trans and ed), rev Stanley Sadie and Fiona Smart, *The Letters of Mozart and his family* (London, 3/1989).

Claudio Annibaldi, '"The singers of the said chapel are chaplains of the pope": some remarks on the papal chapel in early modern times', *Early Music*, xxxix/1 (February 2011), pp.15-24.

Herbert Antcliffe, *The Chorusmaster* (London, [1926]).

James R. Anthony, *French Baroque Music from Beaujoyeulx to Rameau* (New York, 2/1978).

Denis Arnold and Nigel Fortune (eds), *The New Monteverdi Companion* (London, 1985).

Giovanni Maria Artusi, *L'Artusi, overa delle imperfettioni della moderna musica* (Venice, 1600).

Andrew Ashbee, *Records of English Court Music*, 9 vols. (Snodland/Aldershot, 1986-96).

Yaakov Atik, 'The conductor and the orchestra: Interactive aspects of the leadership process', *Leadership & Organization Development Journal*, xv/1 (1994), pp.22–28.

Harold Atkins and Archie Newman, *Beecham Stories* (London, 1979).

Alberto Ausoni, trans Stephen Sartarelli, *Music in Art* (Los Angeles, 2009).

Carl Philip Emanuel Bach, *Versuch über die wahre Art das Clavier zu spielen* (Berlin, 1753).

Ernst Gottlieb Baron, trans Douglas Alton Smith, *Study of the Lute* (Apros, CA, 2/2019).

Christina Bashford, *Public Chamber-Music Concerts in London, 1835-50: Aspects of History, Repertory and Reception*, PhD thesis (King's College, London, 1996).

William Bathe, *A Briefe Introduction to the Skill of Song* (London, 1600).

Jon Baxendale and Francis Knights (eds), *Will Forster's Virginal Book* (Tynset, 2023).

Amanda Bayley, 'Ethnographic Research into Contemporary String Quartet Rehearsal', *Ethnomusicology Forum*, xx/3 (December 2011), pp.385-411.

Bernard Beckerman, *Shakespeare at the Globe* (New York, 1962).

Hugh Benham, *Latin Church Music in England c.1460-1575* (London, 1977).

Joseph Bennett, 'The Conductor in Music', *The Musical Times and Singing Class Circular*, xxxvi/629 (1 July 1895), pp.437-440.

Marcelle Benoit, 'Paris, 1661-87: the Age of Lully', in Price (1993), pp.239-269.

Margaret Bent, 'Resfacta and Cantare Super Librum', *Journal of the American Musicological Society*, xxxvi (1983), pp.371-391.

Karol Berger, 'Musica Ficta', in Brown and Sadie (1989a), pp.107-125.

Hector Berlioz, trans Rachel Scott Russell Holes Holmes, *Memoirs of Hector Berlioz* (London, 1884).

Richard Bethell, *Vocal Traditions in Conflict* (Hebden Bridge, 2019).

Bonnie J. Blackburn, Edward E. Lowinsky and Clement Miller (eds), *A Correspondence of Renaissance Musicians* (Oxford, 1991).

Donald H. Boalch, rev Charles Mould, *Makers of the Harpsichord and Clavichord, 1440-1840* (Oxford, 3/1995).

Anthony Boden and Paul Hedley, *The Three Choirs Festival: A History* (Woodbridge, 2/2017).

Joe Bolger, *The disembodied voice of Early music singing*, PhD thesis (King's College London, 2021).

Susan Boynton and Eric Rice (eds), *Young Choristers 650-1700* (Woodbridge, 2008).

_____, 'Introduction: Performance and Premodern Childhood', in Boynton and Rice (2008), pp.1-18.

Roger Bowers, 'Trinity College, MS o. 3. 58', in Fenlon (1982), pp.88-90.

_____, 'University Library, Pembroke College MS 314', in Fenlon (1982), pp.103-106.

_____, 'University Library, MS Buxton 96', in Fenlon (1982), pp.114-117.

_____, 'University Library, MS Nn. Vi. 46', in Fenlon (1982), pp.118-122.

_____, 'To chorus from quartet: the performing resource for English Church Polyphony, c. 1390-1559', in Morehen (1995), pp.1-47.

_____, 'Chapel and Choir, Liturgy and Music, 1444-1644', in Massing and Zeeman (2014), pp.259-286.

Michael Bowles, *The Conductor: His Artistry and Craftsmanship* (London, 1961).

Matthew Bradley and Juliet John (eds), *Reading and the Victorians* (London, 2015).

Richard Bratby, *Refiner's Fire: The Academy of Ancient Music and the Historical Performance Revolution* (London, 2023).

Roger Bray, 'The Interpretation of Musica Ficta in English Music c.1490-c.1580', *Proceedings of the Royal Musical Association*, cxlvii (1970-1971).

_____, 'Editing and performing *musica speculativa*', in Morehen (1995), pp.48-73.

Philip Brett, ed Joseph Kerman and Davitt Moroney, *William Byrd and his contemporaries: essays and a monograph* (Berkeley, 2007).

Ursula Brett, 'The Polemics of Imperfection', *The Consort*, lxxviii (Summer 2022), pp.71-94.

Paul Broomhead, 'A Study of Instructional Strategies for Teaching Expressive Performance in the Choral Rehearsal', *Bulletin of the Council for Research in Music Education*, No.167 (Winter 2006), pp.7-20.

Sibylle Brosch and Wolfgang Pirsig, 'Stuttering in history and culture', *International Journal of Pediatric Otorhinolaryngology*, lix/2 (14 June 2001), pp.81-87.

Alan Brown (ed), *Byrd: Cantiones Sacrae I (1589)*, Byrd Edition 2 (London, 1988).

Clive Brown, *Classical and Romantic Performing Practice 1750–1900* (Oxford, 1999).

_____, 'Performing 19th Century Chamber Music: The Yawning Chasm between Contemporary Practice and Historical Evidence', *Early Music*, xxxviii/3 (2010), pp.476–480.

David Brown, *Thomas Weelkes: a Biographical and Critical Study* (London, 1969).

Howard Mayer Brown and Stanley Sadie (eds), *Performance Practice: Music before 1600* (Basingstoke, 1989a).

_____, 'Introduction', in Brown and Sadie (1989a), pp.147-169.

_____ (eds), *Performance Practice: Music after 1600* (Basingstoke, 1989b).

John Brown, *A dissertation on the rise ... and corruption of poetry and music* (London, 1763).

David L. Brunner, 'Carefully Crafting the Choral Rehearsal', *Music Educators Journal*, lxxxiii/3 (November 1996), pp.37-39.

Karen L. Bruno, 'Creativity and Artistry in the Children's Choir Rehearsal', *The Choral Journal*, lvi/8 (March 2016), pp.34-42.

Douglas D. Burman and James R. Booth, 'Music Rehearsal Increases the Perceptual Span for Notation', *Music Perception*, xxvi/4 (April 2009), pp.303-320.

Charles Burney, *The Present State of Music in Germany, The Netherlands and United Provinces* (London, 1773).

_____, ed Frank Mercer, *A General History of Music from the Earliest Ages to the Present Period*, 2 vols. (London, 1935).

_____, ed H. Edmund Poole, *Music, Men and Manners in France and Italy 1770* (London, 1974).

_____, *An Account of the Musical Performances in Westminster Abbey and the Pantheon ... in Commemoration of Handel* (London, 1785).

Shai Burstyn, 'In quest of the period ear', *Early Music*, xxv/4 (November 1997), pp.692–701.

_____, 'Pre-1600 music listening: a methodological approach', *The Musical Quarterly*, lxxxii (1998), pp.455–465

Donald Burrows, Helen Coffey, John Greenacombe and Anthony Hicks (eds), *George Frideric Handel: Collected Documents. Volume 1 1609-1725* (Cambridge, 2013).

_____ (eds), *George Frideric Handel: Collected Documents. Volume 3 1734-1742* (Cambridge, 2019).

_____ (eds), *George Frideric Handel: Collected Documents. Volume 4 1742-1750* (Cambridge, 2020).

Thomas Busby, *Concert-room and Orchestra Anecdotes* (London, 1825).

Anna Maria Busse Berger and Jesse Rodin (eds), *The Cambridge History of Fifteenth-Century Music* (Cambridge, 2015).

Charles Butler, *The Principles of Musik* (London, 1636).

Margaret R. Butler,'Time management at Turin's Teatro Regio: Galuppi's *La clemenza di Tito* and its alterations, 1759', *Early Music*, xl/2 (2012), pp.279-289.

Arthur Butterworth, 'Rehearsing and Recording' (2009), http://www.musicweb-international.com/classrev/2009/Apr09/Rehearsing_Butterworth.htm.

James L. Byo, 'Applying Score Analysis to a Rehearsal Pedagogy of Expressive Performance', *Music Educators Journal*, ci/2 (December 2014), pp.76-82.

John Byrt, 'Inequality in Alessandro Scarlatti and Handel: a sequel', *Early Music*, xl/1 (February 2012), pp.91-110.

Augusta Campagne and Elam Rotem, *Keyboard Accompaniment in Italy around 1600: Intabulations, Scores and Basso Continuo* (Basel, 2022).

Philippe Canguilhem, 'Singing upon the Book according to Vicente Lusitano', *Early Music History*, xxx (2011), pp.55–103.

_____, 'Improvisation as concept and musical practice in the fifteenth century', in Busse Berger and Rodin (2015), pp.149-163.

Elena Pons Capdevila, *Arranging the Canon: keyboard arrangements, publishing practices and the appropriation of musical classics, 1770-1810*, PhD thesis (Royal Holloway, 2017).

Neville Cardus, *Sir Thomas Beecham* (London, 1961).

Simon Carrington, 'Small ensemble rehearsal techniques for choirs of all sizes', in Quadros (2003), pp.281-291.

Adam Carse, *The Orchestra in the XVIIIth century* (Cambridge, 1940).

_____, *The Orchestra from Beethoven to Berlioz* (Cambridge, [1948]).

Mary Carruthers (ed), *Rhetoric Beyond Words: Delight and Persuasion in the Arts of the Middle Ages* (Cambridge, 2013).

Tim Carter, 'Listening to music in early modern Italy: some problems for the urban musicologist', in Knighton and Mazuela-Anguita (2018), pp.25–49.

Christine Casey and Melanie Hayes (eds), *Enriching Architecture: Craft and its conservation in Anglo-Irish building production, 1660–1760* (London, 2023).

Cristina Cassia, 'Authorship in sixteenth-century Italian printed keyboard music', in Woolley (2024), pp.32–56.

Mary Ellen Cavitt, 'Descriptive analysis of error correction in instrumental rehearsals', *Journal of Research in Music Education*, li/3 (2003), pp.218–230.

Robert Cawdrey, *A Table Alphabeticall of Hard Usual English Words* (London, 1604).

Christopher Cayari, *Virtual Vocal Ensembles and the Mediation of Performance on YouTube*, PhD disssertation (University of Illinois at Urbana-Champaign, 2016).

Michael T. Clanchy, *From Memory to Written Record: England 1066-1307* (Oxford, 2/1993).

Charles R. Chaffin, 'Perceptions of Instrumental Music Teachers regarding the Development of Effective Rehearsal Techniques', *Bulletin of the Council for Research in Music Education*, No.181 (Summer 2009), pp.21-36.

Richard Charteris, 'Jacobean Musicians at Hatfield House, 1605-1613', *Royal Musical Association Research Chronicle*, xii (1974), pp.115-136.

⎯⎯⎯⎯⎯⎯, 'Giovanni Gabrieli's *Sacrae Symphonae* (Venice, 1597); Some rediscovered partbooks with new evidence about performance practice', *Early Music*, xxiii/3 (August 1995), pp.487-498.

Geoffrey Chew, 'The Provenance and Date of the Caius and Lambeth Choir-Books', *Music & Letters*, li/2 (April 1970), pp.107-117.

Jessie Childs, *God's Traitors: Terror & Faith in Elizabethan England* (London, 2014).

Henry F. Chorley, *Music and Manners in France and Germany* (London, 1841).

Andrew Cichy, 'Lost and found: Hugh Facy', *Early Music*, xlii/1 (February 2014), pp.95-104.

Marcia J. Citron, 'Gender, Professionalism and the Musical Canon', *The Journal of Musicology*, viii/1 (Winter 1990), pp.102-117.

Nir Cohen-Shalit, 'The Romantic Conductor-Scholar: What I Learned from the Archives', in Forment (2024), pp.143-161.

Henry Coleman, *The Amateur Choir Trainer* (London, 1932).

John Conway, C. M. Kosemen, Darren Naish and Scott Hartman, *All yesterdays: unique and speculative views of dinosaurs and others prehistoric animals* (n.p., 2012).

Barry Cooper, 'Rehearsal Letters, Rhythmic Modes and Structural Issues in Beethoven's Grosse Fuge', *Nineteenth-Century Music Review*, xiv/2 (August 2017), pp.177-193.

Philip Copeland, 'Technology for the 21st-Century Choir', *The Choral Journal*, l/5 (December 2009), pp.22-30.

Harold Copeman, *Singing in Latin: Or Pronunciation Explor'd* (Oxford, 2/1996).

Thomas Coryat, *Coryat's Crudities* (London, 1611).

François Couperin, trans and ed Anna Linde, *L'art de toucher le clavecin* (Wiesbaden, [1961]).

Henry Coward, *Choral Technique and Interpretation* (London, 1914).

H. Bertram Cox and C. L. E. Cox (eds), *Leaves from the Journals of Sir George Smart* (London, 1907).

[John Edmund Cox], *Musical Recollections* (London, 1872).

Brian Crosby, 'A Service Sheet from June 1680', *The Musical Times*, lxxi/1648 (June 1980), pp.399-401.

⎯⎯⎯⎯⎯⎯, 'Private Concerts on Land and Water: The Musical Activities of the Sharp family, c.1750-c.1790', *Royal Musical Association Research Chronicle*, xxxiv (2001), pp.1-118

Graham Cummings, 'Handel's Compositional Methods in His London Operas of the 1730s, and the Unusual Case of "Poro, Rè dell'Indie" (1731)', *Music & Letters*, lxxix/3 (August 1998), pp.346-367.

Gareth R. K. Curtis, 'Brussels, Bibliothèque Royale MS. 5557, and the Texting of Dufay's "Ecce ancilla Domini" and "Ave regina celorum" Masses', *Acta Musicologica*, li/1 (January-June 1979), pp.73-86.

Rebecca Cypess, '"It Would Be without Error": Automated Technology and the Pursuit of Correct Performance in the French Enlightenment', *Journal of the Royal Musical Association*, cxlii/1 (2017), pp.1-29.

João Pedro d'Alvarenga, 'On performing practices in mid- to late 16th-century Portuguese church music: the "cappella" of Évora Cathedral', *Early Music*, xliii/1 (February 2015), pp.3-21.

Veronica J. Dark and Geoffrey R. Loftus, 'The role of rehearsal in long-term memory performance', *Journal of Verbal Learning & Verbal Behavior*, xv/4 (1976), pp.479–490.

Thurston Dart, 'Bononcini sets Handel a Test', *The Musical Times*, cxii/1538 (April 1971), pp.324-325.

Hans T. David and Arthur Mendel (eds), rev Christoph Wolff, *The New Bach Reader* (New York, 1998).

Karel Davids, 'Craft Secrecy in Europe in the Early Modern Period: A Comparative View', *Early Science and Medicine*, x/3 (2005), pp.341-348.

Jane W. Davidson and James Good, 'Social and Musical Co-ordination Between Members of a String Quartet: An Exploratory Study', *Psychology of Music*, xxx (2002), pp.186-201.

Jean Charles Davillier, *L'Espagne* (Paris, 1874).

Ruth I. DeFord, *Tactus, Mensuration, and Rhythm in Renaissance Music* (Cambridge, 2015).

Mark Delaere and Pieter Bergé (eds), *'Recevez ce mien petit labeur': studies in Renaissance music in honour of Ignace Bossuyt* (Leuven, 2008).

Julia A. M. Delius and Viktor Müller, 'Interpersonal synchrony when singing in a choir', *Frontiers in Psychology*, 13:1087517 (2023).

Denis Diderot, trans Kate E. Tunstall and Caroline Warman, *Rameau's Nephew/Le Neveu de Rameau* (Cambridge, 2/2016).

Graham Dixon, 'The performance of Palestrina: Some questions, but fewer answers', *Early Music*, xxii/4 (November 1994), pp.666–676.

Robert Donington, *The Interpretation of Music* (London, 1989).

Alfred Dörffel, *Geschichte der Gewandhaus Concerte zu Leipzig* (Leipzig, 1884).

Luke Dollman, 'A gulf of difference: conducting pedagogues Ilya Musin and Jorma Panula', *The Musical Times*, clvii/1936 (Autumn 2016), pp.63-74.

Kevin L. Droe, 'The Effect of Teacher Approval and Disapproval of Music Performed in a Rehearsal Setting on Music Preferences', *Journal of Research in Music Education*, lvi/3 (October 2008), pp.267-278.

George Duborg, *The Violin: Some Account of that Leading Instrument and its most Eminent Professors* (London, 4/1852).

Jessica Duchen, 'Who needs a conductor?', *Sunday Times*, Culture magazine (16 July 2023).

Sandrine Dumont, 'Choirboys and *Vicaires* in the Maîtrise of Cambrai: a socio-anthropological study (1550-1670)' in Boynton and Rice (2008), pp.146-162.

Dennis Duncan, *Index, A History of the* (London, 2021).

Alfred Dürr, 'Performance Practice of Bach's Cantatas', *American Choral Review*, xxix/3-4 (Summer and Fall 1987), pp.25-34.

Alfred Dürr and Traute M. Marshall, 'De vita cum imperfectis', *Bach*, lii/2 (2021), pp.212-225.

Hermann Erler, *Robert Schumanns Leben* (Berlin, 1887).

[Frederick George Edwards] 'Dotted Crotchet', 'Winchester College. Seinte Marie College of Wynchestre', *The Musical Times*, xlv/736 (1 June 1904), pp.360-369.

H. Sutherland Edwards, *Life of Rossini* (London, 1869).

Wilhelm Ehmann, 'Performance Practice of Bach's Motets', *American Choral Review*, xxix/3-4 (Summer and Fall 1987), pp.5-24.

Cliff Eisen, *New Mozart Documents* (London, 1991).

Simon Eliot, 'Reading by Artificial Light in the Victorian Age', in Bradley and John (2015), pp.15-30.

John Ella, *Musical Sketches* (London, 1878).

Henry Ellis (ed), *Original Letters, illustrative of English History* (London, 1824).

Thomas Elyot, *The Book Named the Governor* (London, 1531).

Kathryn Emerson, *The social organisation of the choir rehearsal: How interaction between conductor and choir is used to shape the choir's singing*, PhD thesis (University of Sheffield, 2018).

Dinko Fabris and Michela Grossi (eds), *Prove d'orchestra - Nino Rota e la sua musica da concerto* (Barletta, 2025).

Robert Fahrner and William Kleb, 'The Theatrical Activity of Gianlorenzo Bernini', *Educational Theatre Journal*, xxv/1 (March 1973), pp.5-14.

Edmund Fellowes, *Memoirs of an Amateur Musician* (London, 1946).

Iain Fenlon (ed), *Music in Medieval and Early Modern Europe: Patronage, Sources and Texts* (Cambridge, 1981).

———— (ed), *Cambridge Music Manuscripts 900-1700* (Cambridge, 1982).

————, 'King's College, MS Rowe 1', in Fenlon (1982), pp.137-139.

Ernest Ferand, 'Improvised Vocal Counterpoint in the Late Renaissance and Early Baroque', *Annales Musicologiques*, iv (1956), pp.129-174.

Jane Flynn, 'The education of choristers in England during the sixteenth century', in Morehen (1995), pp.180-220.

David Force, 'A Holding, Uniting-Constant Friend': The Organ in Seventeenth-Century English Domestic Music*, PhD thesis (The Open University, 2019).

Bruno Forment, 'An enigmatic souvenir of Venetian opera: Alessandro Piazza's "Teatro" (1702)', *Early Music*, xxxviii/3 (August 2010), pp.387-401.

———— (ed), *Performing by the Book? Musical Negotiations between Text and Act* (Leuven, 2024).

David Fuller, 'An Introduction to Automatic Instruments', *Early Music*, xi/2 (April 1983), pp.164-166.

Janet Galván and Matthew Clauhs, 'The virtual choir as collaboration', *The Choral Journal*, lxi/3 (October 2020), pp.8-19.

Martin Geck and Alfred Mann, 'Bach's art of church music and his Leipzig performance forces: contradictions in the system', *Early Music*, xxi/4 (November 2003), pp.558-571.

Peter Giles, *The History and Technique of the Counter-Tenor* (Aldershot, 1994).

Paul Glennie and Nigel Thrift, *Shaping the Day: A History of Timekeeping in England and Wales, 1300-1800* (London, 2011).

Elizabeth Gibson, 'Italian Opera in London, 1750-1775: management and finances', *Early Music*, xviii/1 (February 1990), pp.47-62.

Sebastian Giustinian, trans Rawdon Brown, *Four Years at the Court of Henry VIII* (London, 1854).

Jonathan Glixon, 'Music at the Venetian Scuole Grandi, 1440-1540', in Fenlon (1981), pp.193-226.

_____, '*Far il buon concerto*: Music at the Venetian Scuole Piccole in the Seventeenth Century', *Journal of Seventeenth Century Music*, i/1 (1995), section 3.4.

Ruth Goodman, *How to be a Tudor* (London, 2016).

Dana Gooley, *Fantasies of Improvisation: Free Playing in Nineteenth-Century Music* (Oxford, 2018).

Thomas W. Goolsby, 'Eye Movement in Music Reading: Effects of Reading Ability, Notational Complexity, and Encounters', *Music Perception*, xii/1 (Fall 1994), pp.77-96.

_____, 'Time use in instrumental rehearsals: A comparison of experienced, novice, and student teachers', *Journal of Research in Music Education*, 44 (1996), pp.286-303

Stewart Gordon, *Mastering the Art of Performance* (Oxford, 2006).

Brian Gorelick, 'Planning the Perfect Choral Rehearsal', *Music Educators Journal*, lxxxviii/3 (November 2001), pp.28-33 and 60.

Harvey Grace, *Choral Training and Conducting* (London, [1938]).

K. Dawn Grapes, *Dowland* (Oxford, 2024).

James Grassineau, *A Musical Dictionary. being a collection of terms and characters, As well Ancient as Modern. Including the Historical, Theoretical, and practical Parts of Music* (London, 1740).

John Griffiths and Sigrid Wirth (eds), *Teaching & Studying the Lute* (n.p., 2022).

Massimiliano Guido (ed), *Studies in historical improvisation: from* Cantare super librum *to* Partimenti (London, 2019).

James Orchard Halliwell (ed), *The Moral Play of Wit and Science, and Early Poetical Miscellanies* (London, 1848).

Kyle J. Hanson, 'A Rehearsal Refresher', *The Choral Journal*, lviii/10 (May 2018), pp.49-58.

John Harley, *William Byrd: Gentleman of the Chapel Royal* (Aldershot, 1999).

Nikolaus Harnoncourt, trans Mary O'Neill, *Baroque Music Today: Music as Speech* (Portland, 1988)

Sally Harper, *Music in Welsh Culture before 1650: A Study of the Principal Sources* (London, 2007).

John Hart, *An Ortographie, conteynyng the due order and reason, howe to write or paint thimage of mannes voice, most like to the life or nature* (London, 1569).

David G. T. Harris, 'Musical Education in Tudor Times (1485-1603)', *Proceedings of the Musical Association*, 65th session (1938-1939), pp.109-139.

Ellen T. Harris, 'Voices', in Brown and Sadie (1989), pp.97-116.

Frank Ll. Harrison, *Music in Medieval Britain* (London, 2/1963).

Leslie P. Hartley, *The Go-Between* (London, 1953).

Gary W. Harwood and Gregory W. Harwood, 'Robert Schumann's Choice of Repertory & Rehearsal Planning in his Career as a Choral Conductor', *The Choral Journal*, li/2 (September 2010), pp.32-39, 42-51.

Moritz Hauptmann, *Briefe von Moritz Hauptmann an Franz Hauser* (Leipzig, 1871).

_____, *Aus der Musikerwelt* (Berlin, 1875).

Sam Hayden and Luke Windsor. 'Collaboration and the Composer: Case Studies from the End of the 20th Century', *Tempo*, lxi:240 (2007), pp.28-39.

Bruce Haynes, *A History of Performing Pitch: The Story of A* (Lanham ML and Oxford, 2002).

_____, *The End of Early Music* (New York, 2007).

Karen Heenan, *A Wider World* (n.p., 2021).

Stephen Hefling, *Rhythmic Alteration in Seventeenth- and Eighteenth-Century Music* (New York, 1993).

Trevor Herbert and Helen Barlow, *Music and the British Military in the Long Nineteenth Century* (New York, 2013).

Rebecca Herissone, *'To fill, forbear, or adorne': The Organ Accompaniment of Restoration Sacred Music* (Aldershot, 2006).

Val Hicks, 'Attention, Effort and Motivation in Rehearsal and Performance', *The Choral Journal*, xxvi/10 (May 1986), pp.11-16.

John Walter Hill, 'Florence: Musical Spectacle and Drama, 1570-1650', in Price (1993), pp.121-145.

Ferdinand Hiller, 'Ueber das Auswendig-Dirigiren', in *Musikalisches und Persönliches* (Leipzig, 1876).

Joy Hirokawa, 'Teaching Vocal Technique in the Choral Rehearsal', *The Choral Journal*, lvi/4 (November 2015), pp.73-77.

R. Gerald Hobbs and Annie Noblesse-Rocher (eds), *Bible, Histoire et Société: Mélanges offerts a Bernard Roussel* (Turnhout, 2013).

Christopher Hogwood, *Haydn's visits to England* (London, 1980).

Claire Holden, Eric F. Clarke and Cayenna Ponchione-Bailey (eds), *Practice in Context: Historically Informed Practices in Nineteenth-Century Instrumental Music* (Oxford, 2025).

Peter Holman, *Four and Twenty Fiddlers: the violin at the English court, 1540-1690* (Oxford, 1995).

_____, *Before the Baton: Musical Direction and Conducting in Stuart and Georgian Britain* (Woodbridge, 2020).

Imogen Holst, *Conducting a Choir: A Guide for Amateurs* (London, 1973).

Anselm Hughes, *Catalogue of the Musical Manuscripts at Peterhouse Cambridge* (Cambridge, 1953).

Arthur Hughes, Peter Trudgill and Dominic Watt, *English accents and dialects: An introduction to social and regional varieties of English in the British Isles* (London, 5/2012).

John Hunt, *Philharmonic autocrat: the discography of Herbert von Karajan (1908-1989)* (London, 4/2016).

David Ross Hurley, 'Handel's Recomposed Return Arias and Romantic Attraction in Alexander Balus', *Journal of the American Musicological Society*, lxix/3 (Fall 2016), pp.651-698.

David R. M. Irving, *Colonial Counterpoint: Music in Early Modern Manila* (Oxford, 2010).

_____, 'Lully in Siam: music and diplomacy in French-Siamese cultural exchanges, 1680-1690', *Early Music*, xl/3 (August 2012), pp.393-420.

———, *The Making of European Music in the Long Eighteenth Century* (Oxford, 2024).

Stuart Jenks (ed), 'The London Customs Accounts', *Hansischer Geschichtsverein* Lübeck, lxxiv (2016-2023), 45 vols.

Beverly Jerold, 'Why Most *a cappella* Music Could Not Have Been Sung Unaccompanied', *The Choral Journal*, xl/7 (February 2000), pp.21-27.

———, 'A Re-Examination of Tempos Assigned to the Earl of Bute's Machine Organ', *Early Music*, xxx/4 (November 2002), pp.584-591.

———, 'Fontenelle's Famous Question and Performance Standards of the Day', *College Music Symposium*, xliii (2003), pp.150-160.

———, 'Fasch and the Beginning of Modern Artistic Choral Singing', *Bach*, xxxv/1 (2004), pp.61-86.

———, 'Bach's Lament about Leipzig's Professional Instrumentalists', *Bach*, xxxvi/1 (2005), pp.67-96.

———, 'Choral Singing before the Era of Recording', *The Musical Times*, cxlvii/1895 (Summer 2006), pp.77-84.

———, 'Intonation Standards and Equal Temperament', *Dutch Journal of Music Theory*, xii/2 (May 2007), pp.215-227.

Ann Howard Jones, 'A point of departure for rehearsal preparation and planning', in Quadros (2003), pp.272-280.

James H. Johnson, *Listening in Paris: a cultural history* (Berkeley, 1995).

Andrew Johnstone, '"As it was in the Beginning": Organ and Choir Pitch in Early Anglican Church Music', *Early Music*, xxxi/4 (November 2003), pp.506-525.

Benjamin Jowett (trans), *The dialogues of Plato* (Oxford, 3/1892).

Youyoung Kang, 'Monteverdi's Early Seventeenth-Century "Harmonic Progressions"', *Music Analysis*, xxx/2-3 (July-October 2011), pp.186-217.

Julius Kapp, *Geschichte der Staatsoper Berlin* (Berlin, 1937).

Nicholas Kenyon, *The Life of Music* (New Haven and London, 2021).

Daniel J. Koury, *Orchestral Performance Practices in the Nineteenth Century: Size, Proportions, and Seating* (Rochester, NY, 1986).

Adolph Kielblock, *The Stage Fright or How to Face an Audience* (Boston, 1891).

Andrew Kirkman, *Music and Musicians at the Collegiate Church of St-Omer: Crucible of Song, 1350-1550* (Cambridge, 2020).

Hermann Klein, *Thirty Years of Musical Life in London (1870-1900)* (London, 1903).

———, *The Golden Age of Opera* (London, 1933)

J. Merrill Knapp, 'Handel's *Tamerlano*: The Creation of an Opera', *The Musical Quarterly*, lvi/3 (July 1970), pp.405-430.

David Knight, *The organs of Westminster Abbey and their music, 1240-1908*, PhD thesis (King's College, London, 2001).

Tess Knighton and David Fallows (eds), *Companion to Medieval and Renaissance Music* (London, 1992).

Tess Knighton and Ascensión Mazuela-Anguita (eds), *Hearing the city in early modern Europe* (Turnhout, 2018).

Francis Knights, 'Zechariah Buck of Norwich', *The Musical Times*, cxxxi/1764 (February 1990), pp.107-109.

_____, 'John Richardson's Cathedral Tour of 1869', *The Organ*, lxix/272 (Spring 1990), pp.8-12.

_____, 'A Restoration Version of Gibbons' Short Service', *Organists' Review*, lxxvi: 271 (June 1990a), pp.97-100

_____, 'Magdalen College MS 347: An Index and Commentary', *Journal of the British Institute of Organ Studies*, xiv (1990b), pp.4-9.

_____, 'The Choral Foundation of Corpus Christi College, Oxford', *The Organ*, lxx/275 (Winter 1991), pp.10-14.

_____, 'The historic chapel music manuscripts at Trinity', *Trinity College Annual Report* (2007), pp.55-59.

_____, 'Observations on two 16th century music manuscripts belonging to Sir John Petre', *The Consort*, lxxv (Summer 2019), pp.22-41.

_____, 'Guidelines for the systematic evaluation of early music theorists', *National Early Music Association Newsletter*, iii/2 (Autumn 2019), pp.44-49.

_____, 'J. S. Bach's keyboard works: from performance to research', *Muzikologija*, xxxi (2021), pp.161-180.

_____, 'Thomas Wilson, *Organista Petrensis*', *Early Music Performer*, l (April 2022), pp.16-29.

_____, 'Bach's *Orgelbüchlein* as a keyboard tutor', *National Early Music Association Newsletter*, vii/1 (Spring 2023), pp.21-34.

_____, 'A Register of British keyboard makers, composers, copyists and players, c.660-1630', *National Early Music Association Newsletter*, vii/2 (Autumn 2023), pp.25-108.

Francis Knights and Pablo Padilla, 'Issues in the Historical Performance from Renaissance Choirbooks', *National Early Music Association Newsletter*, viii/2 (Autumn 2024), pp.15-66.

_____, *Formal Methods in Musicology: Models and Computation* (Newcastle, 2025).

Francis Knights, Pablo Padilla and Mateo Rodríguez, '*O Splendor gloriae*: Taverner or Tye?', *Early Music*, xlix/4 (November 2021), pp.565-578.

David Knowles, *The Religious Orders in England: Volume III, The Tudor Age* (Cambridge, 1971).

Heinrich Christoph Koch, 'Kapellmeister', *Musikalisches Lexikon* (Frankfurt am Main, 1802).

Niina Koivunen and Grete Wennes, '"Show us the sound!" Aesthetic leadership of symphony orchestra conductors', *Leadership*, vii/1 (2011), pp.51–71.

Anu Konttinen, 'Conductor education in Finland', *Finnish Musical Quarterly*, iii (2006).

_____, *Conducting gestures: institutional and educational construction of conductorship in Finland, 1973–1993*, dissertation (University of Helsinki, 2008).

H. C. Robbins Landon (ed), *The Collected Correspondence and London Notebooks of Joseph Haydn* (London, 1959).

———, 'The Operas of Haydn', *New Oxford History of Music*, vii (Oxford, 1973), pp.172–199.

Elke B. Lange, Diana Omigie, Carlos Trenado, Viktor Müller, Melanie Wald-Fuhrmann and Julia Merrill, 'In touch: Cardiac and respiratory patterns synchronize during ensemble singing with physical contact', *Frontiers in Human Neuroscience*, 16:928563 (2022).

Colin Lawson (ed), *The Cambridge Companion to the Orchestra* (Cambridge, 2003).

Elizabeth Eva Leach, 'Nature's forge and mechanical production: Writing, reading and performing song', in Carruthers (2013), pp.72-95.

Norman Lebrecht, *Mahler Remembered* (London, 1987).

———, *The Maestro Myth* (New York, 2/2001).

Peter Le Huray, *Music and the Reformation in England, 1549-1660* (London, 1967).

Simon Leipold, Carina Klein and Lutz Jäncke, 'Musical Expertise Shapes Functional and Structural Brain Networks Independent of Absolute Pitch Ability', *The Journal of Neuroscience*, xli/11 (17 March 2021), pp.2496-2511.

Raymond Leppard, 'Music and the conductor', *Journal of the Royal Society of Arts*, cxxi/5207 (October 1973), pp.707-716.

Joseph Lewis, *Conducting without fears* (London, 1945).

Jean Lionnet, 'Performance Practice in the Papal Chapel during the 17th Century', *Early Music*, xv/1 (February 1987), pp.3-15.

Lewis Lockwood, 'Strategies of music patronage in the fifteenth century: the *capella* of Ercole I d'Este', in Fenlon (1981), pp.227-248.

Edward E. Lowinsky, 'On the Use of Scores by Sixteenth-Century Musicians', *Journal of the American Musicological Society*, i/1 (Spring 1948), pp.17-23.

Thomas Lloyd, 'When the Orchestra Arrives', *The Choral Journal*, xl/5 (December 1999), pp.35-46.

John Lumley and Nigel Stringthorpe, *The Art of Conducting* (London, 1989).

Thomas Mace, *Musick's Monument, or a Remembrancer of the best Practical Musick...* (London, 1676).

Laurie E. Maguire, *Shakespearean suspect texts: The 'bad' quartos and their contexts* (Cambridge, 1996).

Alma Mahler, trans Basil Creighton, *Gustav Mahler: Memories and Letters* (London, 1946).

John Mainwaring, *Memoirs of the Life of George Frederic Handel* (London, 1760).

Philip Marr, *The Life and Works of John Alcock (1715–1806)*, PhD thesis (University of Reading, 1978).

Robert Marsden, *Inside the Rehearsal Room: Process, Collaboration and Decision-making* (London, 2022).

Christopher Marsh, *Music and Society in Early Modern England* (Cambridge, 2010).

C. W. Marshall, '"Alcestis" and the Ancient Rehearsal Process ("P. Oxy." 4546)', *Arion*, Third Series, xi/3 (Winter 2004), pp.27-45.

Edward J. Marshall, *Do choirs have accents? A sociophonetic investigation of choral sound*, PhD thesis (University of Glasgow, 2023).

Edward J. Marshall, Jane Stuart-Smith, John Butt and Timothy Dean, 'Variation and change over time in British choral singing (1925–2019)', *Laboratory Phonology: Journal of the Association for Laboratory Phonology*, xv/1 (2024), pp.1-39.

Jean Michel Massing and Nicolette Zeeman (eds), *King's College Chapel 1515-2015: Art, Music and Religion in Cambridge* (London, 2014).

Raluca Matei and Jane Ginsborg, 'Music performance anxiety in classical musicians – what we know about what works', *BJPsych International*, xiv/2 (May 2017), pp.33-35.

Michael Maul, trans Richard Howe, *Bach's famous choir: the Saint Thomas School in Leipzig, 1212-1804* (Woodbridge, 2018).

Marcello Mazzetti (ed), *Basso Continuo in Italy: Sources, Pedagogy and Performance* (Turnhout, 2023).

Harry R. McCarthy, *Boy actors in early modern England: skill and stagecraft in the theatre* (Cambridge, 2022).

Timothy J. McGee, *Medieval and Renaissance Music: A Performer's Guide* (Aldershot, 1990).

Gary E. McPherson, 'Factors and Abilities Influencing Sightreading Skill in Music', *Journal of Research in Music Education*, xlii/3 (Autumn, 1994), pp.217-231.

John C. Meagher, *Pursuing Shakespeare's Dramaturgy: Some Contexts, Resources, and Strategies in His Playmaking* (Madison and Teaneck, NJ, 2003).

Nancy Meckler, *Notes from the Rehearsal Room* (London, 2023).

John Merbecke, *The Booke of Common Praier noted* (London, 1550).

Judith Milhous, 'Lighting at the King's Theatre, Haymarket, 1780–82', *Theatre Research International*, xvi/3 (1991), pp.215-236.

Judith Milhous and Robert D. Hume: 'A Prompt Copy of Handel's *Radamisto*', *The Musical Times*, cxxvii/1719 (1986), pp.316–321.

David Milsom, 'Mendelssohn and the Orchestra', in Reichwald (2008), pp.85–100.

John Milsom, 'Sacred songs in the chamber', in Morehen (1995), pp.161-179.

_____, 'Notes from an erasable tablet', in Delaere and Bergé (2008), pp.195-210.

Jennifer Mishra, 'A Century of Memorization Pedagogy', *Journal of Historical Research in Music Education*, xxxii/1 (October 2010), pp.3-18.

Nicholas Mitchell, 'Choral and Instrumental Pitch in Church Music 1570-1620', *The Galpin Society Journal*, xlviii (March 1995), pp.13-32.

Jean-Paul C. Montagnier (ed), *The Polyphonic Mass in France, 1600–1780: The Evidence of the Printed Choirbooks* (Cambridge, 2017).

_____, 'Choirbooks and Musical Practice', in Montagnier (2017), pp.34-66.

John Morehen, 'Ornaments in organ scores' (unpublished essay, c.1968).

_____ (ed), *English Choral Practice, 1400-1650* (Cambridge, 1995)

_____, 'The "burden of proof": the editor as detective' in Morehen (1995), pp.200-220.

Thomas Morley, *A Plaine and Easie Introduction to Practicall Musicke* (London, 1597).

Alan Mould, *The English Chorister: A History* (London, 2007).

Kenneth C. Murray, 'Effective Rehearsal Time: What Research Has to Offer', *The Choral Journal*, xx/5 (January 1980), pp.11-13.

Thomas Neal, 'Between Practice and Print: Performing Palestrina's *Missarum liber quartus* (1582) with Alessandro Nuvoloni's *Basso principale co'l soprano* (1610)', in Mazzetti (2023), pp.105-139.

Jennifer Nevile (ed), *Dance, Spectacle and the Body Politick, 1250-1750* (Bloomington, 2008).

———, '"I had to fight with the painters, master carpenters, actors, musicians and the dancers": rehearsals, performance problems and audience reaction in Renaissance spectacles', *National Early Music Association Newsletter*, vi/1 (Spring 2022), pp.7-25.

Seishiro Niwa, '"Madama" Margaret of Parma's patronage of music', *Early Music*, xxxiii/1 (February 2005), pp.25–38.

Caitlin Nolan, *Music of the Paston Household: Case Studies of Circulation and Adaptation in the Lutebook GB-Lbl Add. MS 29247*, PhD thesis (Newcastle University, 2023).

Michael Noone and Graeme Skinner, 'Toledo Cathedral's Collection of Manuscript Plainsong Choirbooks: A Preliminary Report and Checklist', *Notes*, Second Series, lxiii/2 (December 2006), pp.289-328.

Marten Noorduin, 'The Rehearsal Practices of the London Philharmonic in the Early to Mid-Nineteenth Century', in Holden, Clarke and Ponchione-Bailey (2025), pp.66-83.

John Norman, *Box of Whistles: The History and Recent Development of Organ Case Design* (London, 2007).

Grant O'Brien, *Ruckers: A harpsichord and virginal building tradition* (Cambridge, 1990).

Pat O'Brien, 'Just how secret were those Muses?', *Lute Society of America Quarterly*, xlii/1 (2007), pp.11-14.

Paul O'Dette, 'Teaching Historical Lute Technique in the 21st Century: Exceptions to the Normal Rules of Renaissance Lute Fingering', in Griffiths and Wirth (2022), pp.23-42.

Eamonn O'Keeffe, *Musical Warriors: British Military Music and Musicians during the French Revolutionary and Napoleonic Wars*, DPhil thesis (University of Oxford, 2022).

———, 'Military music and society during the French wars, 1793–1815', *Historical Research*, xcvii (2024), pp.108–128.

Mary Oleskiewicz, 'The Flutes of Quantz: Their Construction and Performing Practice', *The Galpin Society Journal*, liii (April 2000), pp.201-220.

Adriana Olmos, Nicolas Bouillot, Trevor Knight, Nordhal Mabire, Josh Redel and Jeremy R. Cooperstock, 'A High-Fidelity Orchestra Simulator for Individual Musicians' Practice', *Computer Music Journal*, xxxvi/2 (Summer 2012), pp.55-73.

Greta Olson, 'Required early seventeenth-century performance practices at the Colegio-Seminario de Corpus Christi, Valencia', *Studies in Music*, xxi (1987), pp.10–38.

Arthur W. J. G. Ord-Hume, *Clockwork music: an illustrated history of mechanical musical instruments from the musical box to the pianola, from automaton lady virginal players to orchestrion* (London, 1973).

Noel O'Regan, 'The performance of Palestrina: some further observations', *Early Music*, xxiv/1 (February 1996), pp.144–156.

———, 'Choirboys in Early Modern Rome', in Boynton and Rice (2008), pp.216-240.

Ateş Orga, *The Proms* (London, 1975).

Nicholas Orme, *Tudor Children* (New Haven and London, 2023).

Richard Osborne, *Herbert von Karajan: A Life in Music* (Boston, 2000).

Jessie Ann Owens, *Composers at Work: the craft of musical composition* (New York, 1997).

Simon Palfrey and Tiffany Stern, *Shakespeare in Parts* (Oxford, 2010).

Claude V. Palisca, *The Florentine Camerata: Documentary Studies and Translations* (New Haven, 1989).

Vincent J. Panetta, jr (trans and ed), *Treatise on Harpsichord Tuning by Jean Denis* (Cambridge, 1987).

Christopher Page, *Discarding images: reflections on music and culture in medieval France* (Oxford, 1993).

William Thomas Parke, *Musical Memoirs* (London, 1830).

Andrew Parrott, 'Rehearsal time', in Thomson (1978), pp.34-37.

_____, *The essential Bach choir* (Woodbridge, 2000).

_____, *Composers' Intentions? Lost Traditions of Musical Performance* (Woodbridge, 2015).

_____, *The Pursuit of Musicke: Musical Life in Original Writings & Art* (n.p., 2022).

Caitlin Parry, 'The Institutional decline of music in Wales between c.1567 and c.1760', *National Early Music Association Newsletter*, viii/2 (Autumn 2024), pp.67-83.

Lewis Emanuel Peterman, 'Michel Blavet's Breathing Marks: A Rare Source for Musical Phrasing in Eighteenth-Century France', *Performance Practice Review*, iv/2 (Fall 1991), article 4.

Johann Samuel Petri, *Anleitung zur praktischen Music* (Leipzig, 2/1782).

Stephen J. Pettitt, *Philharmonia Orchestra: A Record of Achievement* (London, 1985).

R. Hans Phaf and Gezinus Wolters, 'Attentional Shifts in Maintenance Rehearsal', *The American Journal of Psychology*, cvi/3 (Autumn 1993), pp.353-382.

Robert Philip, *Performing music in the age of recording* (New Haven, 2004).

Venceslaus Philomathes, *Musicorum libri quattuor* (Vienna, 1512).

Ken Pierce, 'Choreographic Structure in Baroque Dance', in Nevile (2008), pp.182-208.

Klaus Pietschmann and James Steichen, 'Musical institutions in the fifteenth century and their political contexts', in Busse Berger and Rodin (2015).

Alejandro Enrique Planchart, 'Choirboys at Cambrai in the Fifteenth Century', in Boynton and Rice (2008), pp.123-145.

Irene Plant, *Ancient Drama: Stagecraft and Signcraft*, PhD thesis (King's College, London, 1999).

Barbara Pollack and Harriet Simons, 'The Psychologist and the Conductor: Solving Rehearsal Problems Using Awareness of Personality Types', *The Choral Journal*, xxxvi/10 (May 1996), pp.9-16.

Cayenna Ponchione-Bailey and Eric F. Clarke, 'Digital Methods for the Study of the Nineteenth-Century Orchestra', *Nineteenth-Century Music Review*, xviii (2021), pp.19-50.

_____, 'Technologies for investigating large ensemble performance', in Timmers, Bailes and Daffern (2022), pp.119-128.

Robert Ponsonby, 'The Art of the Conductor: Pierre Boulez in Conversation', *Tempo*, lxii/243 (January 2008), pp.2-15.

Pamela L. Poulin, 'A View of Eighteenth-Century Musical Life and Training: Anton Stadler's "Musick Plan"', *Music & Letters*, lxxi/2 (May 1990), pp.215-224.

Ferdinand Praeger, *Wagner as I knew him* (London, 1892).

Peter Prelleur, *The Modern Musick-Master, or The Universal Musician* (London, 2/1731).

Curtis Price (ed), *The Early Baroque Era* (Basingstoke, 1993).

David Price, *Patrons and musicians of the English Renaissance* (Cambridge, 1981).

Humphrey Proctor-Gregg, *Beecham Remembered* (London, 1976).

Lee Prosser, 'Experiments with historic light in Kensington Palace's early eighteenth-century interiors', in Casey and Hayes (2023), pp.138-159.

André de Quadros (ed), *The Cambridge Companion to Choral Music* (Cambridge, 2012).

Johann Joachim Quantz, trans Edward R. Reilly, *On Playing the Flute* (London, 1966).

François Raguenet, trans Johann Galliard, *A comparison between the French and Italian musick and opera's. Translated from the French; with some remarks. To which is added A critical discourse upon opera's in England, and a means proposed for their improvement* (London, 1709).

Siegwart Reichwald (ed), *Mendelssohn in Performance* (Bloomington, 2008).

Charles Reid, *Thomas Beecham* (London, 1961).

Edward R. Reilly, 'Quantz and the Transverse Flute: Some Aspects of His Practice and Thought regarding the Instrument', *Early Music*, xxv/3 (August 1997), pp.428-438.

Gordon Reynolds, *The Choirmaster in action* (London, 1972).

Thomas William Reynolds, *A Study of Music and Liturgy: choirs and organs in monastic and secular foundations in Wales and the borderlands, 1486-1645*, PhD thesis (Bangor University, 2002).

A. Madeley Richardson, *Choir Training based on Voice Production* (London, [1899]).

David Richman, 'The King Lear Quarto In Rehearsal and Performance', *Shakespeare Quarterly*, xxxvii/3 (Autumn 1986), pp.374-382.

Felix Richter, 'The Rise and Fall of the Compact Disc' (17 August 2022), https://www.statista.com/chart/12950/cd-sales-in-the-us.

Michael F. Robinson, *Opera before Mozart* (London, 3/1978).

Michael Scott Rohan (ed), *The Classical Video Guide* (London, 1994).

Romain Rolland, *Adelphi Collected Works of Romain Rolland* (2020).

Ellen Rosand, 'Venice 1580-1680', in Price (1993), pp.75-102.

John Rosselli, 'The Castrati as a Professional Group and a Social Phenomenon, 1550-1850', *Acta Musicologica*, lx/2 (May-August 1988), pp.143-179.

Mireya Royo, *La Capilla del Colegio del Patriarca: vida musical y pervivencia de las Danzas del Corpus de Juan Bautista Comes (1603–1706)*, PhD thesis (University of Oviedo, 2015).

_____, 'Instruments in the liturgy of the Real Colegio Seminario de Corpus Christi, València, in the 17th century', *Early Music*, xlix/1 (February 2021), pp.35–48.

Katherine Rundell, *Super-Infinite: The Transformations of John Donne* (London, 2022).

Dolly Rutherford (trans), *Rachmaninov's recollections, told to Oskar von Reisemann* (London, 1934).

Raymond Russell, rev Howard Schott, *The Harpsichord and Clavichord* (London, 2/1973).

Stanley Sadie and Neal Zaslaw, *Mozart: The Early Years 1756-1781* (Oxford, 2006).

Walter Salmen (ed), trans Herbert Kaufman and Barbara Reisner, *The Social Status of the Professional Musician* (New York, 1983).

James Saunders, *English Cathedral Choirs and Choirmen, 1558 to the Civil War: An Occupational Study*, PhD thesis (University of Cambridge, 1997).

Roger Savage and Matteo Sansone, '*Il Corago* and the staging of early opera: four chapters from an anonymous treatise *circa* 1630', *Early Music*, xvii/4 (November 1989), pp.495-511.

David G. Schaal, 'The English Background of American Rehearsal-Direction Practices in the Eighteenth Century', *Educational Theatre Journal*, xii/4 (December 1960), pp.262-269.

Anton Schindler, trans Ignaz Moscheles, *Life of Beethoven* (London, 1841).

Harold C. Schonberg, *The Great Conductors* (London, 1977).

Floris Schuiling, '(Re-)Assembling Notations in the Performance of Early Music', *Contemporary Music Review*, xxxix/5 (2020), pp.580-601.

Robert Schumann, trans Fanny Raymond Ritter, *Music and Musicians* (London, 1891).

Heinrich W. Schwab, 'The Social Status of the Town Musician', in Salmen (1983), pp.33-59.

Christopher Seaman, *Inside Conducting* (Rochester, NY, 2013).

Ephraim Segerman, 'Tempo and tactus after 1500', in Knighton and Fallows (1992), pp.337-344.

_____, 'A re-examination of the evidence on absolute tempo before 1700', *Early Music*, xxiv/2 (May 1996), pp.227-249.

_____, 'A re-examination of the evidence on absolute tempo before 1700', *Early Music*, xxiv/4 (November 1996), pp.681-690.

Justine Sergent, Eric Zuck, Sean Terriah and Brennan MacDonald, 'Distributed Neural Network Underlying Musical Sight-Reading and Keyboard', *Science*, New Series, xxlvii/5066 (3 July 1992), pp.106-109.

William Shakespeare, *Troilus and Cressida* (London, 1609).

Tim Shephard, 'The Studiolo, Identity, and Music', in *Echoing Helicon: Music, Art and Identity in the Este Studioli, 1440-1530* (2014), pp.4-29.

Richard Sherr, *Music and Musicians in Renaissance Rome and Other Courts* (Aldershot, 1999).

_____, 'The papal chapel in the late fifteenth century', in Busse Berger and Rodin (2015), pp.446-462.

David Skinner, 'Davy [Davys], Richard', www.oxfordmusiconline.

Nicholas Slonimsky, *Nicholas Slonimsky's Book of Musical Anecdotes* (New York, R/2002).

Askold V. Smirnov, 'Johann Gottfried Wilhelm Palschau: reconstructing the composer's biography', *National Early Music Association Newsletter*, vi/1 (Spring 2022), pp.56-66.

Anne Smith, *The Performance of 16th-Century Music* (Oxford, 2011).

Fiona Smith, *Original Performing Material for Concerted Music in England, c.1660-1800*, PhD thesis (University of Leeds, 2014).

Don L. Smithers, in 'The Original Circumstances in the Performance of Bach's Leipzig Church Cantatas, "Wegen Seiner Sonn- und Festtägigen Amts-Verrichtungen"', *Bach*, xxvi/1-2 (Spring-Summer 1995/Fall-Winter 1995), pp.28-47.

E. Speyer, *Wilhelm Speyer, der Liedercomponist, 1790-1878* (Munich, 1925).

John Spitzer and Neal Zaslaw, *The Birth of the Orchestra: History of an Institution, 1650-1815* (New York and Oxford, 2004).

Louis Spohr, *Autobiography* (London, 1878).

Andrew Steptoe, 'Stress, Coping and Stage Fright in Professional Musicians', *Psychology of Music*, xvii/1 (1989), pp.3-11.

Tiffany Stern (ed), *Rehearsal from Shakespeare to Sheridan* (Oxford, 2007).

―――, 'Rehearsal in Shakespeare's Theatre', in Stern (2007), pp.46-123.

John Stevens, *Music and Poetry in the Early Tudor Court* (Cambridge, 2/1979).

Robert M. Stevenson, *Music in Mexico: A Historical Survey* (New York, 1952).

Graham Strahle, *An Early Music Dictionary* (Cambridge, 1995).

Laurie Stras, *Women and Music in Sixteenth-Century Ferrara* (Cambridge, 2018).

Oliver Strunk, *Source Readings in Music History: I Antiquity and the Middle Ages* (London, 1981).

―――, *Source Readings in Music History: II The Renaissance* (London, 1981).

―――, *Source Readings in Music History: III The Baroque Era* (London, 1981).

―――, *Source Readings in Music History: IV The Classic Era* (London, 1981).

John Strype, *Annals of the Reformation*, 4 vols. (London, 1709-25).

Matthew Swanson, Eva Floyd and David Kirkendall, 'Choral Rehearsals During COVID: Examining Singer Engagement', *The Choral Journal*, lxi/9 (April 2021), pp.75-79.

Christopher Taborsky, 'Musical Performance Anxiety: A Review of Literature', *Update: Applications of Research in Music Education*, xxvi/1 (2007), pp.15-25.

Daniel Taddie, 'Achieving Peak Performance: Rehearsal, Performance Attitudes, and Pre-Concert Routines, *The Choral Journal*, xli/9 (April 2001), p.41.

Michael Talbot, *Vivaldi* (London, 1979).

Ruth Tatlow, *Bach's numbers: compositional proportion and significance* (Cambridge, 2016).

Alexander Wheelock Thayer, *Life of Beethoven* (New York, 1921).

John M. Thomson (ed), *The future of early music in Britain* (London, 1978).

Renee Timmers, Freya Bailes and Helena Daffern (eds), *Together in music* (Oxford, 2022).

Evelyn Tribble, 'Distributing Cognition in the Globe', *Shakespeare Quarterly*, lvi/2 (Summer 2005), pp. 135-155.

Daniel Trocmé-Latter, 'Thieves, Drunkards, and Womanisers? Perceptions of Church Musicians in Early Reformation Strasbourg', in Hobbs and Noblesse-Rocher (2013), pp.383-399.

Thomas Tudway, *A Collection of all the Anthems daily used in Divine Service, throughout the year, in King's College Chapel in Cambridge* (Cambridge, 1706).

Dneya Udtaisuk, *A Theoretical Model of Piano Sightplaying components*, PhD thesis (University of Missouri-Columbia, 2005).

Giorgio Vasari, trans Julia Conaway Bondanella and Peter Bondanella, *The Lives of the Artists* (Oxford, 1991).

Roger Vaughan, *Herbert von Karajan: A Biographical Portrait* (New York, 1985).

John Vicars, *Gods arke overtopping the worlds waves* (London, 1646).

Nicola Vicentino, trans Maria Rika Maniates, *Ancient Music adapted to Modern Practice* (New Haven, 1996).

Richard Wagner, trans Edward Dannreuther, *On Conducting* (London, 1897).

Helen Wallace, *Spirit of the orchestra* (London, 2006).

Peter Walls, *History, Imagination and the Performance of Music* (Woodbridge, 2003).

Chris Walton, *Richard Wagner's Essays on Conducting: A new Translation with Critical Commentary* (Rochester, 2021).

Andrew J. Waters, Geoffrey Underwood and John M. Findlay, 'Studying expertise in music reading: Use of a pattern-matching paradigm', *Perception and Psychophysics*, lix (1997), pp.477-488.

William Weber, 'Did People Listen in the 18th Century?', *Early Music*, xxv/4 (November 1997), pp.678-691.

Max von Weber, *C. M. von Weber, ein Lebensbild* (Leipzig, 1864).

Rob C. Wegman, 'Concerning Tempo in the English Polyphonic Mass, c. 1420-70', *Acta Musicologica*, lxi/1 (January-April 1989), pp.40-65.

_____, *Born for the muses: the life and Masses of Jacob Obrecht* (Oxford, 1994).

_____, 'Sense and Sensibility in Late-Medieval Music: Thoughts on Aesthetics and "Authenticity"', *Early Music*, xxiii/2 (May 1995), pp.298-312.

_____, 'From Maker to Composer: Improvisation and Musical Authorship in the Low Countries, 1450-1500', *Journal of the American Musicological Society*, xlix/3 (Autumn 1996), pp.409-479.

_____, '"And Josquin Laughed...": Josquin and the Composer's Anecdote in the Sixteenth Century', *The Journal of Musicology*, xvii/3 (Summer 1999), pp.319-357.

_____, 'Different Strokes for Different Folks? On Tempo and Diminution in Fifteenth-Century Music', *Journal of the American Musicological Society*, liii/3 (Autumn 2000), pp.461-505.

_____, '"Musical Understanding" in the 15th Century', *Early Music*, xxx/1 (February 2002), pp.46-66.

_____, 'Johannes Tinctoris and the "New Art"', *Music & Letters*, lxxxiv/2 (May 2003), pp.171-188,

Felix Weingartner, trans Ernest Newman, *On Conducting* (London, 1906).

L. G. Wickham Legg (ed), *A Relation of A Short Survey of 26 Counties* (London, 1904).

Arthur L. Williams, 'Planning an Instrumental Rehearsal', *Music Supervisors' Journal*, xviii/2 (December 1931), pp.23-25.

Nora J. Williams, 'Writing the Collaborative Process: Measure (Still) for Measure, Shakespeare, and Rape Culture', *PARtake: The Journal of Performance as Research*, ii/1 (2018).

Magnus Williamson, *The Eton Choirbook: Its Institutional and Historical Background*, DPhil thesis (University of Oxford, 1997).

Hugh Willmott and Adam Daubney, 'Of saints, sows or smiths? Copper-brazed iron handbells in Early Medieval England', *Archaeological Journal*, clxxvii/1 (2019), pp.336-355.

John Wilson (ed), *Roger North on Music: Being a Selection from his Essays written during the years c.1695-1728* (London, 1959).

Walter L. Woodfill, *Musicians in English Society from Elizabeth to Charles I* (Princeton, 1953).

Leslie Woodgate, *The Chorusmaster* (London, 1944).

Andrew Woolley (ed), *Studies on Authorship in Historical Keyboard Music* (Abingdon, 2024).

Alison Wray, 'The sound of Latin in England before and after the Reformation', in Morehen (1995), pp.74-89.

_____, 'English pronunciation, c. 1500-c. 1625', in Morehen (1995), pp.90-108.

Craig Wright, 'Performance Practices at the Cathedral of Cambrai 1475-1550', *The Musical Quarterly*, lxiv/3 (July 1978), pp.295-328.

_____, 'Antoine Brumel and patronage at Paris', in Fenlon (1981), pp.37-60.

David Wulstan, *Tudor Music* (Iowa City, 1986).

Cornelia Yarbrough and Katia Madsen, 'The Evaluation of Teaching in Choral Rehearsals', *Journal of Research in Music Education*, xliv/4 (1998), pp.469-481.

Anne Bagnall Yardley, 'The Music Education of Young Girls in Medieval Nunneries', in Boynton and Rice (2008), pp.49-67.

Franklin B. Zimmerman, 'Performance Practices and Rehearsal Techniques', *College Music Symposium*, ix (Fall 1969), pp.101-111.

Magdalena Zira, *The Problem of the Chorus in Contemporary Revivals of Greek Tragedy and Directorial Solutions in the Last Forty Years*, PhD thesis (King's College London, 2019).

INDEX

A

Ableton Live. 175
Absenteeism. 44, 56
Académie Royale de Musique . . 101, 139
Academy of Ancient Music. . 153
Accent. 123
Accompaniment 78
Adam, Adolphe. 135
Admiral's Company. 184
Albrechtsberger, Johann Georg. . 79
Alcock, John 62
Alembert, Jean le Rond d' . . 111
Alleyn, Edward 184
Amateur music 125
Amsterdam 143
Amsterdam Royal Concertgebouw Orchestra. 158
Annibaldi, Claudio 103
Ansani, Giovanni 10
Antcliffe, Herbert 166
Archives. 32
Arnell, Richard 161
Arnold, Samuel 20
Artaria, Mathias 36
Artusi, Giovanni Maria. . . . 115
Ashwell, Thomas 45
Associated Board 180

Attendance 55
Atlas, The 149
Auditions 38
Augsburg 88
Aztec sacred music 82

B

Baas, Baldiun 188
Bach, Carl Philipp Emanuel . 130
Bach, Johann Sebastian . . . 11, 19, 25, 31, 33, 88, 110, 120, 136, 161, 191, 194
Bacon, Nicholas. 125
Bajón 42
Baldinucci, Filippo 187
Baltimore 131
Bancroft, John. 61
BandLab. 175
Banister, John 17
Barbirolli, John 155
Bardi, Giovanni de'. 111, 115, 121
Bar numbers 34
Baron, Ernst Gottlieb 8, 120
Bartók, Béla 137, 138
Bartoni, Pompeo 71
Bassano 54, 98
Bathe, William 46
Batten organ book 78

Battistelli, Giorgio. 188
Bayley, Amanda. 180, 181
Bayly, Lewis 7
BBC Symphony Orchestra . . 165
Beecham, Thomas 160-162
Beethoven, Ludwig van. . . 10, 36, 37, 131, 132, 134, 136, 137, 154, 158, 163, 192
Behaviour 59, 62
Bellucius, Cesare 33
Benham, Hugh 26
Bennett, Joseph . . . 144, 145, 151
Berg, Alban 165, 166
Bergen op Zoom 55
Berger, Karol 105
Berlin 24, 133, 139, 142
Berlin Philharmonic Orchestra . 162
Berlioz, Hector . . . 133, 136, 140, 143, 145, 146
Bernacchi, Antonio. 102
Bernini, Gian Lorenzo 187
Bernstein, Leonard 161
Bertoldi, Francesca 102
Besozzi 98
Bianco, Mattia. 75
Biber, Heinrich 192
Birnbaum, Johann Abraham . . 31
Blavet, Michel. 46
Blow, John. 32
Boleyn. 59
Bonacchi, Ronaldo 188
Bononcini, Giovanni 87
Book of Perditions 83
Borne, John 71
Bottrigari, Ercole . . . 57, 95, 113
Boulez, Pierre. 164-166
Boult, Adrian 142, 169
Bowen, Jemmy 120
Bowers, Roger. 51
Bowles, Michael. 168
Boyce, William . . . 23, 32, 98, 99

Braddon, John 62
Brahms, Johannes. 145, 161
Bray, Roger 26, 84
Breitkopf & Härtel 137
Britten, Benjamin. 161
Brown, John. 62
Browne, John 190
Bruceña, Diego de 54
Bruhl, Carl Friedrich Moritz Paul von 140
Brussels Opera 140
Brussels 5557 106
Bucer, Martin 60
Buck, Zechariah. 129
Bülow, Hans von 134
Burckard, Johannes. 60
Burgos Cathedral . . . 7, 147, 148
Burney, Charles . . . 10, 20, 32, 59, 64, 71, 72, 75, 76, 84, 90, 99, 101, 107, 109
Busby, Thomas 137
Bustamante, Francisco de. . . . 54
Butler, Charles 114
Butterworth, Arthur 155
Byrd, William 30, 90, 126

C

Caldara, Antonio 43
Cambrai Cathedral . . 8, 46, 60, 62, 63, 81, 98, 120
Cannabich, Rosa 75
Cannons. 125
Cantelli, Guido 136, 154
Canterbury Cathedral 71
Cardinal College, Ipswich . . 100
Cardus, Neville 160
Carlton House 20
Carrington, Simon 167
Carse, Adam 131, 144, 146
Carter, Thomas 20
Cartwright, Thomas 112

Carver, Robert 118
Casola, Bassano 90
Castello, Dario 90
Castil-Blaze 132
Cavitt, Mary Ellen 82
Cayari, Christopher 174
Cazzati, Mauritio 52
Cecil, William 125
Cellini, Benvenuto 108
Cheltenham Festival 154
Cherbury, Lord Herbert of . . . 87
Chailly, Riccardo 162
Chapel Royal . . 59, 62, 71, 87, 98
Chapelle-Musique 42
Charles V, Emperor 53
Chichester Cathedral . . 45, 53, 56, 61, 62, 103
Choirbook 25, 28
Choristers 58, 72
Christian IV, King 43
Cibber, Susannah 186
Cimello, Giovan Tomaso 12
Clauhs, Matthew 174
Clement VII, Pope 108
Clementi, Muzio 114
Clive, Catherine 185
Coleman, Charles 17
Coleman, Henry 166
Colosimo, Clara 188
Concerto delle donne 81
Concerts Spirituel 10
Conducting 95, 152
Conservatorio of S. Onofrio, Naples 107
Conway, John 16
Copeland, Philip 175
Corbeli, Jean 99
Cordier, Jean 52
Corelli, Arcangelo 112
Cornysh, William . 59, 74, 106, 118
Corsi, Jacopo 48
Coryat, Thomas 71, 100
Costa, Michael 140, 142
Couperin, François 112, 120
Covent Garden Theatre, London . . 20, 122, 143
Coward, Henry 168
Cracow 47
Crane, William 59
Crawe, James 44
Curtis, Gareth 107

D

Dallam, Thomas 79
Dance 101, 187
Darmstadt 134
David, Ferdinand 133
Davidson, Jane 180
Davillier, Jean Charles 148
Davy, Richard 59, 93
Defesch, William 27
Delaney, Mary 48
Delius, Frederick 161
della Robbia, Luca 96
de Rore, Cipriano 30
Diction 123
Diderot, Denis 64
Didier, Guillaume 56
Diezl, Joseph 32
Digital orchestras 175
Digital workstations 175
Discipline 62
Dittersdorf, Carl Ditters von 46, 91
Doles, Johann Friedrich 54
Dollman, Luke 166
Donne, John 81
Doré, Gustave 47, 48
Dorico software 176
Douai 48
Drama 184
Dresden 133, 135, 143, 144
Dropbox 175

219

Drury Lane Theatre, London. 122
Dublin. 24
Duborg, George. 147
Dufay, Guillaume 70
Dunstable, John. 190
Dupreille, Charles Albert. . . . 75
Durham. 125
Durham Cathedral . . . 45, 57, 58, 79, 84
Dürr, Alfred. 31

E

Earle, John 61
Edwards, H. Sutherland . . . 139
Edwards, Tom. 87
Elizabeth I, Queen 54
Ella, John 132, 143
Ely Cathedral 57
Elyot, Thomas. 124
Employment 50
English Concert. 153
Engramelle, Marie-Dominique-Joseph. 9
Ensemble size 130
Erasmus, Desiderius 60
Errors 31, 56, 82, 136
Essex Record Office. 28
Esterházy, Prince Nicolaus . 32, 57, 64, 86, 108
Ethelred, Bishop 111
Eton Choirbook. . . 1, 28, 31, 190
Eton College 28, 49, 57, 59, 189, 194
Etymology. 13
Évora Cathedral. 56, 118
Exeter Cathedral 52, 60

F

Fabri, Annibale Pio 102
Facy, Hugh 48
Farinelli, Giovanni Battista . . 115
Fayrfax, Robert 28, 84, 190
Fellini, Federico. 199
Fellowes, Edmund H.. 9
Ferlendis, Giuseppe. 93
Ferrara 81
Ferrara, Duke of 71
Festa, Andrea 30
Fétis, François-Joseph 132
Fevre, Robert le 111
Finland 166
Finnissy, Michael 180
Fioroni, Jean Andrè. 99
First Symphonic Orchestra, Russia 153
Florence Cathedral . . . 70, 96, 97
Forkel, Johann Nikolaus 88
Frederick the Great 86
Froberger, Johann Jakob . . . 112
Furtwängler, Wilhelm . . 154, 189
Fux, Johann Joseph 43, 114

G

Gaffurius, Franchinus. . . . 32, 35
Gallini, Giovanni Andrea Battista 24
Galván, Janet 174
Gardane, Angelo 30
Gardner, William 139
Garnet, Henry. 126
Geck, Martin 31
Geminiani, Francesco 122
German College, Rome. 42
Gesner, Johann Matthias 19
Gewandhaus Orchestra, Leipzig . 101, 133, 134, 136
Gilling Castle 125
Girard, Narcisse. 145
Gloucester Cathedral 61
Gluck, Christoph Willibald. 20, 46, 91, 173

Goethe, Johann Wolfgang von . 91
Gonzaga. 42, 52
Gonzaga, Scipione 58
Good, James. 180
Google Drive 175
Grace, Harvey. 166
Grassis, Paride de 124
Graz 72
Greene, Maurice 98
Grelot, Guillaume-Joseph . . . 21
Grétry, André Ernest Modeste 122
Guido of Arezzo 72, 87
Guines, Duc de 81
Gutheil-Schoder, Marie 158

H

Habeneck, François Antoine . 131, 140, 143
Hallé, Charles 145
Hallé Orchestra 155
Hammond, Lieutenant 69
Handel, George Frideric 17, 20, 23, 30, 34, 38, 48, 87, 98, 102, 125, 186
Hanson, Kyle J. 168
Hanssens, Charles 140, 141
Harnoncourt, Nikolaus . 70, 72, 73
Harpsichord 89, 139
Harrison, Frank Ll. 190
Harrold, Thomas 61
Harsnett, Samuel 56
Hartley, Leslie P. 5
Hasse, Johann Adolph 72
Hawkins, John 120
Haydn, Joseph 18, 21, 24, 32, 55, 63, 108, 109, 115, 116, 122, 186, 190
Haydn, Michael 93
Hayes, William 17
Haymarket Theatre, London 21, 53
Hengrave Hall 125
Henry VIII, King . 59, 77, 91, 100

Henslowe, Philip 184
Hiller, Ferdinand 136
Hiller, Johann Adam 69
Hobson, Nicholas 58
Hodges, Walter 185
Hoensbroech, Raphael von . . 153
Hogarth, William 27
Holman, Peter 98, 99
Holst, Imogen 167
Holz, Karl 36
Hooper, Edmund 107
Horwood, William 44
Howard Jones, Ann 167
Howells, Herbert 147
Hübner, Johannes 59
Hutchinson, Lucy 17

I

Improvisation 14, 92
Ingatestone Hall 125

J

Jerold, Beverly 115
Jesuit Cappella, Cracow 47
Johnson, Edward 125
Johnson, Samuel 13
Jommelli, Niccolò 20
Jordan, James 169
Josquin des Prez . 38, 90, 102, 120
Jullien, Louis-Antoine 130

K

Kähler, Willibald 159
Kapsberger, Giovanni Girolamo 192
Karajan, Herbert von . . . 153, 154
Kärntnerthor Orchestra, Vienna 140
Kassel 143, 156
Katz, Shelley 175
Kemble, John Philip 122

Kendall, Thomas 57, 59
Kennedy, John F. 161
Ketyll, William 57
Kielblock, Adolph. 85
Kienzl, Wilhelm. 157
King's College, Cambridge . 28, 41, 45, 58, 103, 194
King's Theatre, London . . 132, 152
Klein, Hermann. 160
Koch, Heinrich Christoph . . . 99
Kohon, Benjamin 157
Konttinen, Anu 166
Kreutzer Quarte. 180
Kurz, Selma 157
Kusser, Johann 19, 110

L

Labi, Elizabeth 188
Lange, Maria Aloysia Antonia Weber 48
La Scala, Milan 133
Lassus, Orlande 43
Laud, William 7
Lawson, Colin 167
Leach, Elizabeth Eva 39
Leadership 177
Le Cerf de la Viéville 19
Leconfield Castle 43
Legge, Walter 154
Le Grand, Adam 62
Legrenzi, Giovanni 72
Le Huray, Peter 7
Leighton, Kenneth 147
Leipzig 19, 143
Lentall 100
Leo, Leonardo 10
Leppard, Raymond 154, 155
Lewis, Joseph 167
L'Heritier, Jean 12
Lichfield Cathedral 62
Lighting 48, 191

Lilliat, John 46
Lincoln Cathedral 44
Lipinski, Charles 133
Lloyd, John 28
Lloyd, Thomas 36
Lobo, Alonso 54
Locatelli, Pietro 113
Logic Pro software 175
London . 21, 23, 48, 53, 64, 72, 80, 114, 125, 133, 160, 189
London Philharmonic Orchestra 161
London Philharmonic Society 143, 146
London Waits 107
Longotabarro 88
Loughton, Thomas 62
Loosemore, George 29
Lowe, Edward 9
Ludlow Parish Church 92
Lully, Jean-Baptiste 19, 64, 95, 188
Lumley, John 168
Lute 117

M

Maazel, Lorin 135, 136
Mace, Thomas 43, 70, 123
Maffei, Giovanni Camillo 47
Magdalen College, Oxford . 28, 79
Mahler, Alma 134
Mahler, Gustav . 24, 156-160, 166
Mainwaring, John 87
Málaga Cathedral 54
Manesse Codex 95
Manheit, Jacques 157
Manila 49, 119
Mann, Alfred 31
Mannheim 75, 76
Marchand, Heinrich 109
Margaret of Parma 58
Maria Theresa, Empress 23

Martin, Gregory 124
Martin, Thomas. 7
Marwood, Richard 62
Mattheson, Johann . . 19, 110, 115
Mead, John 56
Mechanical instruments 9
Medici. 188
Meinardus, Ludwig. 145
Meiningen. 134
Meisner 124
Memory. 80
Mendelssohn, Felix . 91, 133, 134, 143-146
Mengelberg, Willem 157
Merton College, Oxford 61
Merulo, Claudio 22
Mewe, Richard 56
Meyerbeer, Giacomo 133
Mico, Richard. 125
Microsoft Teams 172
Miglietti, Ugo 58
Milan 24, 64, 68, 80, 99
Military music 149
Monachus, Guillelmus 112
Monteverdi, Claudio . . 38, 75, 90, 102, 188, 192
Morehen, John 6
Morley, Thomas. . 57, 89, 92, 106
Moscheles, Ignaz 131
Motolinia, Fray 81
Motz, Georg. 114
Mouton, Jean 14, 15
Mozart, Leopold . . 7, 24, 39, 47, 64, 75, 80, 88, 93, 110, 122
Mozart, Wolfgang Amadeus . . . 7, 10, 22, 24, 38, 39, 64, 71, 81, 87, 88, 93, 101, 109, 124, 136, 158, 192, 193
Munich 43, 64
Murray, William 58
Musescore software. 176
Musica ficta. 105

Musical jokes 192
Musical Times, The. 130
Music education 72
Music minus One. 172, 173
Music notation software . . . 176
Musin, Ilya 166, 169

N

Naples 20, 75, 108, 113, 122
Naumburg. 14
NBC Symphony Orchestra . . 154
Nenita. 21
Newalke Collegiate Church . 103
New College, Oxford 79
New Philharmonia Orchestra 135
New York 131
Neissen, Heinrich von 95
Nicolai, Otto 133
Niemetschek, Franz. 93
Nikisch, Arthur 142, 160
North, Francis. 69, 87
North, Roger . . 8, 17, 47, 79, 87, 121, 122
Norwich Cathedral . . . 56, 69, 92, 129
Notre Dame de Paris 81

O

Obrecht, Jacob 55, 56
Odo of Cluny 89
Odo of Saint-Maur 63
Olmütz 157
OneDrive 175
Opera 17, 63
Orchestra of the Age of
    Enlightenment 153
Organ 76, 78, 118
Ornamentation 120
Orpheus Chamber Orchestra . 53
Ospedale della Pietà, Venice . . 72

P

Page, Christopher 70
Paisiello, Giovanni 24
Palestrina, Giovanni Pierluigi da 29
Pallavicino, Benedetto 30
Palschau, Johann Gottfried
    Wilhelm 9
Panula, Jorma 166
Paris 10, 38, 42, 72, 81, 95,
    109, 111, 131-133, 136
Parke, William Thomas 65
Parrott, Andrew 8, 113
Partbooks 25, 28
Pasqualigo, Pietro 71
Paston manuscripts 117
Payer, Hieronymus 143
Peacham, Henry 89
Pellegrini, Vincenzo 83
Pensions 57
Performance anxiety 85
Performance standards 130
Performer stipends 43
Pergolesi, Giovanni Battista . 173
Peri, Jacopo 48
Peterborough Cathedral . . . 167
Peterhouse, Cambridge 34
Petre 28
Petri, Johann Samuel . . . 22, 123
Phaf, Hans 179
Pfaffe 54
Philharmonia Orchestra, London
    154, 162
Philharmonic Orchestra, London
    120, 133
Philip II, King 53
Philip, Robert 11
Philomathes, Venceslaus . 96, 122
Piano 139
Picasso, Pablo 187
Piccioni, Giovanni 80
Pipelare, Matthaeus 14
Pitch 117
Plato 80
Playford, John 21
Playing by ear 80
Pliny the Elder 36
Ponsonby, Robert 164
Practice schedules 44
Praeger, Ferdinand 146
Prague 43, 129
Prelleur, Peter 50
Prieur, Dreux 103
Pringsheim, Klaus 158
Proof-reading 38
Pro Tools software 175
Prynne, William 76
Puchberg, Michael 24
Pugnani, Gaetano 98
Purcell, Henry 120, 121, 19

Q

Quadros, André de 167
Quantz, Johann Joachim . . 43, 47,
    54, 73, 86, 101, 110, 112, 114, 117,
    121, 122

R

Raaff, Anton 124
Rachmaninov, Sergei 158
Radio 151
Raguenet, François . . . 20, 90, 95
Rameau, Jean-Philippe 64
Ramm, Friedrich 93
Ramsey Abbey 51
Ramsey, Robert 29
Raphael (Raffaello Sanzio
    da Urbino) 187
Ravel, Maurice 164
Redford, John 18
Redoutensaal 24
Rehearsal etiquette 110

Rehearsal etymology 13
Rehearsal letters. 23
Rehearsal spaces 47
Rehearsals, audiences at 23
Rehearsals, historical descriptions 18
Rehearsals, numbers of 107
Reichardt, Johann Friedrich . . 10, 75, 114, 123, 191
Renart, Miguel 119
Repertoire, selecting 192
Reynier 55
Reynolds, Gordon 167
Ricci, Marco. 6
Richardson, A. Madeley . . . 166
Richardson, John 69
Richmond Palace 71
Richter, Hans 152
Rinuccini, Ottavio 48
Rochlitz, Johann Friedrich . . 101, 110, 134, 139
Rome 42, 72, 135
Rosbaud, Hans 164
Rosenmüller, Johann 39
Rose Theatre, London 184
Rossini, Gioachino . 133, 139, 161
Rota, Nino. 188
Rousseau, Jean-Jacques 76
Rovetta, Giovanni. 72
Royal Albert Hall, London . . 130
Royal Hall, Harrogate. 155
Ruckers 117

S

Sagudino, Nicholas 71, 132
Sainte-Chapelle, Paris. 103
Saito, Hideo. 169
Salisbury Cathedral. . . 7, 61, 69, 73, 112
Salzburg. 7, 22, 93, 109
San Giovanni in Laterano, Rome 58

San Petronio, Bologna 52
San Rocco, Venice 56
Santa Maria della Visitazione degli Orfani. 72
San Vito, Ferrara 95
Savonarola, Girolamo. 60
Scarlatti, Alessandro 114
Scheibe, Johann Adolph . 31, 110
Schein, Samuel 14
Scherchen, Herman. 169
Schindler, Anton 132
Schlimbach, Christian Friedrich 22
Schmidhammer, Arpad. . . . 159
Schoenberg, Arnold 159
Schubert, Franz 134
Schumann, Robert . 134, 137, 144, 145, 163
Schumann-Heink, Ernestine . 157
Schuppanzigh, Ignaz . . . 114, 122
Scuolo dello Spirito Santo, Venice 53
Seaman, Christopher 169
Seidl, Anton. 146
Sendrey, Alfred 157
Senleches, Jacob de 39
Sensheim, Count 24
Shaftesbury, Earl of 186
Shakespeare, William . . . 91, 102
Sharp family. 125
Shaw, Thomas 122
Sherr, Richard. 7, 75, 83
Shield, William 122
Siam, King of 113
Sibelius software 176
Sibelius, Jean 161
Sight-reading 87, 89, 91, 154, 183
Silvestri, Constantin 161
Sing-Akademie, Berlin 129
Sisear, Juan 54
Sistine Chapel, Rome . . 14, 51, 60, 82, 86, 99, 103, 187
Smart, George. 55, 142

SmartMusic software 176
Smith, Fiona 32
Smith, William 79
Somis, Giovanni Battista 98
Sound recording . . . 11, 151, 154
Soundtrap software 175
Southwark Cathedral, London 167
Southwell, Robert 126
Spinone, Benedetto 30
Spirituel-Concerte, Vienna . . 134
Spohr, Louis . . 133, 135, 139, 143
Spontini, Gaspare 133, 142
Stadler, Anton . . . 21, 72, 87, 110, 113, 121
Stage fright 85
St Aignan, Paris 59
Saint Aubert, Abbey of 71
St Mark's, Venice 98
St Paul's Cathedral, London 18, 61
St Petersburg 88
St Omer 56
Steffani, Agostino 120
Stein, Johann Andreas 88
Steptoe, Andrew 85
Stevens, John 42
Stokowski, Leopold 165
Storace, Stephen 109
Stringthorpe, Nigel 168
Strada, Anna Maria 102
Stravinsky, Igor 161
Strype, John 83
Stubs, John 61, 114
Susato, Tylman 42
Sutton, John 118
Symphonova Instrument . . . 175
Syon Abbey 82, 111

T

Table book 25
Tamburini, Antonio 86
Taverner, John 190

Tchaikovsky, Pyotr Ilyich . . . 152
Teatro di San Carlo, Naples . . . 20
Teatro Regio Ducale, Milan . . 64
Technology 171
Telemann, Georg Philipp . . . 173
Tempo 121
Tercero, Lucas 54
Text underlay 106
Thakar, Markand 169
Thomasschule, Leipzig . . 46, 108
Three Choirs Festival 129
Tiffany, Louis Comfort 159
Tinctoris, Johannes 39, 113
Toledo Cathedral 54, 148
Tomkins, Thomas 12
Toscanini, Arturo 152
Tosi, Pier Francesco 114
Trinity College, Cambridge. 29, 78
Tuning 21, 113
Turin 98
Türk, Daniel Gottlob 115
Turk's Head Tavern, London . . 23

U

Úbeda, Vicente 55

V

Valderrábano, Enriquez de . . . 36
València 55, 56, 76, 119
Vanneo, Stephano 82
Vanzhura, Ernest 88
Vasari, Giorgio 96
Vaughan Williams, Ralph . . . 161
Venice . 30, 53, 58, 64, 71, 72, 100, 108, 124
Veracini, Francesco Maria 98, 115
Verdelot, Philippe 22
Viadana, Ludovico . . . 74, 78, 89
Vicars, John 76
Vicentino, Nicola 112

Vienna 20, 46, 72, 84, 123, 139, 158
Vienna Philharmonic Orchestra 165
Vienna Symphony Orchestra.   163
Villella, Ferdinando. 188
Villiers, George 185
Vimeo 176
Virtual Choir 174
Vivaldi, Antonio 72, 108
Vledrezelle, Gerardus de 56
Vogler, Georg Joseph 88

W

Wagner, Richard . . 132, 135, 145, 146, 160, 161
Wallerstein, Prince Oettingen von 109
Walond, William 62
Weber, Bernard Anselm . . . 139
Weber, Carl Maria von 133, 140, 143
Weber, Mme 88
Webern, Anton 165
Weckmann, Matthias 112
Weelkes, Thomas 45, 61
Wegman, Rob 55
Weimar 88
Weingartner, Felix 136
Weiss, Josef 157
Wells Cathedral 13, 61, 62
West Dereham 125
Westminster Abbey, London 57, 83
Whitacre, Eric. 174
Whitehall Chapel, London . . . 23
Whythorne, Thomas 52
Wilbye, John 125
Willaert, Adrian. 30
Will Forster's Virginal Book . . 30
Williams, Arthur 189
Williamson, Magnus 57
Winchester College 73
Wolsey, Thomas. . . . 22, 91, 100
Wolters, Gezinus 179

Wood, Henry 134, 162, 169
Woodgate, Leslie 166
Worcester Cathedral 103
Wright, Craig 59, 70
Wulstan, David 12

Y

Yong, William. 57
York Minster 59
York Waits. 58
Young, James Howard 175
Yousician software 176
YouTube. 176

Z

Zenobi, Luigi 82, 100, 111
Zimerman, Krystian 161
Zoom software 172
Zweig, Stefan 157